AWAKENING

Rachel B. Vogelstein and Meighan Stone
A Council on Foreign Relations Book

AWAKENING

#MeToo and the Global Fight
for Women's Rights

PUBLICAFFAIRS

New York

PublicAffairs
Hachette Book Group
1290 Avenue of the Americas, New York, NY 10104
www.publicaffairsbooks.com
@Public_Affairs

Printed in the United States of America

First Edition: July 2021

Published by PublicAffairs, an imprint of Perseus Books, LLC, a subsidiary of Hachette Book Group, Inc. The PublicAffairs name and logo is a trademark of the Hachette Book Group.

The publisher is not responsible for websites (or their content) that are not owned by the publisher.

Print book interior design by Amy Quinn.

Founded in 1921, the Council on Foreign Relations is an independent, national membership organization and a nonpartisan center for scholars dedicated to producing and disseminating ideas so that individual and corporate members, as well as policymakers, journalists, students, and interested citizens in the United States and other countries, can better understand the world and the foreign policy choices facing the United States and other governments. The Council does this by convening meetings; conducting a wideranging Studies program; publishing *Foreign Affairs*, the preeminent journal covering international affairs and U.S. foreign policy; maintaining a diverse membership; sponsoring Independent Task Forces; and providing up-to-date information about the world and U.S. foreign policy on the Council's website, www.cfr.org.

THE COUNCIL TAKES NO INSTITUTIONAL POSITION ON POLICY ISSUES AND HAS NO AFFILIATION WITH THE U.S. GOVERNMENT. ALL STATEMENTS OF FACT AND EXPRESSIONS OF OPINION CONTAINED IN ITS PUBLICATIONS ARE THE SOLE RESPONSIBILITY OF THE AUTHOR OR AUTHORS.

Library of Congress Control Number: 2021933116

ISBNs: 978-1-5417-5862-9 (hardcover), 978-1-5417-5861-2 (ebook)

LSC-C

Printing 1, 2021

To Sage and Parker,
my life's greatest gifts,
and to the women who persist.

—R.B.V.

To every activist who survives and speaks,
Maureen and Dan for your constant friendship,
and my beloved son Moses, as he becomes a new man.

—M.S.

Stories matter. Stories have been used to dispossess and to malign. But stories can also be used to empower, and to humanize. Stories can break the dignity of a people. But stories can also repair that broken dignity.
—Chimamanda Ngozi Adichie, *TED Talk: The Danger of a Single Story*

She had resolved never to take another step backward.
—Kate Chopin, *The Awakening*

CONTENTS

'me too.' founder and activist Tarana Burke (second from right) helps lead a march for survivors of sexual assault in Los Angeles, California, in November 2017. Credit: Reuters/ Lucy Nicholson

FOREWORD

Tarana Burke

Fifteen years ago, I was a community organizer and cultural worker in Selma, Alabama, running an organization for young girls. I was all too familiar with the messages they were hearing every day: you're not good enough, smart enough, important enough. So I made it my mission to change those messages—to help groups of Black and brown girls find their voices, celebrate their unique potential, and recognize their power as leaders.

It didn't take long to see the pattern that was taking shape. Every time we gathered together, stories would spill out. I sat in community centers, classrooms, and church basements, listening to thirteen- and fourteen-year-olds matter-of-factly describe their experiences with sexual violence, abuse, and assault. Because I'm a survivor myself, my heart ached for them. I wanted to say something deep and profound—something that captured our shared pain and trauma. I wanted to tell them that this had happened to me, too.

That's how 'me too.' began: as shared language between survivors. It was a signal to these girls that they were in a space where they could focus on their healing without having to be performative or guarded. It was empowerment through empathy.

If you had asked me back then, I would have told you that I believed our survivor-led movement had the potential to move the world. But I never could have imagined that #MeToo would become a hashtag translated into dozens of languages, spark a global reckoning, and become a connective framework for movements across the globe. The spark ignited more than a decade ago has caught fire in ways beyond my wildest dreams.

For me, reading the stories of the women in *Awakening* is an inspiring experience—and a humbling one. I'm stunned by the defiance of women like Mozn Hassan, a lawyer in Egypt who has been repeatedly targeted and surveilled by an authoritarian regime because of her outspoken feminist advocacy, including her support of #AnaKaman, or #MeToo. By the fortitude of survivors like Khadijah Adamu and Fakhrriyyah Hashim in Nigeria, who have broken with taboo and organized publicly with #ArewaMeToo, at enormous personal risk. I'm awed by the determination of computer science graduate Luo Xixi, who was inspired by #MeToo's viral moment in the United States to break her silence after thirteen years and name the professor who had harassed her. And the defiance of Swedish actress and writer Cissi Wallin, who decided to speak publicly and remains determined to help protect others, even after she was found guilty of defaming the man she accused. I admire the resilience of Pakistani singer and actress Meesha Shafi, who came forward about a colleague in the entertainment industry, proclaiming, "It is not easy to speak out . . . but it is harder to stay silent." In parts of the globe where #MeToo is seen as a form of treason, where legal systems fail women over and over again, where "sex for grades" is accepted as part of life, where standing up for women's rights is dangerous, where survivors face crushing stigma, and even in places the world views as feminist utopias, the activists in this book are expanding the definition of courage. I am honored to be in common cause with each of them—and with so many others whose names we might never know.

What this global movement has achieved is incredible—and so is its use of technology to empower women to work together across countries and cultures. As someone who came of age in the era when faxing flyers across the city was considered cutting-edge organizing, it's extraordinary to witness the ways activists around the world are tapping into their collective power through social media. Through private Facebook groups, Twitter, Instagram, YouTube, WhatsApp chats, and Zoom, survivors are using every tool at their disposal and inventing new ones. Even with the challenges social media presents for issues around safety and privacy, it makes it possible to amplify voices that have been silenced for far too long. The result is a movement to end sexual violence that—as it must be—is intersectional and inclusive, centering the experiences of survivors of color.

Ask any organizer and they'll tell you that one of the hardest things to do is to create lasting, meaningful culture change. This book covers years of efforts to do just that. Ikram Ben Said, a Tunisian activist and founder of Aswat Nissa, summed it up perfectly when she said, "This didn't happen in a vacuum. This is the result of at least twenty, thirty years of the older generation of feminists who were really talking about gender-based violence and sexual harassment in public space, in private space." Now, we're seeing the beginnings of real justice in court systems around the globe. Perpetrators are starting to face consequences. Advocates have changed and strengthened laws against sexual assault. And in places like Brazil, Lebanon, Mexico, the United States, and Sri Lanka, women are running for public office in record-breaking numbers. Even the backlash to 'me too.' is a sign of just how much cultural standards have changed.

None of this means that our work is finished. Recently, a pandemic, a global economic crisis, and an overdue reckoning with racism have shown just how much we still have to do to address injustice and inequality in the United States and around the world. As we look to the future of #MeToo, a debate is unfolding: Should we focus on the immediate crisis? Or should we set our sights on the root causes? I believe the answer can't be "either/or"—it has to be "both/and." We can—we have to—support the people who are impacted by sexual violence on a daily basis and work to dismantle the systems that allow it to happen in the first place. That's what our *Survivor's Agenda*—a policy blueprint informed by survivors of sexual violence—aims to do. Like the activists in this book, we need to use every tool we have.

I started the 'me too.' movement because I wanted the girls in the program I ran and survivors everywhere to be empowered to create their own tools both for their own healing and for dismantling the systems that allowed them to be harmed. There are so many of us who carry this burden, who have been holding our trauma in the pit of our stomach for years. I dream of a day when we no longer have to experience our trauma, when we have the joy and healing we deserve. Fifteen years later, I close my eyes and imagine a generation of young people around the world who have been learning about respect, boundaries, and consent for as long as they can remember; it's second nature to them. They are free from sexual harassment and assault.

This book shows that, around the world, we've come farther than ever before. I'm humbled to be in partnership with leaders globally fighting to realize this vision.

AUTHORS' NOTE

Rachel's Story

On the afternoon of November 9, 2016, I stood weeping in the aisle of a commuter train with several other women I had only just met, en route home from New York. Hillary Clinton—someone I admired and had served for two decades, the first American woman ever to win a presidential major party nomination, who had long symbolized the rising power of women in America and around the world—had just lost the US presidential election to an avowed misogynist, one who boasted of groping women without their consent and degraded them for sport.

A train attendant approached.

"Ladies," he inquired earnestly, "is everything OK?"

I marveled at his imperviousness to the shattering loss that had united the diverse group of women with whom I huddled. Surely he had to know that everything was not OK. Not in a world where the most powerful person on the face of the planet would, once again, be male, as had been true since the dawn of civilization. And not just any male, but an alpha chauvinist who had been credibly accused of sexual harassment and assault by multiple women, threatening to undo decades of progress toward women's equality at home and abroad.

I was incredulous that the attendant didn't recognize our pain. Our disappointment. Our dejection that this step toward the equal future we'd envisioned for our ourselves—and for our children—still was not to be.

What I couldn't yet perceive, as I slumped back into my seat, was that the sadness we felt was shared by women around the world, and would quickly morph into rage, helping to spark a global outcry that would catalyze a movement for women's rights far more powerful and widespread than at any moment in history.

Back in my office at the Council on Foreign Relations, a think tank in Washington, DC, my gloom diminished over the next months as I marveled at the rise in women's activism that ensued—activism whose roots predated the events of 2016 but was fueled by them, ultimately traveling across borders, over the internet, onto the streets, and into the halls of power. Together with a team of researchers in the Council's Women and Foreign Policy program, I began chronicling this international surge in the women's movement, starting with the Women's March in January 2017, the largest global women's protest in history; the explosion of the #MeToo movement later that same year, which spread to more than one hundred countries; and the growth in women's political participation in the 2018 elections and beyond. We carefully monitored breakthroughs in region after region, country after country, as women buoyed by the strength and courage of their sisters were inspired to come forward in droves and demand change.

The coverage and popularization of this movement in the United States astonished me, despite the fact that I had spent my career advocating for women's rights. Initially, I had worked on women's issues domestically— volunteering at a domestic violence shelter in New York, and fighting for women's legal rights at the ACLU Reproductive Freedom Project and as a young lawyer at the National Women's Law Center. I labored to close the gender gap in the political arena, helping Hillary Clinton, who was then the First Lady, become the first woman ever elected to the US Senate and statewide office from New York, in 2000; the first woman to prevail in a contested presidential primary, in 2008; and the first woman to win a major US party nomination for president, in 2016, along with more than sixty-five million votes in the general election. I worked on global women's issues as well, partnering with courageous women's rights defenders while serving in the Secretary of State's Office of Global Women's Issues during the Obama administration, as a member of the White House Council on Women and Girls, and later at the Clinton Foundation in New York, where I sought to elevate the status of women at the United Nations and on the US foreign policy agenda, given the wealth of evidence that doing so advances prosperity, stability, and security at home and abroad.

In all these roles, the raison d'être for my job as a women's rights advocate was often questioned—despite the reality that women are paid less than men everywhere in the world, remain dramatically underrepresented in capitals and boardrooms, comprise the majority of the world's poor, and face an epidemic of violence that affects one in three women in their lifetimes. When I shared that I was a women's rights lawyer in a roomful of newly minted attorneys after my admission to the bar, the leader in charge of our training was incredulous. "Full time?" he asked, as if there wouldn't be enough work to keep me busy all day. "Haven't women already achieved equality?"

At the White House, at the State Department, and on Capitol Hill, officials from both sides of the aisle routinely considered concerns about the treatment of 50 percent of the global population to be a distraction from the crucial economic and security issues of the day, ignoring not only how those issues affect women, but also their critical role in addressing them. Even after Secretary of State Hillary Clinton, whom I served, declared global women's issues a priority to US security—an assessment based on reams of data showing that the inclusion of women promotes stability and reduces conflict—government leaders continued to question their importance. A senior US official, in an interview with the *Washington Post*, derisively referred to women's issues as a special interest and "pet rock," and insisted that such issues had to "take a back seat to other priorities."[1] In politics, blindness to gender inequality was endemic: in each of the political campaigns on which I served, voters of all persuasions regaled me with countless reasons why they couldn't support the woman I was trying to elect—which they claimed had nothing to do with her gender—including her appearance, her voice, her marriage, and even her tenacity and intelligence, which were held against her as she was again and again pronounced "unlikable" for possessing qualities that are routinely rewarded in male leaders. In the media, the issues on which I worked daily—mistreatment of and discrimination against women in the workplace, in their homes, in public, and in private—were seldom considered worthy of putting above the fold.

Following the 2016 election, the #MeToo movement, and the ensuing rise in women's activism, the questions I faced about the importance of women's issues began to fade, replaced by urgent entreaties from all quarters—reporters, colleagues, family members, friends, neighbors, my children's teachers—about how to address the persistent gender inequalities to which so many had finally awakened. In the United States, allegations of harassment and assault that normally would have escaped scrutiny or been disbelieved—or never been lodged in the first instance—suddenly dominated daily headlines and nightly newscasts. People began having open conversations about gender-based violence, discrimination, and power imbalances over dinner tables and around water coolers. And women from all walks of life joined in the movement by speaking out and rising up, claiming their rights and demanding change—fighting not only sexism, misogyny, and gender-based violence, but also racism and xenophobia, economic inequality, environmental ruin, and so much more.

While the recognition of American women's activism grew, however, the US media continued to overlook the concomitant uprisings led by women around the world. As the domestic #MeToo movement dominated US headlines, I hosted a talk at the Council on Foreign Relations to highlight the scourge of gender-based violence around the world, featuring Nobel Peace Prize laureate Nadia Murad, a courageous Iraqi women's rights defender who had survived sexual slavery at the hands of ISIS and later served as a UN ambassador on human trafficking. On the margins, I met up with other activists and scholars, trading stories about the international rise in women's activism we had been tracking in our own work and decrying its absence from the mainstream media, which was failing to capture the birth of a new wave of the global women's movement, of which the US movement was only one part. Determined to share what I'd learned and to analyze the cumulative effect of this activism, I embarked on a journey to the front lines of this global movement—one that culminated in a partnership with my Council colleague Meighan Stone on this book.

Having the opportunity to share these stories has been a privilege—and an inspiration. Never could I have imagined, as a fledgling women's rights lawyer, or in the dark days following my train ride in November 2016, that I would soon have a chance to chronicle a resurgence of the global women's movement, one that promises to be the most far-reaching in history. I could not have known the strength I would personally draw from the persistence displayed by millions of sisters marching online and off around the world. The courage and determination of the women you will read about in these pages offer a lesson in how pain, hardship, and oppression can spur hope, progress, and change. To honor these women, I am more determined than ever to ensure that this progress extends to women everywhere in the world, of every race, ethnicity, class, creed, and country—and I hope their example will inspire many more to enlist in the global fight for gender equality.

—November 2020

Meighan's Story

On September 27, 2018, I huddled with a group of women around a make-shift video stream set up in a hallway at a *New York Times* conference in Brooklyn. We were gathered there for the *Times*'s inaugural summit on gender, power, and policy. But breaking news had stolen our attention: Brett Kavanaugh, President Donald Trump's nominee to the Supreme Court, and Dr. Christine Blasey Ford, the woman who had accused him of assaulting her, were testifying before the Senate Judiciary Committee.

Megan Twohey, the Pulitzer Prize–winning *Times* journalist who had broken the Harvey Weinstein sexual abuse story with Jodi Kantor, sat nearby with her young daughter. Former chief of staff to Michelle Obama Tina Tchen, Katie McGrath, and other leaders of the US-based #TimesUp movement for workplace equity stood side by side with Melinda Gates's advisers, other activists, and former prime ministers. I found a seat in the only place left, on the floor. With my work taking me everywhere from refugee camps to rural health clinics, I've always found the ground as fine a place as any to sit.

The scene was reminiscent of an old photo—people gathered around a storefront black-and-white television, watching, say, a man land on the moon. But this TV event felt commonplace and extraordinary at the same time. Far too many American women have stories to share about sexual assault. Far rarer are stories about a powerful man being publicly held to account.

I sat quietly as Dr. Ford began her testimony, about the day three decades before when she believed, she said, that Kavanaugh "was going to rape me."

I thought of myself as a teenage girl, one who'd been raped and would have no day in court. I thought of how ashamed I felt walking up for altar-call prayers at my evangelical Christian church, asking that God might heal me of what I thought was my fault.

In that hallway, women held each other as Dr. Ford said her most un-shakable memory was the mocking of her male attackers. "Indelible in the hippocampus is the laughter. The uproarious laughter between the two. They're having fun at my expense." The room fell completely silent then, except for the sound you hear when women allow themselves and one another to cry in community, when we know no men are present. That we're safe together.

When I returned to Washington, DC, still ruminating on the out-of-control anger in Kavanaugh's testimony—anger that should have disquali-fied him on grounds of judicial temperament alone—I took myself down to the Supreme Court to protest. There, a trifecta of female senators—Kamala Harris, Mazie Hirono, and Kirsten Gillibrand—delivered speeches and led cheers from the front of the austere building: *Shame! Shame! Not fit!* The crowd, a huge gathering of angry women asking for nothing more than a credible investigation into credible claims, engaged in the kind of call and response that feels so familiar to those of us who attend a certain kind of church, urging the speaker to *Go on, say that. Amen.*

I remembered being a girl in small-town Virginia, hearing adults talk about the nomination of Sandra Day O'Connor: *a woman has no place on the Supreme Court.* Three years later, Geraldine Ferraro would run for vice president, and I'd hear more of the same. *No place.*

I grew up in a family rife with generations of alcoholism, addiction, and abuse. In 2017, while at the Harvard Kennedy School as a fellow, I attended a fancy dinner one night where an attendee beamed with pride as she told me her daughter was doing a spring service trip to help those poor people who live in trailer parks. I breathed deeply and smiled as I told her my grandparents had lived in a trailer park. I'd wanted that woman at Harvard to know, in the gracious way that cuts someone clean off at the knees, that daughters of people like that were in the room, too, sitting right next to her.

If I'm honest, this work probably started for me when I was around seven years old, when I watched my father throw my mother out of our car. As she cried on the ground and her blood crept across her pressed, white dress, I desperately looked out the window for anyone to show up and help. No one did. So I got out of the back seat, shaking, and started shouting for him to stop, barely aware of how small or powerless I was. Quite a few times, the neighbors called the police to come to my house when I was a child, but I noticed they always left without really intervening. I share this in an attempt to dissolve any pretense of a superior "us" studying a lesser "them"—to underscore that these injustices happen here, in America, not just in some foreign place. They are committed by people we know or love, and may even forgive—like my father, whom during the writing of this book I held as he died, praying God's grace over him.

Carrying secrets and trauma, I never expected to amount to much. But through some luck of fate and hard work, I've earned my keep in a succession of jobs I never dreamed of having, have had seats in places I never thought of belonging. All along, the work I've done has always been about changing who has a place in the room. Especially in rooms where real decisions get made—about power, money, freedom, rights—without the presence of those they will ultimately affect.

In 2013, I started working for Nobel Peace Prize laureate Malala Yousafzai, and ultimately served as president of her nonprofit organization, the Malala Fund, which fights for girls' rights to learn and lead without fear. Thirteen years earlier, in the year 2000, world leaders had gathered at the United Nations and revealed their ambitions for girls around the world, declaring how many years of education they thought girls deserved as a human right: six. In 2015 the world's leaders were gathering again, at the UN's Sustainable Development Goals summit, to set a new global goal for girls' education. The consensus going in was that maybe, by the year 2030, we could get to nine years. But at the Malala Fund, we decided to start fighting for a different number: twelve. Twelve years of education for every girl. We met with parliaments and politicians, we released reports, we built the modeling spreadsheets. We ran the numbers, we did the work.

And in the end? We won. One of our greatest moments came when Malala stood up, in the General Assembly on the floor of the UN, to celebrate that we'd helped win the fight for twelve years of education—that we'd lifted global ambitions and signaled the world's belief in girls living in the world's poorest countries by saying this was their human right.

Malala spoke to a room full of the most powerful leaders in the world. But the most important people in the room for me that day were the two girls standing with Malala, the ones we'd fought to make sure were there. The young woman on Malala's right was Salam, whom we'd met while visiting schools in Lebanon. Salam was a Syrian refugee who had to fight for her education every day—not in the removed way we think of when we talk about policy, but in a way that was hard and *personal*. The girl standing on Malala's left was Amina, from Kaduna State in Nigeria, where the terror group Boko Haram has abducted thousands of girls. She and girls like her attended the informal educational programs we were financing at the Malala Fund, under threat of violence every day. They later addressed the press together, from the same stage where the UN secretary-general speaks to the media. To us, it was crucial that people with the power to change lives would have to *listen to these young women* and promise an education to all children, to declare that wars and other forms of violence could not stop them from learning.

After meeting women activists from developing and war-torn countries, in the hallways of too many high-level summits, I knew that the real work happened in their communities, and not at cocktail receptions in safe places. I also knew how often Western women with big checkbooks—who always said how inspiring these women were—sent them back home to threats and threadbare existences without a dime. *Don't let them off so easy as to just inspire them*, I would say to Malala on our many long flights as we talked about strategy. *Make them change.*

Because of my work with Malala, I've had the honor of crossing paths or working with women human rights defenders around the world. Sadly, it's not so large a sisterhood, because the work is hard and heartbreaking. You will lose friends; your family might be imprisoned or threatened in retribution for your work. You will lose your job, and will long for that old sense of simply feeling safe and free when you walk down the street. You may become an exile from your beloved country, or wind up in the hospital recovering from a beating.

Over the years, many women activists have confided in me that they've been physically or sexually assaulted. Raped by family members, subjected to female genital mutilation, sexually assaulted in retaliation for their work or simply for asking for their freedom. Female democracy protestors in Hong Kong alleged that they were sexually assaulted while detained by pro-Chinese government forces. Egyptian women survived horrific sexual assaults for daring to stand for their rights in Tahrir Square during the Arab uprisings. Even Rosa Parks—who, contrary to popular belief, was not just a tired woman on a bus—began her work by investigating the brutal sexual assaults of Black women in the segregated American South, driven by her own experience surviving a 1931 rape attempt by a white male neighbor. It's not surprising to me that these tragic attacks occurred. It is overdue that we tell these stories—and that we stop pushing the violation of women's bodies to the margins of human rights policy and our accounts of historic social change.

It's important to me to emphasize that *Awakening* is not about women around the world being "awakened" to Western feminism, nor is it a book about Western white feminists "teaching" women in other countries about their own liberation. Where we offer suggestions on how donor governments and global organizations can best support these women's work, it's just that: an acknowledgment of the imperative to support them, in the way *they* deem most helpful.

Our goal with *Awakening* was to center the victories of women working locally in their communities, to document the challenges they've overcome, to feature their own words, recorded from interviews and time spent together in their countries. These brave activists—many accidental heroines, all of them women of agency, ready to fight for their rights and humanity no matter how high the cost—don't need saving, period.

Ultimately, I like to think of this as a book about men—or about those in power who seek to block women's progress—being awakened to the fact that women simply won't stand for it anymore. They may be delayed, deferred, even imprisoned and assaulted. But they will keep coming nonetheless. And the sooner you awaken to the fact that half the population will not be silenced or subjugated, the better your nation's future will be.

I'm honored to share the words and stories of the women in these pages, and especially grateful to have written about women from countries like Nigeria, Egypt, Tunisia, and Pakistan, places with rich feminist histories, where women often face seemingly impossible cultural and religious barriers to achieving equality. Perhaps because of my own conservative faith background, I feel some solidarity with women from nations and religious communities that are often misunderstood, due to either lack of knowledge or deliberate discrimination. When people attack Islam's proscriptions for Muslim women, I ask them if they've spent much time in America's churches—like the one where I was told by a pastor in my marriage classes that I had to submit to my husband, because it was God's will. That in entire Christian denominations, women are still not allowed to teach men, or preach from the pulpit at all. When it comes to reforming our communities, the tough truth is, we all have work to do.

I carry these women in my prayers constantly. I think of them all the time, and have many of their photos in my office. They keep me intellectually honest. They keep me working hard. Today, my own faith is best expressed in service, as pronounced by one of my treasured verses from Scripture: "Faith without works is dead." If there is anything I've learned from my work, it's that words in a G7 communiqué, summit agreement, or unenforced law are not worth the pages they're printed on until they measurably impact people's lives. Real change demands a fight, requires constant pressure and vigilance.

I pray that this book will be some small, humble contribution to the global cause of women's dignity and freedom—and that these women's works will be blessed.

—November 2020

Women protest the alleged rape and murder of a twenty-seven-year-old woman in Hyderabad, India, in December 2019. The alleged suspects were later killed in an extrajudicial police killing and were never tried in court. Credit: Reuters/Vinod Babu

INTRODUCTION

In 2006, THE YEAR TWITTER WAS BORN, TARANA BURKE BECAME THE MOTHER OF a movement.

That year, she was working as an activist and camp counselor in Selma, Alabama, when a young girl named Heaven told her she'd been sexually abused. Heaven was so meek and vulnerable, the abuse she recounted so devastating, that Tarana couldn't find the words to comfort her just then. But as the girl walked away, Tarana shuddered. Heaven's story—the shame she'd shared—was excruciatingly familiar to Tarana, who was also a survivor of sexual abuse. In that moment, she quietly admitted to herself: me too.[1]

Thus began Tarana's movement: a campaign to help other Black and brown girls and women, survivors like herself and Heaven, to find both solidarity and justice.[2] Together, these women would see their work grow from a grassroots effort into a momentous initiative with global impact. Together, they would fight to disrupt the systems perpetuating sexual violence worldwide. For good.

A decade later—in the wake of a sweeping *New York Times* investigation detailing allegations of sexual harassment and abuse against the Hollywood mogul Harvey Weinstein—Tarana's campaign, now propelled by the hashtag #MeToo, went viral across the United States, with more than twelve million posts on Facebook in less than twenty-four hours. In two days, nearly half of American Facebook users knew someone who had posted "MeToo."[3]

As the movement spread throughout the United States, so too did exposés about abusive behavior by powerful men across multiple industries, many of whom were forced to resign through grassroots online efforts: The *Today Show* host Matt Lauer. CBS chief executive Les Moonves. The famed architect Richard Meier. Wayne Pacelle, president of the Humane Society.

1

The chef and restaurateur Mario Batali. Peter Martins, artistic director of the New York City Ballet. The political pundit Mark Halperin. Members of Congress on both sides of the aisle. The list went on—and is still growing.[4]

But you know that story.

This book tells the story you don't yet know—one that has unfolded far beyond the United States. In 2017, as the American media focused on sexual harassment and discrimination at home, the #MeToo movement ignited globally, reaching hundreds of millions of people on every continent. This movement—powered by technology and reaching across borders, races, ethnicities, classes, and religions—calls for an end to sexual abuse against people of all genders. It has also awakened the world to the monumental scale of discrimination and violence against women, provoking the most widespread cultural reckoning on women's rights in history.

In many countries, the #MeToo movement is not new. Instead, it has been fueled by years of local activism by courageous women leaders, many of whom have deployed modern communication methods to organize and campaign for change. In other places, #MeToo has inspired women to raise their voices publicly for the first time. And in far too many nations, women who have come forward under the guise of the #MeToo movement have put not only their reputations and livelihoods, but also their lives, on the line.

Women like Khadijah Adamu, a twenty-four-year-old pharmacist and blogger from northern Nigeria. In February 2019, Khadijah decided to share the account of her assault at the hands of a boyfriend who had threatened to kill her. On Twitter, she told her story—and named her attacker. Because she lives in Kano, a city where sexual and domestic abuse laws are rarely enforced, she didn't expect justice, or even support. But three hundred miles away, in Nigeria's capital, Abuja, the entrepreneur and sexual assault survivor Fakhrriyyah Hashim saw Khadijah's tweet. Risking her safety and reputation, she posted in solidarity and coined the hashtag #ArewaMeToo, adding the Hausa word "Arewa," for the northern region. Soon, a groundswell of online and real-time activism began, powered by Khadijah's taboo-defying honesty and Fakhrriyyah's hashtag. Rejecting cultural expectations of silence and shame, women from all over the country joined the movement. "There's been an awakening of people's consciousness," Fakhrriyyah later proclaimed in an interview.[5]

It's a pattern we've seen repeated all over the world. Today, in over one hundred countries, women like Khadijah and Fakhrriyyah are using the #MeToo hashtag as a rallying cry to demand change and fight the violence they face every day—and they are winning.

Awakening travels to the front lines of a networked movement that is fundamentally shifting how women organize to demand equality in some of the most challenging places in the world to be a woman. This book documents the stories of brave women in Africa, Asia, Europe, Latin America, and the Middle East who are raising their voices, creating new models of power, and transforming justice and equity for women. These activists' transnational, digital campaign has accelerated the global women's movement to powerful and disruptive effect, creating the conditions for unprecedented social, economic, and legal progress.

Historically, revolutions have begun when groups discover that their grievances are not individual, but collective and systemic.[6] Women, however, are often excluded from or underrepresented in the very places where that organizing occurs: media, government, universities, businesses. Where women cannot go, they cannot speak; when women cannot gather, they cannot address injustices. To accelerate the movement for power and equality, they needed a place to share stories and amass participants, one that would be safe even in communities that prevented women from speaking or appearing in public.

In short: they needed the internet.

Today, social media has become an alternative public square for women, especially in countries where their physical spaces and activism are constrained by state control, cultural norms, or violence. The Turkish academic Zeynep Tufekci, whose work is focused on the confluence of technology and society, has written about what she calls the "affordances" of the internet and their powerful propulsion of modern networked movements.[7] In the case of #MeToo, the low cost of digital connectivity has increased the speed, scale, and diversity of a movement that is simultaneously transnational and hyperlocalized—creating, in turn, the seeds for a global breakthrough in the fight for women's rights.

Access to electronic communication has accelerated the speed and scale of change across borders, inspiring unprecedented activism for gender equality.

In prior eras of the women's movement, transnational gains were won only after lifetimes of organizing. In the early 1900s, the global fight for women's suffrage was painstakingly slow. International suffrage marches took months or even years of planning by telegram and steamship, and it took a century for women globally to win the right to vote. In the late twentieth century, the campaign to recognize women's rights under a human rights doctrine took decades. International conferences to promote women's rights were held intermittently, only every five years, beginning with the first United Nations World Conference on Women in 1975 and culminating in the historic 1995 Fourth World Conference on Women in Beijing, at which delegates finally enshrined the principle that "women's rights are human rights" into international law.[8]

Today, in contrast, the women's movement employs social media to mobilize millions in a matter of weeks, or even days. The historic Women's March of 2017, the largest coordinated global women's protest in history, was organized digitally on every continent only ten weeks after the contentious US election that elevated the avowed misogynist Donald Trump to the presidency over Hillary Clinton, the first woman to win nomination to that office by a major party. That same year, in less than one month, the #MeToo hashtag was employed over seventy-seven million times on Facebook alone.[9]

Modern communication tools such as email, social media, and smartphones have also diversified the global women's movement, granting purchase to anyone with access to an internet connection. Whereas movement leaders in earlier eras tended to be wealthy and privileged or professional activists, today millions of women of every race, ethnicity, creed, and class have raised their voices online. Even though some parts of the world still lack reliable internet connectivity, and many fewer women than men have access to this technology around the world, the overall growth in online penetration has been dramatic enough to facilitate the engagement of more voices than ever before.[10] This overdue inclusivity has significantly strengthened the global women's movement, amplifying the voices of marginalized and economically disenfranchised women who in eras past were pushed out or ignored.

The democratization of the women's movement has also changed what it means to be a feminist organizer in the #MeToo age—and how power is wielded. Many traditional gatekeepers of "old power"—the media, those educated in rarefied institutions, members of the elite—have been relieved of their duties. In the modern era, digital "foot soldiers" are as important to the movement as establishment leaders. Collective action spurred by internet organizing creates a current that the scholars Jeremy Heimans and Henry Timms describe as "new power," which is participatory and open to all.[11] Under this model, a Tunisian doctoral student like Rania Said studying overseas can help lead an open-source #MeToo campaign and mobilize women in her home country—many of whom she may never meet in person—whose shared activism can outpace efforts by larger, traditional organizations.

The online era of the women's movement has also expanded transnational organizing. Through social media, women around the world have shared near-universal experiences of discrimination and harassment, helping many survivors see that they are far from alone. The undeniable effect of the sheer volume of women coming forward has also showed them the collective power of their voices. The movement's global reach has helped create an inclusive language of shared experience that extends beyond any one community or region. Today, the #MeToo hashtag has been translated into dozens of languages and searched online on Twitter, Facebook, and other platforms in all 193 countries.[12]

At the same time, the internet facilitates a hyperlocalization of the global #MeToo campaign, making the movement much more effective. The context in which women are fighting gender inequality is different in every region of the world, and as the #MeToo movement ignited, local organizers made the campaign entirely their own, highlighting specific cases of harassment or discrimination and defining the legal, economic, or political reforms needed in their own communities.

Awakening investigates how women are pursuing change across cultures, profiling activists and leaders in seven countries: Brazil, China, Egypt, Nigeria, Pakistan, Sweden, and Tunisia. Though our research confirmed the rise of the #MeToo campaign in dozens of other nations, we selected these seven to reflect the proliferation of the movement in places with different ethnicities, religions, populations, and systems of government—from small social democracies to large communist autocracies. While the status of women and strength of the women's movement in these geographically diverse countries vary considerably, together they offer a comprehensive snapshot of the promise and perils of the #MeToo campaign around the world.

Over the course of two years, in cafés and government offices and at conferences and over Zoom, we traveled to the front lines of the #MeToo movement in these seven countries, interviewing women who are organizing in the face of systemic injustice, government repression, and personal threats—all of whom shared how they had harnessed the power of the global #MeToo campaign to promote gender equality locally. Each chapter in this book explores how and why the #MeToo movement has progressed across different regions and reveals collective lessons about how change is sought, fought, and won around the globe.

In Brazil, the #MeToo movement has inspired a new, diverse generation of women to use digital organizing and political power to run for office and resist the rising tide of reactionary populism. In China, where the government brutally represses women's rights activism, the sheer number of people active in the #MeToo movement initially overwhelmed government censors, boosting awareness of gender inequality. In Egypt, #MeToo activists remained resolute even as an authoritarian president alleged that their campaign amounted to terrorism, slander, and "fake news." In northern Nigeria, as #ArewaMeToo took off, Muslim and Christian survivors found common ground and united across religious lines. In Pakistan, women leaders drew upon years of advocating for freedom from violence to fight digitally for legal solutions to sexual harassment and assault. In Sweden, home to some of the most progressive gender equality protections in the world, women across every major industry have still had to organize online to call for an end to persistent discrimination in the workplace, from sexual harassment and pay inequality to women's underrepresentation in leadership positions. And in Tunisia, #EnaZeda activists have shifted from fighting for freedom to crafting and enforcing a legal framework to protect women from assault and harassment.[13]

. . . .

What will this global, digital wave of the women's movement achieve? Media coverage of #MeToo to date has focused on the avalanche of high-profile ousters of men in the highest echelons of politics, culture, and business who were accused publicly of sexual harassment and assault. But the #MeToo movement has wrought more than a wave of resignations—in fact, a fundamental recalibration of the treatment and status of women and girls is underway.[14]

Though #MeToo has become an international rallying cry, the leaders at the forefront of the movement have expanded the agenda far beyond the issue of sexual harassment and abuse. Much as Rosa Parks and civil rights organizers took on the larger cause of racism in 1955 by targeting one specific injustice—segregated buses—today's women's activists are using the momentum created by #MeToo to campaign against entire systems of inequality.

Globally, #MeToo has become much more than a viral moment—and the online conversation has contributed to an equally robust movement offline. Since the #MeToo hashtag went viral, record numbers of women candidates from all backgrounds have sought political office in nearly every major election, in countries as diverse as Afghanistan, India, Iraq, Ireland, Lebanon, Malawi, Sri Lanka, and the United States. In the private sector, women are pushing for workplace protections and better policies on harassment, parental leave, and pay equity.[15]

Legal standards are also rapidly changing. In just two years, courts around the world have handed down sentences that reflect the definitive cultural shifts the #MeToo movement has already wrought—and not just for Harvey Weinstein. In Egypt, South Korea, and Sweden, landmark cases on sexual violence have all resulted in victories for the accusers. The Indian lawyer and activist Vrinda Grover has likened the #MeToo movement to an unstoppable wave, observing that "until now, we have seen consequences only on the women who complained. This time, the consequences are for those who have committed the misconduct."[16]

The digital wave is also inspiring policy reform. In Spain, following digitally organized nationwide protests in 2018 over meager sentences handed down to convicted rapists, the government amended the penal code to make rape convictions easier. In Morocco, dialogue triggered by #MeToo reenergized support for stalled legislation that now prohibits sexual harassment, domestic violence, and forced marriage. And in Japan—a country that previously had no legal prohibition on sexual harassment—an online petition prompted the labor ministry to convene public discussions on harassment in the workplace, which led to passage of a new workplace law.[17]

Progress hasn't happened everywhere. The #MeToo movement has been layered on top of long-standing and evolving fights for women's equality that vary considerably among nations, which in part explains the variation in effects and consequences revealed in this book. Yet even in nations where women haven't yet won legal or legislative victories, the #MeToo movement has disrupted the silence and stigma surrounding sexual assault and harassment in ways that already have shifted the culture—and women's willingness to come forward for redress. In Senegal, for instance, two women in Dakar started the hashtag #Nopiwouma (Wolof for "I will not shut up") to encourage women to speak out about harassment and assault; they received a flood of private messages from women around the country, almost all saying it was the first time they'd spoken about their experiences. The value of being able to come forward and share one's story—even without ultimate accountability for one's perpetrator—has bestowed a new form of power. In some places, the outpouring of personal stories caused not only men, but also women, to reevaluate hardwired cultural predispositions in favor of the accused. The notion that we should "believe women"—meaning, as Tarana Burke has explained, to start from a place in which we do not assume dishonesty or fault when survivors come forward, and to fairly investigate all claims, including those lodged against the powerful—is becoming more widely accepted.[18]

To be sure, the #MeToo movement is not immune from structural and cultural barriers limiting its reach. This book also explores the rising backlash against women's economic, political, and social equality—fueled by online activism, which has proved to be a double-edged sword. The same tools that have aided transnational activism by #MeToo supporters have been employed by forces seeking to silence women's voices and shield perpetrators from consequences. While the internet has in many instances provided a safe space for women to collaborate out of the public eye, it has also reproduced many of the dangers that women face in the real world through its use as a dangerous tool with which to track, target, harass, and defame women who dare to raise their voices. And the rise of a new class of misogynist leaders—including Jair Bolsonaro in Brazil, Rodrigo Duterte in the Philippines, Vladimir Putin in Russia, Recep Tayyip Erdogan in Turkey, and Donald Trump in the United States—emboldened those fighting to preserve the status quo.[19]

Yet, as with other successful movements for social change, this backlash is a sign of progress—a sign that norms are, in fact, changing, rendering those who cling to them even more determined to stem the tide. Despite opposition at the highest levels, the #MeToo movement has achieved unprecedented momentum. Although the story of #MeToo is still unfolding, we believe the "new power" that characterizes the digital wave of the women's movement— its speed and scale, diversity, transnational reach, and hyperlocalization— creates the conditions for historic progress on gender equality.

In the final chapter of this book, we propose an agenda to safeguard the gains that have been made and to ensure that progress continues in the face of a rising backlash. This agenda captures insights from visionary champions for gender equality—from Secretary of State Hillary Clinton and Nobel Peace Prize laureate Malala Yousafzai to the highest-ever ranking African woman in the United Nations, Deputy Secretary-General Amina Mohammed, and the first women heads of state in Chile, Liberia, and Australia. We talk to women leaders from the pinnacle of power to the grassroots, many of them "firsts"— first party leader, first minister of defense, first female US presidential candidate of a major party, first woman to speak out in her community, first woman to argue a precedent-setting legal case. Informed by their experiences, we've developed a framework for action we refer to as the "Five Rs"—redress for survivors, legal reform, increased representation, sufficient resources, and recalibration of global norms—which will ultimately transform laws, economies, and communities around the world.

Lastly, we want to be clear from the start: this book is not about the heroic arrival of white, Western feminism to other countries. In the nations we profile, women have long organized for their own equality, and in many countries the rise in online activism predated the popularization of the #MeToo hashtag.[20] The only heroines in these pages are the women themselves—most, if not all, of whom have paid a tremendous price for their work, bringing great integrity, sacrifice, and creativity to the struggle for equality in their communities. It is from this truth that we approach this book and the women at the center of it with humility. We honor their contributions not just because it's right and overdue, but because all of us who care about gender equality—in whichever country we reside—have work to do and can learn from the fight these leaders have waged.

This vision of sisters working together across nations to fight harassment and discrimination grows stronger every day. And it is exemplified by the fitting coda to the story of Harvey Weinstein, the American man whose crimes helped spark the outrage that ignited the global #MeToo movement. For decades, Weinstein wielded "old power" to successfully silence women into hiding his abuse. By the time of his rape trial in Manhattan, that silence had given way to a global collective of women claiming "new power." On January 10, 2020, more than one hundred women of every race, ethnicity, age, and ability campaigned for justice outside the courthouse where Weinstein was being tried, drawing inspiration from activists far from the US. From Lower Manhattan to the Trump International Hotel and Tower at the south end of Central Park, they joined together for public performances of "Un Violador en tu Camino," or "A Rapist in Your Path," a defiant anthem composed by the Chilean feminist art collective Las Tesis that—like the #MeToo hashtag—had gone viral, spreading from Chile to Colombia to India to Turkey and, ultimately, to the United States.[21]

In New York, surrounded by a scrum of media cameras, the crowd of women chanted, "The rapist is you."

> *Y la culpa no era mía, ni dónde estaba ni cómo vestía*
> *El violador eras tú*
> *El violador eres tú*
> *Son los pacos*
> *los jueces*
> *el Estado*

> *And it's not my fault, not where I was, not how I dressed*
> *And the rapist was you*
> *And the rapist is you*
> *It's the cops*
> *It's the judges*
> *It's the system*

This book is about women fighting that system and winning—around the world.

Whether that victory means being heard online, protesting in the street for the first time, winning an unprecedented legal case, changing a law, or simply surviving a structure stacked against them, the world has awakened to the power of women's voices. We hope you will celebrate these women's victories. We hope you will know their names.

Awakening is a testament to these women's stories, and to the promise of a new model of power. Propelled by technology and driven by millions more women than ever before, the digital wave of the global women's movement has the potential to fundamentally revolutionize gender roles—and transform the world we leave to the next generation.

Street mural of Brazilian politician and human rights activist Marielle Franco, with the slogan Lute Como ("Fight Like Marielle Franco"), by graffiti artist and women's activist Panmela Castro, in Rio de Janeiro, Brazil, 2018. Credit: Rede NAMI

Chapter One

BRAZIL: SOWING SEEDS

#MeuPrimeiroAssedio

You cannot cover up the sun with a sieve.

—Brazilian proverb

In October 2016, when the US presidential contest between Hillary Clinton and Donald Trump dominated headlines in newspapers across the globe, a quieter political revolution was afoot a continent away, in Rio de Janeiro. At its center: an election for Rio city council. Among its candidates: an unknown thirty-seven-year-old political activist named Marielle Franco.[1]

Marielle was an unlikely competitor in a political system ruled by white men. A descendent of African slaves who was born to a family of migrants from the northeast of Brazil, one of its poorest regions, she hailed from Maré, a favela, or slum, in Rio's North Zone.[2] She was raised in poverty, put to work at the age of eleven, became a single mother by nineteen, and labored as an underpaid preschool teacher to support herself and her daughter while pursuing her own education. She also faced discrimination as a Black woman and, when she came out later in life, as a lesbian. But Marielle was driven. Despite her challenging circumstances, she won a scholarship to a private university and vowed to use her education on behalf of the disenfranchised, especially Black favela women with whom she was raised and who remained shackled by discrimination and violence. She made good on her promise, obtaining a master's degree in public policy and becoming a vocal critic of government neglect of the impoverished, advising city council members on the needs of a community often ignored by those in power.

Marielle's unexpected rise left her determined to open doors for others— and she put herself on the line to do so. In 2016, inspired by a rising tide of women's activism online and in the streets decrying discrimination against women, she took the improbable step of seeking election to the male-dominated city council for which she served as a staffer, campaigning for inclusivity in representation under the slogan "I am because we are." Though her campaign was historic, no one expected a Black, lesbian human rights activist from the favelas to win political office in a country controlled by wealthy white men. Brazil had long struggled with racism, a legacy of Portuguese colonizers who, upon arriving in 1500, enslaved indigenous people to help fuel the economy, and then began trafficking in the African slave trade. By 1850, Brazil had an estimated four million African slaves—more than seven times the number in the United States. Brazil was the last country in the Western world to abolish slavery, in 1888, and had notoriously neglected its Afro-Brazilian population ever since, the majority of whom were concentrated in slums on city peripheries, far from the centers of power.[3]

Marielle's race also ran counter to the history of underrepresentation of women in the national and local legislatures of Brazil. Although women made great strides forward in health and educational attainment after the birth of the modern women's movement in the 1970s—ultimately winning equality with men under the Brazilian constitution that was ratified after a series of coups and military dictatorships in 1988, and electing their first female head of state in 2010—they continue to face discrimination and underrepresentation in the economic and political sphere. Today, Brazil ranks only 92nd out of 153 countries on the World Economic Forum's Global Gender Gap index, in part because of the continued dominance of men in positions of power. At the time of Marielle's campaign, elective office was especially elusive for Black women, who comprised nearly a third of the Brazilian population but held only 3 percent of state and federal elected positions.[4] In this context, Marielle's run was improbable; her staff predicted she would earn about seven thousand votes at best, eking out a respectable loss.

Instead, that October, she won nearly fifty thousand votes in a landslide, receiving the fifth-highest vote total of the fifty-one candidates elected and besting more than fifteen hundred others, due in part to outreach to marginalized populations and the overwhelming turnout of women voters. "People used to look at her and say, 'She represents me,'" remembered Anielle Franco, Marielle's sister. "'That's me right there in the public arena.'"[5] Marielle's election was a warning shot, signaling the growing power of women's voices in Brazil and around the world—and threatening those desperate to preserve the status quo.

. . . .

The activism that fueled Marielle's rise was ignited by the Brazilian #MeToo movement, which had begun back in 2013, long before the hashtag campaign was popularized in the United States, and had birthed a season of political activism known as the Women's Spring.[6] As in other countries, this new wave began online—sparked, in this case, by a twenty-eight-year-old journalist in São Paulo named Juliana de Faria.

Juliana had faced sexual harassment throughout her life, in childhood and in the workplace. But she could not persuade the newspapers or women's magazines for which she wrote to publish stories on the topic. The editors—almost all white men—insisted that "women don't want to read about these issues," she recalled during an interview in a bustling coworking space in downtown São Paulo.[7]

Juliana disagreed. Like so many other women around the world, her experiences with sexual harassment and violence had shaped her life—what she wore, where she went, with whom she traveled and worked—and she knew the same was true for others in whom she confided. The first time she was harassed on the street by a man, walking home from a bakery, she was only eleven years old. To this day, she said, she can still feel the humiliation and distress. "He said things to me that you could never print in the paper," she said, averting her eyes. "I was too young to fully understand what had happened, but I felt violated and I started to cry." Upon seeing her tears, an older lady consoled her, but then laughed after learning what had happened. "Oh, dear, don't be silly," Juliana recalled her elder saying. "You should take it as a compliment." Juliana understood then that she was expected to accept this behavior—from this man, from any man. She didn't dare tell her family, for fear of condemnation.

Across Latin America, discrimination, harassment, and violence against women are endemic to machismo culture, and Brazilian women are particularly at risk: they face the highest incidence of femicide—the killing of a woman because of her gender—in the region, and one of the largest rates in the world. Legislators in Brasília only recently passed legislation, in 2006, recognizing all forms of violence against women as criminal, establishing special domestic violence courts, and opening shelters for abused women. The law was named for Maria da Penha, who was paralyzed after being shot by her husband in the 1980s and campaigned for twenty years for stronger legal protections.[8] Despite the law, the cultural acceptance of discrimination against women has persisted, leaving women without recourse and often blamed for the violence and harassment they face.

Juliana became determined to challenge these norms, especially after reports began circulating on the internet in 2013 that a famous female TV presenter had been groped by a powerful director. Although the incident made the news, it was covered as a humorous story. "Lots of men were defending the guy," Juliana recalled. They argued that "she was asking for it, because of what she was wearing—because she is the kind of woman you could do that to." Those supporting the groper included not only harassers but also men Juliana respected professionally, who had wives and sisters and daughters but nevertheless defended this man. Juliana concluded that these men were not malicious—after all, she knew many of them—but instead simply didn't appreciate how millions of women experienced such behavior. "They are not monsters," she insisted. "They are the men of our society. We work with them, we are raised by them, we are friends with them." In the face of continued rejection each time she tried to pitch an article on harassment, she resolved to find a different way to send a message to these men.

Like so many of her activist peers, Juliana eventually turned to the internet, founding a website and creating a hashtag—#ChegadeFiuFiu, or "No More Catcalling"—that quickly went viral on Facebook and Twitter.[9] Recognizing that attempts to address sexual abuse in academic and legal circles hadn't received traction, Juliana kept her campaign relatable to young people, at first even eschewing the word "harassment": "I thought the word was too heavy for the moment," she recalled. Instead, she used humorous graphics, illustrations, and irreverent posts. She remembered being pleased when the campaign account she'd created reached one hundred followers.

Then her hashtag began to spread. Thousands of women started posting from all across Brazil, sharing stories about their daily experiences. "The more we published, the more they would write us," Juliana said. "They really wanted to talk about it—almost as if sharing their story would help them take power over what had happened." She soon became overwhelmed by the women's devastating accounts and enlisted the help of two colleagues to sift through them. At first the deluge shocked her, but she quickly recognized that the validation these posts afforded inspired even more to share. "It made me feel like I was in the right place, like I wasn't crazy, or the only one who hated it," she recalled. The volume of stories posted online started to be reported on by the same publications that had refused to publish Juliana's stories on harassment just weeks before.

The response was striking—and so was the backlash. "We received lots of criticism," Juliana said. "Rape threats. Thousands of messages. Horrible things said about me and my colleagues." Some critics took umbrage at the characterization of men's behavior as harassment, arguing that many women enjoyed catcalls. "You may not like it, but there are a lot of women who do," several wrote. "Women want it to feel good, to feel empowered." In response, Juliana and her team decided to survey women about their experiences with harassing behavior. The vast majority reported that they did not like it and would adjust their clothing or travel choices—not taking a bus or walking alone at night, for example—to avoid it. The numbers were impossible for the mainstream media to ignore: a staggering 98 percent of respondents had experienced either sexual harassment or assault.[10]

Notwithstanding the data, some disputed that the problem was as widespread as women reported, claiming that harassment happened only in certain neighborhoods or communities. To help demonstrate the pervasiveness of the abuse, Juliana and her colleagues used visualization technology to create a crowdsourced map of the location of those being harassed, modeled after a similar website launched by Hollaback!, an advocacy organization based in New York City whose work had been profiled at South by Southwest, a media conference that garners international news coverage.[11] With this tool, women experiencing harassment could anonymously pin their location on the map to report it; as a result, Brazilians who thought that harassment was not an issue at their workplace, on their street, or in their university could see the problem in real time. Data and information technology were critical to these efforts. "With the internet and social media, I could have my own platform without filters," Juliana recalled. "I understand that not everyone is online or has the same access to the internet—but a lot of people do." Online activism even spilled into the streets. Women in the south of Brazil began printing and posting stories of harassment on street poles, so those without internet access could read them.

The #ChegadeFiuFiu campaign also prompted recognition of the link between women's concerns about violence and their underrepresentation in politics.[12] Women's activism on a host of issues was rising both online and off—including in the political arena, where the exclusion of women correlated with the failure of government leaders to take women's experiences with discrimination and violence seriously. "In the end, it became a conversation about women's mobility," Juliana said. "With street harassment, men think that the public space is theirs. And we don't have enough representation in public policy to change it."

This growing chorus hit a crescendo two years later, in October 2015, when another cultural moment captured national interest. The television show *MasterChef Junior*, a popular children's cooking competition, featured a twelve-year-old contestant named Valentina Schulz who attracted widespread attention that quickly turned sexual, despite her young age. Thousands of men began posting graphic comments online about the middle schooler, shocking the program's many followers. "If it's consensual, is it pedophilia?" one asked. "Let me keep quiet to not be jailed," another wrote. Like many others, Juliana was sickened at the pedophiliac fantasizing about this young girl, which echoed her first experience with sexual harassment, at the age of eleven. So she decided to create a new hashtag—#MeuPrimeiroAssedio, or "My First Harassment"—and invited others to share stories of their first encounters with sexually abusive behavior.[13]

The response was a tsunami, equivalent in size to the outpouring by millions around the world who would go on to tweet #MeToo just two years later. In 2015, #MeuPrimeiroAssedio was searched eleven million times on Google; it became the fifth-most-searched phrase on the platform in Brazil that year. Women bravely shared stories of their initiation into a culture of sexual harassment and violence, reporting abuse that began as young as age six. The Portuguese hashtag soon traveled across Latin America under a Spanish translation, #MiPrimerAcoso, reaching countries from Chile to Mexico, and eventually spreading to Western Europe and Southeast Asia.

Industry-specific campaigns began as well, with women detailing misogyny in the workplace under #MeuAmigoSecreto ("My Anonymous Friend") and in the classroom under #MeuQueridoProfessor ("My Dear Teacher"). The #ChegadeFiuFiu ("No More Catcalling") hashtag launched two years before had laid the groundwork for this breakthrough moment. The viral spread of #MeuPrimeiroAssedio also reflected the proliferation of women's online activism across the region, where the hashtag #NiUnaMenos, or "Not One Less"—a campaign against femicide originating in Argentina, following the murder of a pregnant fourteen-year-old at the hands of her boyfriend—had also caught fire.[14]

For Juliana, the avalanche of #MeuPrimeiroAssedio posts was electrifying, but also crushing. While it was incredibly validating to see hundreds of thousands of women raising their voices, the stories they told were harrowing. Juliana and the two colleagues she had recruited mined the stories for data, determining that the average Brazilian woman had experienced sexual harassment for the first time between the ages of nine and ten years old. They also found empirical evidence that these abuses usually occurred close to home.[15] "What we learned from this is that we were never safe anywhere," she said in our interview. "It wasn't just the street: we were also being harassed, or violated, or even raped in our houses." Absorbing so many personal stories of abuse was gut-wrenching. "People I know—my friends, my aunts—started telling me about violent experiences they had," Juliana recalled, her throat catching. "It was overwhelming."

For Brazilian feminist leaders, the #MeuPrimeiroAssedio campaign was a breakthrough not only because of the number of people it reached, but also because of the new populations it brought into the movement. Antonia Pellegrino, a highly educated, Rio-based political activist who blogged at the popular newspaper *Folha de São Paulo*, had been working to diversify the women's movement and elevate in the political discourse the voices of Brazilian women who were too often overlooked—women from the favelas like Marielle Franco, who were targeted not only because of their gender, but also for their race, religion, or socioeconomic status. "Everyone has a story to tell," Antonia said in an interview in her breezy apartment overlooking Guanabara Bay near Copacabana Beach.[16] "Including me. Being a woman in Brazil is being a victim of violence." But, she recognized, her experience as a privileged white woman paled in comparison with the over-lapping discrimination faced by women of color and those at the bottom of the economic ladder. "If you are a Black woman, a poor woman, you likely have been through more violence than I have," she said. With social media as a medium of communication, without censors or filters, these voices were finally beginning to break through.

As with the #ChegadeFiuFiu campaign, online activism sparked through #MeuPrimeiroAssedio quickly translated into calls for greater rights and representation for women in the political sphere. Only a few days after #MeuPrimeiroAssedio went viral, women's activists caught wind of the pend-ing introduction of a bill to circumscribe women's right to abortion in Brazil, which was already restricted to instances of rape, life endangerment, or fetal deformity. The new legislation—proposed by Eduardo Cunha, an evangelical Christian and powerful leader of the federal House chamber, and an antago-nist of President Dilma Rousseff, Brazil's first female president—would have limited reproductive rights even for rape survivors and criminalized a form of contraception known as the morning-after pill. Within a week, thousands of women who'd been activated through the #MeuPrimeiroAssedio network started organizing under the hashtag #MulheresContraCunha ("Women Against Cunha") to protest this attack on their rights.[17] Soon, online activism was converted into public protest aimed at defeating the bill, with women marching in cities across the country. "We already had a huge debate about harassment on the internet," Antonia Pellegrino recalled. "So we were ready to go to the streets." The spread of women's voices from the internet to the public sphere was "an awakening—more to women than men," she said, em-phasizing women's growing recognition of their collective strength. "But it was an awakening for some men, too."

The media, which had previously prohibited journalists like Juliana de Faria from writing about these issues, began covering them extensively. But the attention, though welcome, was still being filtered through the voices of the white men who dominated the media landscape. "It was funny," Manoela Miklos, an academic and nongovernmental organization (NGO) activist who collaborated with Antonia and Marielle, said during an inter-view over coffee in a São Paulo café, chuckling. "All the white men would say in their columns, 'Women are trying to say something. We should hear them.' And yet, how can they, if everyone is reading only what men have to say?"[18] When, she wondered, would the moment come that women would get to speak for themselves? She and Antonia devised an answer: Brazilian women ought to do more than merely protest in the streets. They needed to occupy the entire narrative.

Although achieving gender parity in journalism was a long-term proposition, Antonia, Manoela, and others began employing technology to take action in the short term. They quickly assembled a campaign over Facebook requesting that every male columnist in the four biggest newspapers in Brazil, as well as the most popular male bloggers, invite women to write in their places. "As privileged women, we had access to many of the men who had columns," Antonia said. She and Manoela capitalized on those connections to ensure that a diverse group of women could have their voices heard. Some editors questioned the need for a media occupation, but many of the male columnists readily agreed to cede their platforms. Antonia remembered calling one friend on a Saturday evening to tell him she wanted to occupy his Monday column. "OK, great!" he replied. "I'm going to the beach." Other male columnists affirmatively took the cause on themselves, disturbed by the stories women were sharing online and in the streets.

"We wrote to the author of the most-read blog in Brazil, which, naturally, is about soccer," Manoela said. "He wrote us back during a championship game and said, 'OK, I got it. You'll see.'" He ended up publishing a piece immediately after the game, written by his daughter, who had posted a few weeks earlier about her first experience with harassment, an encounter she had never told him about. Manoela was stunned, knowing that millions of men would log on after a championship match to read his postgame analysis and instead find his daughter's heartfelt post about machismo and abuse. "I think I cried the whole day just reading that," she recalled. The media occupation, which crossed several platforms, went on for weeks. "It was huge," Manoela said. "It was bigger than anything we ever would have expected."

As readership for stories on women's activism grew, so too did media interest in publishing more women's voices. *Folha de São Paulo*, the country's biggest newspaper, approached Antonia and Manoela about writing a blog for the paper's website. The women said yes, but on one condition: they would curate the blog, which would feature writing from a diverse group of women around the country, rather than write it themselves. "We recognized our white privilege," Antonia said. "And we wanted to have a platform that could open voices, so that women from the favela could publish as well." Antonia and her colleagues began soliciting pieces for the blog, which ran for the next three years, shaping the national debate and spotlighting new perspectives too often excluded from the popular dialogue. "We had a mass of powerful women writing about issues that were very important," Antonia said. "Black women, favela women—women like Marielle Franco, who published three pieces with us." Once again, technology was critical to introducing new voices to different audiences. "It was how we invited other women in," Manoela reported. "It's the way to intersectionality."

As people from a range of backgrounds—Afro-Brazilians, indigenous women, favela women—entered the public debate, so too did their concerns about discrimination and violence, which mobilized even more to speak out. The shift was exemplified in 2016 by the explosive reaction to a graphic video posted online. The video showed the brutal gang rape of a sixteen-year-old girl by more than thirty men in a Rio de Janeiro favela—an assault that left the girl exposed, bloodied, and unconscious. Brazil's culture of victim blaming was so strong that the girl, who spoke out anonymously on a prime-time television show, was initially subjected to a wave of misogynist backlash. She received thousands of death threats online. She was blamed by people who said she was responsible for the crime because she was inebriated or wearing a short skirt. But unlike in years past, this wave was soon overwhelmed by a deluge of women's outrage. Women organized simultaneous demonstrations in cities around Brazil to protest violence against women and rape culture. Organizers campaigned under the hashtag #MexeuComUmaMexeuComTodas— "Mess with One, Mess with All of Us"—suggesting that women from a range of backgrounds would no longer tolerate being blamed for abuses committed against them, regardless of where the crime took place or who was victimized.[19] The response to the campaign rivaled the attention garnered by #MyFirstHarassment.

By the time the #MeToo campaign began sweeping the globe, the Brazilian national dialogue had already been engulfed by a vigorous debate about violence and abuse committed by men, and the legal and political rights of women. But while this debate predated #MeToo, it was also shaped by it.

"When that happened, it was so important for us," Antonia recalled. "Because it showed Brazil: 'See? Across the world, this is not normal anymore.'" The validation of the global community was vital to the Brazilian women who had faced backlash while leading the charge online, in the streets, and in politics. "We already had this boiling bubble. We had all of these debates happening," Antonia said. "But #MeToo was kind of the first time I think we saw our power. It inspired us—and it was a turning point."

. . . .

It was in the context of this unprecedented surge in women's activism in Brazil that Marielle Franco rose to elected office, as advocates who had focused on occupying the #MeToo media narrative increasingly turned their attention to occupying political power. The growing recognition of the injustices women faced—especially women subject to multiple forms of discrimination—"catapulted women into the electoral arena," said Dr. Kristin Wylie, a professor at James Madison University and an expert on Brazilian politics.[20] "And it fueled Black women especially—in part because the costs of not running had gotten too high." The power of women's rage was being channeled to gain power in predominantly male spaces, including state and local parliaments.

At the height of the online and street protests, a faction of educated Black women who had benefited from a generation of affirmative action policies in public and federal schools began to organize. In late 2015, activists planned a march in Brasília, the nation's capital, gathering more than ten thousand Black women from across the country to highlight the particular challenges facing this population: not only alarming rates of discrimination, harassment, and violence, but also concerns about housing, public safety, and access to government services. Women took first to the streets, then to the campaign trail. In addition to Marielle Franco in Rio, a handful of other Black activists became candidates in 2016 local and state campaigns, including Talíria Petrone of Niterói and Áurea Carolina in Minas Gerais, both regions of southeastern Brazil. Many of these women led marches in states and cities before deciding to run.[21] Although Black women had sought elected office before, the difference this time was that these candidacies—fueled by online activism—were finally gaining mass appeal, as evidenced by both public opinion and the number of votes won.

The 2016 campaign was also fueled by Brazilian women who were drawn to the polls to express outrage over the recent impeachment of the country's first female president, Dilma Rousseff, which exposed a growing backlash against women's advancement. President Rousseff was ostensibly voted out of office for using public bank funds to finance government social programs. But many male politicians had done this in the past without incident. Feminists, even those who had opposed some of Rousseff's policies, united against her sudden expulsion. Thousands took to the streets in protest, and new groups like Mulheres Pela Democracia (Women for Democracy) appeared overnight. They pointed out the hypocrisy behind Rousseff being pilloried for corruption when more than half the members of the Brazilian legislature—and the members of the impeachment commission itself—were also under investigation. Her impeachment was largely seen as a political attack with gendered overtones. "The feminist movement was showing its capacity for resistance and mobilization," the sociologist Maria Betania Ávila wrote of the protests.[22] She called the outcry over Rousseff's ouster "a confrontation with the patriarchy."

Even with this surge in women's political activism, when Marielle Franco won her city council seat in a landslide, it was a shock. "Before 2016, it was impossible to think of someone like Marielle in a position of power," said Dani Monteiro, who at the time was Marielle's community relations organizer. "The struggles of a young Black woman like her, like me—they start when you step out of the house. Harassment. Urban violence. Mobility. Even public bathrooms." Marielle's triumph was not only being elected but doing so while championing an agenda for favela women, tackling issues that had long been excluded from political discourse. Upon assuming office, she denounced gender-based violence and police brutality in urban slums, defended reproductive rights, fought corruption and racism, and demanded better conditions for the poor.[23] She also encouraged other women to follow in her footsteps, becoming a symbol to young women who marveled at her rise. "She was an inspiration," explained Dani, who later ran for office because of Marielle's example. "Suddenly you're no longer invisible in a space where we had always been invisible."

Marielle's drive to fight for change was part of her DNA. "She was always a leader for everything in our family," Anielle Franco, Marielle's younger sister, said during our interview, which took place on the margins of a business convention in downtown São Paulo. "I remember that if the lights cut off for some reason, Marielle would go and try to get candlelight for us, so we could keep studying." Marielle had long been determined to use any power she could amass to benefit those with whom she was raised. "Even when we were growing up, she would look at me and say, 'We're going to change this place,'" Anielle recalled with a smile. "She would never be quiet. She stood up for us in so many ways." Her family didn't expect Marielle to be elected. But once she was, they recognized her achievement as a transformative moment for the entire community. "People started looking at her and said, 'Wow, if she can do it, maybe I can do it as well.'"

Marielle decided that pulling women up the ladder along with her required more than advocating for strong public policies through her platform. It meant throwing open the doors of democracy to more women like herself. "When Marielle was elected, she made an open invitation to a group of Black women activists, creating a lab for open democracy, participatory law projects, and training for those who wanted to seek political office themselves," explained Ana Carolina Lourenço, a dynamic young Black woman who had volunteered for Marielle's campaign. The network began to discuss how Black women could amplify their power in the 2018 elections. This was the genesis of Black Women Decide, a campaign "to show that we are the biggest demographic group in Brazil, and that the electoral process could be decided by Black women," said Ana Carolina, who went on to lead the effort. She and her partners organized a lecture series to encourage members of other underrepresented groups to run for office and seize political power. They planned to complement those efforts with an online campaign, propelled by the surge in internet activism, to build a more open environment for Black women in politics.

But on the afternoon of March 14, 2018—just over a year after Marielle had assumed office—tragedy struck. That day, Ana Carolina and her cofounders formally launched the Black Women Decide campaign.[24] After giving a presentation to the group's sponsors, Ana Carolina traveled to Santiago, Chile, for a speaking engagement, while her cofounders hosted a celebratory event with Marielle, called Young Black Women Moving Power Structures, at the House of Black Women in the Lapa neighborhood of downtown Rio de Janeiro. Marielle delivered a fiery speech urging Afro-Brazilian women to join her in the political arena. "There were over fifty women there," said Dani Monteiro, Marielle's community relations organizer. Marielle was pleased, but implored her staff to recruit even more, saying the time had come for Black women to rise together. "She ended the event by patting us on the shoulder and insisting, 'Don't rest on your laurels,'" Dani recalled. "'Don't think that just because you did a good job today there won't be more work tomorrow.'"

Marielle and her adviser, Fernanda Chaves, piled into her white Chevrolet with her driver, Anderson Gomes, to head home. As they approached northern Rio, another car pulled up next to their vehicle, and an assassin opened fire.[25] The gunman unleashed thirteen rounds from a submachine gun—instantly killing Marielle, who suffered four shots to her head, as well as her driver. Fernanda, who survived, went into hiding in Europe shortly thereafter.

Anielle, Marielle's sister, was at home with Marielle's daughter and their mother, who was ironing clothes, when the phone started ringing off the hook. "One of my friends said it was on the news that they had killed her," Anielle said. "So I told my family." She paused and looked down. "I thought for a second I would lose my mom and my niece in the same day. Because they just fell on the ground."

Anielle rushed to the murder site to see her sister, but the authorities had already arrived and wouldn't let her near. "The last image I have of my sister was her hand hanging out of the car and the blood dripping," Anielle recalled in a quiet voice. "But I couldn't get close to her." She was allowed only to retrieve Marielle's bags from the floor of the car, and her ring and glasses. At home, Anielle confirmed for her family that the news was true. "I didn't cry that day," she said. "Or the next day. Because I saw my mom, my niece, my daddy so devastated that I didn't have the courage to cry in front of them." Anielle cast her eyes upward. "I tried to stay strong. Like she would have been."

Marielle's family and friends were traumatized and devastated. "I was in shock for at least ten minutes," recalled Dani, Marielle's staffer, who had accompanied Marielle to her final event only minutes before the attack. "I lost track of time. I would keep on remembering her asking me to be at the office tomorrow. How can I be if she won't be there? She was always there. She always complained for everybody else to be there." Dani paused and gazed out her office window. "But she wasn't there. She was never there again."

Marielle's brazen assassination was meant to send a message. Although the crime remains unsolved as of this writing, investigators suspect that the shooters were militia members linked to right-wing political leaders who opposed her platform. Her killing was intended to silence her—and other progressive women assuming political power and demanding reform across Brazil. "Marielle represented a threat to the status quo," said Renata da Silva Souza, her former chief of staff. "They wanted us to feel intimidated, to stay away from politics—to understand our role."[26]

To those close to Marielle, what happened next was even more unexpected than her election, or even her assassination: her killing had the opposite of its intended effect. Word of her murder spread quickly over the internet, her story telegraphed to those far outside the reach of Rio's municipal lines. Rather than being silenced, Marielle's voice was suddenly louder than ever. Thousands gathered in the streets across Brazil to protest her killing and mourn her death.[27] Anielle still marvels at the reaction. "I've never seen so many people in my life," she recalled.

Thanks to the internet, stories of Marielle's courageous advocacy also traveled far beyond Brazil's shores, reaching prominent activists and leaders around the world. "Viola Davis and Spike Lee called!" Anielle exclaimed. "Angela Davis called me to have dinner at her house. A square was named after Marielle in France." Anielle smiled. "We always saw Marielle's strength, her power. But we could never imagine that she would go global."

Back in Santiago, Ana Carolina, the founder of Black Women Decide, struggled to take action while in mourning. "None of us slept the night of Marielle's murder," she said. "I didn't sleep for days." But she quickly started to organize protests with like-minded sympathizers in Chile, where women and student activists were already fighting violence against women under the hashtag #NiUnaMenos, or "Not One Less." "We had just launched our website for Black Women Decide, and within twenty-four hours, we decided to press forward—to show that four shots were not going to stop the Black women who constitute more than 27 percent of Brazil." Ana Carolina's advocacy even reached the leaders of the US-based Black Lives Matter movement, who tweeted Marielle's name under their #SayHerName hashtag honoring Black victims of violence, fueling even more international interest.[28] Suddenly the message of Black Women Decide was everywhere. "This idea that the underrepresentation of women in Brazil had a connection to violence and harassment," Ana Carolina said, "was clearer than ever with what happened to Marielle."

In the weeks that followed, Ana Carolina and her colleagues continued to grieve—and organize. In April, in honor of Marielle, Black Women Decide launched a group to support political education for Black women in Rio and São Paulo. "The first meetings were pretty much therapeutic," Ana Carolina recalled. But one by one, many of Marielle's former staffers and associates were persuaded to step up and run in the 2018 election, to send a message to her assassins: they wouldn't back down. "Our movement was about the quality of democracy," Ana Carolina said. "And the best solution to Marielle's murder was to amplify the number of votes and support for Black women in politics in Brazil."

In the wake of Marielle's death, a wave of Black women decided the best way to honor her legacy was to run for office themselves. Dani Monteiro, Marielle's community organizer, had been contemplating a run for city council before the assassination, but afterward, "it was as if I had to make the decision again," she recalled. "Before, it was a chance for expansion. But now it had become a necessity. I couldn't back off, because if I did that, it would mean that we lost Mari and then retreated." Renata da Silva Souza, Marielle's former chief of staff, helped gather hundreds of women with the potential to become candidates—and then decided to become one herself, running for council over the strong objections of her loved ones. "Of course, everyone in my family was against it," she said. "My mother used to think of Marielle as another daughter, and she feared for my life. But I had to take that decision. We couldn't step back after facing such huge violence." Tainá de Paula, another candidate for city council who aspired to become the first female mayor of Rio de Janeiro, agreed. "The moment that we lost Marielle, we lost everything," she said in an interview, her eyes welling up.[29] "And we lost our fear as well."

The 2018 election turned out to be historic, shepherding a record number of Black women into political office, including Renata da Silva Souza—who was elected as a state councilor with a record 63,937 votes, the most for any candidate among Rio's left-wing parties—and Dani Monteiro, who was raised in the favelas and was elected state councilor at the age of twenty-seven. The activist Talíria Petrone, a close friend of Marielle, was elected to the national legislature in the House chamber. That year, the proportion of women in Brazil's parliament jumped from 10 to 15 percent—a national record.[30] "We were like hydras," Dani said. "When a head is cut off, three others appear in its place."

But although the 2018 election was momentous for the millions of women who in recent years had marched, protested, and tweeted to demand their rights, it also galvanized the forces leading the backlash against Marielle and her mission. Voters came out in droves, installing as president Jair Bolsonaro, a Donald Trump doppelgänger who rode a wave of racist, misogynist populism to the top of Brazil's political system. Bolsonaro had previously threatened violence against gay people and blamed working women for a supposed rise in homosexuality; he had also publicly called women ignorant, and told one female congresswoman that she was too ugly to rape. Bolsonaro's election gave credibility to the surge of antiwoman, antigay, antiminority sentiments growing on the Brazilian right—the very forces that killed Marielle and threatened to eradicate the social, political, and legal gains that so many Brazilian women had fought for and won. In 2018, a record number of women had finally come into power—but they faced a conservative groundswell.[31]

Today, under the Bolsonaro administration, with women's rights under constant attack, female officeholders in Brazil understand that their assumption of political power is more important than ever before. "Our greatest risk today is institutional rupture and the degradation of democracy," said Jandira Feghali, one of the longest-serving women in the Brazilian parliament and an author of the Maria da Penha legislation outlawing violence against women.[32] She now criticizes its underenforcement. "When you weaken democracy, the first ones to suffer are women and vulnerable populations." But even in the face of Bolsonaro's assault on women's rights, gay rights, and the rights of minorities and indigenous people, the women elected in a wave after Marielle are determined to press forward. "Our plan is to occupy power so that we can subvert power," Renata da Silva Souza said from her office in the Rio municipal chamber. "We want real changes that will promote social equality with respect to gender, race, and class. To repossess power for women—for the least favored populations."

Though Anielle—who recently established the Marielle Franco Institute to carry on the work for which her sister gave her life—still grieves, she takes solace in the continued activism that Marielle helped ignite, even as the Brazilian government retreats from the issues she championed. "I think her death woke up the people that were quiet," she said in an interview before delivering a talk in São Paulo. "I'm one example. I was never on the mic before. Now I'm about to give a speech to a convention of businessmen. And so many other women got elected, or now want to get into politics, because of her." Renata, now a powerful legislator in her own right, agreed, while acknowledging the challenges her agenda faces under a right-wing populist government. "Sometimes I think Marielle's murder had a collateral stronger, bigger effect than if she were here still talking to us today," she said. "It was as if a tectonic plate moved and shook people to do something. So many women today, who were not necessarily in political parties, they understand that they have to do something from where they are. And having so many of us mobilize to engage in politics is the exact opposite of what they were aiming for." Renata smiled. "They thought they killed Marielle by burying her, but they planted a seed."

Perhaps that is the greatest legacy Marielle left behind: not only inspiring a diverse wave of women to run and win, but also motivating legions of others—including those who were disenfranchised, poor, Black, or trapped in dilapidated favelas—to make their voices heard, both online and at the voting booth. Marielle not only spoke for these women; she was one of them. "She was different," Anielle said. "Even though I miss her, I understand that she had to do it. She was person to person—body to body. She wouldn't ever send her assistant. She always said, 'I'm going in with you.'" Marielle's insistence on dignity and safety for women from all walks of life inspired her legions of supporters. "It was the women who clean houses, the waitress, the teacher, the custodian—those were the women in front of our house, saying, 'I'm so happy, because now we have someone who looks like me,'" Anielle said. "Whoever killed her realized that."

These days, Brazilian women's rights advocates describe the political situation under Bolsonaro as bleak and seek greater support for their work from international leaders and donors. While Marielle inspired several of those closest to her to rise above their fears and run for office, many others who previously spoke out online or took to the streets remain afraid. "We're a country that is killing its human rights defenders," Manoela Miklos, who organized the #MeToo media occupation, said about Marielle's death. "Everybody always got threats, especially online. But when Mari was killed, the stakes became concrete. Should we have complained so much? Should we have put her out there? What costs are we willing to take?" Shortly after Marielle's death, Manoela left Rio, moving back to São Paulo to pursue a PhD. "I couldn't face it for a while," she said. "It made me second-guess everything."

But others take solace in the dramatic expansion of the women's movement during Marielle's life, and are convinced that progress cannot be reversed, even in the midst of a difficult political season. Dani Monteiro, now a young state legislator, reflected on how technology had changed Brazilian feminism. "It's why movements like #MeToo are so powerful," she said in an interview in her office in Rio's municipal building. "When you join a Facebook group with women who talk about the harassment and violence they went through, you will find rich women, poor women, white women, Black women, married women, divorced women, single women, women who had an abortion, women who would never have an abortion. In short: women." She leaned forward, placing her hands on her desk. "The internet has the power of letting you read that woman's story. And even if you notice there is a social class difference, you can see the gender oppression is the same." This recognition, she believes, cannot be undone and will only continue to grow.

Even Manoela, who is still grappling with Marielle's death, sees that the legacy she left behind is larger than her loss. "Marielle put a public face to an awareness for women from all kinds of backgrounds about what it means to be a feminist—and about the priorities for the women's movement," she said. "Marielle became an idea, an icon for all the things that she stood for. She gave her cause a new scale when she was alive. And sadly—but also, I think she would be proud—she gave it a global scale after she died. And that is something that makes me feel a little bit confident that her legacy will be bigger than any of us."

Dani also believes that the reforms Marielle and so many others fought for have already changed the future, even in the face of a challenging present, because of the numerous young women who have risen to power in her wake—herself included. "Young people are growing up with access to information and rights that no other generation has had before," she said. "Think of what the #MeToo movement has brought. We can now hear five-year-old girls saying, 'Don't touch my body. Only if I consent.' I think we now have a foundation to grow a lot more, to sow a lot more. This is the generation. They are the ones planting the future."

After the phrase "MeToo" was banned by the Chinese government, women replaced the characters for #MeToo with homophones and images, using an emoji version made up of pictures of a bowl of rice (pronounced "mi") and a bunny ("tu"). March 2018. Courtesy of CNN.

Chapter Two

CHINA: SMALL FIRES

#我也是
#米兔

A single spark can start a prairie fire.

—Mao Tse-tung

In 2004, a young computer science student in her twenties named Luo Xixi was pursuing her PhD at Beihang University in Beijing, writing her thesis under the renowned professor Chen Xiaowu, a forty-five-year-old academic and leader of the China Computer Federation. Luo felt lucky to be in a prestigious program and to have a prominent scholar like Chen as her adviser. In a country like China, where university professors command the highest level of esteem, it is hard to exaggerate the power of one's supervisor; respect for authority is critical to a student's success. One day, Chen pulled Luo aside to request that she care for his sister's houseplants while she was away. She was honored by the trust her professor placed in her. He offered to drive her to his sister's apartment off campus. She declined. But Chen insisted.[1]

When they arrived at the apartment, Chen locked the door behind them. Luo froze. "I will always remember this detail," Luo emphasized in an interview with us, "because that was the moment I started to feel afraid." Soon, he lunged at her. He declared that his wife was too conservative in the bedroom and forced himself on Luo over her protestations. He relented only once she began crying, saying she was a virgin. When he stopped, he warned Luo not to tell anyone what had happened.

For the next thirteen years, she didn't—except to her parents. They, like Chen, asked her to pretend that nothing had happened. "Their response was: you worked so hard to get into this PhD program, so you should stay quiet because your career and your future is more important," she recalled, noting that they offered this advice out of care and concern for her. Luo didn't want to lose her chance to earn her PhD and become the respected academic she dreamed of being. So she complied. "What I didn't expect," she said, her voice cracking, "is that my supervisor would become mean—always making my work difficult, giving me trouble, and making me cry." She paused. "I realized I made a mistake." Her supervisor's retaliation for Luo's refusal of his advances quickly became intolerable—and seemingly unending, as earning her degree would take at least six years.

The only solution Luo could think of to avoid ending her career entirely was to ask her department chair—a former high-level official in the Chinese Ministry of Education—for permission to drop out of her PhD program and downgrade to a master's degree, thereby reducing the number of years she would need to report to Chen. To win approval for such an unorthodox move, she had to confide in her department chair about the reason behind her request. "I still remember wandering outside his office for several hours, until after midnight, just trying to muster enough courage to enter the building, to knock on that door," she said quietly.

Luo's department chair listened to her story. "The first thing he said," Luo recalled, "is 'Don't tell.'" The official acknowledged that Chen had done something wrong in his sister's apartment, but discounted her professor's campaign to interfere with her studies. "He said I am probably thinking about it too much." Her voice welled up. "In that moment, I felt so ashamed of myself." The department chair insisted that she complete her PhD program under Chen. "I didn't have a choice," she said. "Without support to switch my program, the only other thing I could do is quit."

Luo soldiered on, determined not to forfeit her career, even while Chen persisted in his campaign against her—for years. "He gave me so much trouble," she remembered. "I cried a lot." Luo was diagnosed with depression and unsure if she could continue. Then, a lifeline appeared: the launch of a new program that would permit her to study abroad, in the United States, if she could score well on the GRE exam. "I could not prepare for my exam in the lab, because Chen would know," she recalled. "But at night, when I went back to my dormitory, I would study until two a.m. to prepare for my GRE. I slept very little." She was determined to escape.

Luo performed well on the exam and was selected to study in the United States at the renowned Rensselaer Polytechnic Institute. Chen tried his hardest to stop her from going, but Luo appealed to her department chair, who helped her this time, signing the paperwork permitting her to go. She spent the final two years of her PhD program in the US and became a software engineer, moving to San Francisco to work for Cisco, where she started a family. But she gave up her dream of being a university professor, having endured years of abuse in the hallowed halls of academe. And even though she kept quiet about her harrowing experience, she never forgot the harassment she'd endured at the hands of a professor—or her fury.

Years later, in October 2017, just days after the #MeToo hashtag went viral in the United States and began to proliferate around the world, Luo was inspired to break her silence. She had followed the allegations against the Hollywood producer Harvey Weinstein, which not only dominated headlines in the US but also motivated female students in Chinese chat rooms to post anonymous stories of sexual abuse inflicted upon them by powerful superiors. Among those named in the chat rooms was Chen Xiaowu, her former professor. Luo, horrified to read allegations that he had abused many other students, finally decided to speak up about what had happened to her thirteen years before. She posted an account of her professor's attack on Zhihu.com, a Quora-like question-and-answer website.[2]

Nothing happened.

On January 1, 2018, Luo decided to post her story again—this time on Weibo, the most popular Chinese social media platform in a country where government censorship limits people's movements on the internet and both Facebook and Twitter are banned. Luo, determined to be heard, implored readers to join her in protest of sexual abuse, raise their voices, and "stand up bravely and say: no."[3] Luo took the unprecedented step of signing her name, becoming the first Chinese woman to out herself publicly while also naming her assailant—a milestone under a system in which the mainstream media refused to report on anonymous allegations.

Luo's post from the shores of San Francisco reverberated across China, receiving an unprecedented three million hits on Weibo in twenty-four hours.[4] Before long, a rush of women began identifying themselves as they wrote publicly about the sexual harassment they'd faced on Chinese campuses and across the nation. Never before had so many Chinese women dared to voice their experiences of abuse openly. But the roots of the Chinese #MeToo campaign had been planted well before Luo's courageous post crossed the Pacific into Asia—by brave Chinese feminists who'd pushed for change, often at great personal risk, in a nation that routinely censors and persecutes human rights defenders.

. . . .

The fight for women's equality in China has a storied history, dating to the seventeenth-century Qing dynasty. It was not until the early twentieth century, however, that the role of women began to change, in the wake of the Xinhai Revolution, in 1911, in which several women's militias formed, laying the groundwork for greater political activism and civic engagement.[5] In the early era of modern Chinese communism, the status of women rose under the leadership of Chairman Mao Tse-tung, the communist revolutionary who famously proclaimed that "women hold up half the sky." When Mao assumed power and established the People's Republic of China, in 1949, the government promoted gender equality in an effort to establish the largest female workforce in the world, enacting laws to foster women's economic participation, including reforms to family law, childcare provisions, and regulations guaranteeing equal pay. Even during the subsequent Cultural Revolution, gender equality was a valuable norm deployed to increase female labor force participation, with propaganda lionizing so-called iron girls, who performed the same hard labor as men.

Following Mao's death in 1976, as Chinese politician Deng Xiaoping rose to power and ushered in market reforms in the 1970s and 1980s—opening the door to new economic and cultural ideas—the status of women in China declined. Confucian ideals prizing the role of women as mothers and wives returned, shaped by Western standards that prioritized women's physical appearance. "Over more than two decades of reform," the historian Gail Hershatter wrote, "the female body was reconfigured as alluring, vulnerable, dependent, and inferior." Although investment in women's education grew during this period, so did sexism, said Wang Zheng, a professor of women's studies and a China scholar at the University of Michigan, in an interview with journalist Shen Lu.[6]

The subsequent loss of status among Chinese women is striking. Starting in 1990, even as the global gender wage gap narrowed, in China it grew by ten points for urban women and a staggering twenty-three points for rural women. Between 1990 and 2010, the percentage of Chinese men who believed that men belonged in the public domain and women should remain in the household rose by nearly 10 percentage points.[7] The modern real estate boom also left women behind, in part because of regulatory and cultural norms that excluded them from owning property. And although the Chinese government finally bowed to the economic pressure of an aging population and lifted its notorious one-child policy, which had been enforced through brutal violations of women's reproductive rights, the Chinese demographic crisis has put pressure on women to conform to societal expectations of marriage and childbirth, fueling social stigma, workplace discrimination, and widespread harassment.

Today, China ranks only 106th out of 153 countries on the World Economic Forum's Global Gender Gap index. This poor showing rankles a generation of women who have benefited from higher education but face pervasive limitations in the professional sphere. In many cases, discrimination against women not only persists but is perfectly legal: although the Chinese constitution recognizes equal rights for women, its civil code lacks specific prohibitions against sexual harassment and gender discrimination. As a result, employers routinely post jobs for male-only candidates, refuse to hire women of reproductive age, and ignore sexual harassment in the workplace, while universities frequently tolerate abuses by professors against their students.[8]

In recent decades, Chinese activists have addressed women's decline in status by expanding their efforts, particularly in the wake of the UN Fourth World Conference on Women, which the Chinese government agreed to host in Beijing in 1995. At the summit, delegates and activists from 189 nations gathered to adopt the most ambitious agenda for women's rights in history, calling for the "full and equal participation of women in political, civil, economic, social, and cultural life." The Chinese government was wary of global delegates to the conference, concerned that the influence of women's activists from abroad would threaten government control. It even censored the keynote speech delivered by Hillary Clinton, then the First Lady of the United

States, in which she famously recognized that "women's rights are human rights." Yet after the conference, in the face of international pressure to improve the status of women, the Chinese government allowed the formation of more NGOs focused on women's issues, which delicately began to address persistent problems like domestic violence. Most of the Chinese women's advocates who organized after the 1995 conference were nonetheless careful not to confront the government directly, mindful of its harsh crackdown on prodemocracy protesters, including the 1989 Tiananmen massacre.[9]

Beginning in 2012, however, the debate on gender equality moved from the shadows to the headlines, as a new generation of digitally linked young feminists arrived on the scene. These young women were exasperated with the slow progress won by the older generation of advocates, who'd been wary of alienating repressive government forces. Ironically, the impatience of this rising generation of feminists was a byproduct of China's repressive population-control policies, which, by limiting the number of children parents could have, elevated the importance of girls in their families. "We have a lot of opportunities—much more than my parents' generation," observed Liwen Qin, a journalist who pioneered internet news to help circumvent censorship.[10] "Before, parents would say, 'Oh, I wish I had a son,' that constant humiliation reminding you that you are less worthy as a girl. But with the 1980s generation, parents didn't have a choice—they could only have one child. So a girl growing up would have higher self-respect, and get many more resources." These circumstances, according to Liwen, cultivated fertile ground for the #MeToo movement. "Today, we see a lot of well-educated women who embrace feminism," she said. "They even study it—including in the US—and then they use social media to spread their ideas." Even in a country where censorship and government repression are persistent threats, this generation would not be content to work within the system or keep quiet—especially when they had new media tools to make their voices heard.

Young Chinese feminists, primarily concentrated in Beijing and Guangzhou, began to come together via social media, creating a coalition of about one hundred women called Young Feminist Activism. Most participants worked at NGOs or held other full-time jobs but made time to campaign for gender equality. One godmother of the new wave was Lu Pin, the founder of Feminist Voices, the best-known feminist website in China, which by 2018

had over 180,000 followers on Weibo and an additional 70,000 on the popular social media platform WeChat, significant numbers in a country where
political activism is inherently dangerous.[11]

Lu, a fiery and fearless leader, recognized that the government would not
permit traditional protests or street demonstrations on issues like gender-
based violence, harassment, and discrimination. So to raise awareness of gender inequality, she worked with her allies to conceive of "performance art"
highlighting these concerns: public stunts to draw attention to critical issues,
captured on social media to ensure that the messages would spread. One of
their first efforts, to highlight the scourge of domestic violence, took place
on Valentine's Day 2012, on a busy commercial street in Beijing. To protest
the violence that too often characterizes marital life for women in China, the
activists Li Maizi, Xiao Melli, and Wei Tingting dressed in wedding dresses
stained with fake blood, and video and images of the performance quickly
went viral. Though women's advocates had fought for decades for legislation
to outlaw domestic violence, it had stalled for years. Only after the 2012 protest and a series of other eye-catching stunts did the legislation move forward,
in 2015. The performances had spread around the internet, quickly helping
to transform the debate. "These activists definitely did things no one else
had done before," said Don Yige, a China scholar at the University of Puget
Sound, in an interview with the journalist Shen Lu, "turning women's rights,
once an elite issue, into a widely discussed public topic."[12]

The month after the Valentine's Day protest, Lu Pin and her team seized
on another subject to highlight discrimination against women, one relatable
to women across the nation: inequitable bathroom facilities, which resulted
in long lines for women while men breezed in and out without wait. Protesters traveled to Guangzhou to launch an "Occupy Men's Toilets" campaign,
demanding the construction of restrooms that would result in equal wait
times for women and men. The lighthearted approach proved effective, attracting widespread support and attention on social media, and opening an
aperture for dialogue on more challenging issues. "If you fight for sexuality,
or bodily integrity, it's hard," Li Maizi observed. "Occupying a men's room
is easier to understand. People agree with it—there's no controversy."[13]

Indeed, public support was in much shorter supply in response to campaigns on controversial issues, including sexual harassment—a concept that

had been largely absent from the public discourse until later in 2012, when Li's fellow activists led a campaign on subways to protest sexual harassment in the public sphere. Li's comrades took over a Shanghai subway station— chanting the slogan "I can be slutty, you can't harass me"—to protest persistent groping on public transportation and social norms that too often faulted women for their behavior or sartorial choices when they faced sexual harassment or abuse. Countless people expressed outrage at the slogan, condemning the women for defying cultural norms about female modesty and daring to claim a right to sexual agency. But the shock value of the campaign helped introduce the concept of sexual harassment to the public, creating a vocabulary that laid the groundwork for the eventual spread of the #MeToo movement in China. "Many people at the time said that this idea of sexual freedom without abuse is wrong, and that women should be 'responsible' for themselves," recalled the activist Liang Xiaowen, then a university student who participated in the campaign.[14] "But over the next six years, many people on social media started explaining why victim blaming is wrong—the power relations behind it—and how sexual harassment is essentially discrimination against women." By the time Luo Xixi posted her story of harassment at the hands of Professor Chen, in 2018, the opposition to victim blaming by the younger generation in China had increased considerably.

This rise in feminist activism in 2012 attracted attention not only from the public but also from the government, whose growing fear of the power wielded by women's activists led to greater surveillance of both individuals and NGOs. Liang Xiaowen—who in addition to joining the Occupy Men's Toilets and subway campaigns had also shaved her head to protest university admissions policies favoring men—was paid a visit by the police on her graduation day. They insisted that she terminate her involvement in the feminist movement, which they alleged was influenced by "hostile Western forces." Liang knew that the government was monitoring her, but the campus visit shook up her family members, who were already wary of the attention she had attracted. That Liang and her parents feared for her safety, when all she'd done was peacefully express her opinions, was an indication of how dangerous human rights activism could be in China, even when protests targeted conventional social norms rather than the state. "When citizens stand up to take action and organize," said Wang Zheng, a US-based women's studies professor and China scholar, "they are defined as enemies of the state, funded by hostile forces from abroad."[15]

Notwithstanding the intimidation, feminist activism continued to provoke widespread discussion on social media, creating many converts to the cause. Lu Pin, the activist who started working on these issues after the 1995 Beijing Conference, recalled that the number of Chinese women self-identifying as feminist during the summit was small enough that she felt she knew everyone. But as activism traveled across the internet, public awareness increased dramatically, especially among young people, becoming a potent force. "There are so many feminists in China now," Lu said in an interview with SupChina. "And it is impossible for the government to crack down on everyone."[16]

For a time, the "performance art" campaigns led by young feminists provoked not only greater attention, but also policy change. In 2013, for the first time, the Ministry of Education prohibited gender-biased test score cut-offs or gender quotas in admission, taking an important step to level the educational playing field for women. In 2015, China finally enacted its long-sought anti–domestic violence law, becoming one of the last countries in the world to do so. The next year, the Ministry of Housing and Urban-Rural Development required equitable construction of bathroom stalls in all new or renovated public restroom facilities. "The protests were a great way to get people to pay attention and discuss the issues," Lu Pin said in an interview with the journalist Shen Lu, comparing the public activism and online campaigns waged by young feminists to the quiet, cautious advocacy pursued by women's advocates in decades prior. "As the debate continued, you'd find potential supporters of your agenda, and it could affect policymaking."[17]

This success, however, was tempered by rising attacks on feminist activists by a government increasingly threatened by their power to sway public opinion. By 2015, the authorities started responding more aggressively, concerned that student activism on behalf of gender equality could be deployed to foster demands for government change. Rather than trying to clamp down on the tens of thousands of newly self-identified feminists who had become involved in social media campaigns, the Chinese government decided to send a message by making a public example of a select few, on a day when the ominous message would be unmistakable: International Women's Day, celebrated around the world on March 8 each year.

That year, dozens of young Chinese feminists in ten cities decided to mark the day by handing out stickers at public transit hubs, protesting sexual harassment. The women organized over WeChat. Zheng Churan, one of the organizers, who was twenty-five years old at the time, knew they were being monitored but didn't think that the relatively tame protest would provoke a response. "The police went to Li Maizi's house beforehand and threatened her not to take action," she later remembered in an interview with journalist Mona Eltahawy. "They called me to tell me that too. But it was such a minor thing—just stickers. So we thought it would be OK."[18]

It was not OK. Late on the evening of March 6, ten men showed up at Zheng's house to question her. "We've known you for a long time," they told her, and dragged her to the police station in Beijing. At first they allowed her to go home, returning with her to search all her electronics—"my phone, my computer, even USBs," she recalled. But they didn't set her free. Instead, on the morning of International Women's Day, they incarcerated her in Beijing along with four other prominent activists—all of whom were full-time NGO workers—on the dubious grounds of "picking quarrels and creating a disturbance," a pretense often used to lock up human rights activists. In addition to Zheng, the government incarcerated Li Maizi, who had kicked off the domestic violence wedding-dress protest years before; Wu Rongrong, founder of the Weizhiming Women's Center in Guangzhou; Wei Tingting, director of the Ji'ande LGBTQ-rights organization in Beijing; and Wang Man, a leading gender equality and antipoverty activist.[19] A dozen other women were detained and questioned in cities across the country.

Unlike in decades past, when news about the suppression or disappearance of women's rights leaders created barely a ripple on the world stage, the arrests were instantly and digitally transmitted around the world. Liang Xiaowen, who was questioned the night the activists were incarcerated, recalled being on the phone with Zheng when she was taken away—and immediately posting what had happened on the internet. "Zheng called me that night," she said.[20] "She insisted that they didn't have a warrant and couldn't come into her house. It went on for a while. So I sent out word on WeChat that she was being apprehended." After posting, Liang fled. "I thought I too was in danger," she said quietly. But as news of the arrests spread over social media, word soon traveled to capitals around the world. A chorus of critics protested, dubbing the incarcerated women the "Feminist Five."

Within weeks, the news escalated to the highest levels, with world leaders—including former secretary of state Hillary Clinton, US ambassador to the United Nations Samantha Power, and leaders in Canada, the UK, and the European Union—calling on the Chinese government to release the activists. For Li Maizi, one of the jailed women, this support was a lifeline and a testament to the power of a connected global women's movement. "People have different agendas in different countries," she said years later in an interview with us in Washington, DC. "But we share the same solidarity and support for each other." The women remained in jail for over a month, suffering in dire conditions. Wu Rongrong fell ill after being deprived of needed hepatitis medication, and Wang Man suffered a minor heart attack.[21] But after a grueling thirty-seven days, following the international outcry, the government finally conceded to pressure and released them.

Although the Feminist Five were eventually freed, the government's message was unmistakable: feminist activism would no longer be tolerated by the state—and the lives and freedom of those who defied the government were on the line. Several leading Chinese feminists, fearing for their safety, went into hiding or fled the country. At the urging of her parents, Liang Xiaowen—who had been detained but not incarcerated—went to graduate school in the United States, continuing her activism from safer shores. Lu Pin was already in New York at the time of the arrests, to attend the annual UN meeting of the Commission on the Status of Women; after learning that the police had searched her apartment, she knew it would be unsafe for her to return, so she decided to stay put and continue publishing Feminist Voices from the US.[22] Although some of those detained or incarcerated were able to escape China, several others are stuck and still cannot leave. Even after charges have been dropped, those pursuing visa applications have often been denied, told that their cases are not yet closed.

"Women's activism is exponentially more difficult in China, because the retaliation they face is just so much greater," China expert Leta Hong Fincher told us. The women's arrests also betrayed how intimidated the government felt after the renaissance of Chinese women's organizing began to permeate the public consciousness via the internet. This innovative, tech-savvy wave of the women's movement "aroused tremendous fear in the state," observed Wang Zheng, the US-based China scholar. "So the government started to try to control, contain, co-opt, or just outright suppress NGOs—to close civil society space."[23] Officials in Beijing handed down new regulations requiring all NGOs to register with authorities and prohibiting the receipt of foreign funding, effectively shutting down operations for public-interest organizations already strapped for resources. And censors trolled the internet in an attempt to quash public discussion, even banning the word "feminist."

· · · · · · · · · · · · · · · · · ·

Initially, the Chinese government's attempts at censorship worked—but not for long. In 2016, a twenty-one-year-old intern at *Nanfang Daily*, a newspaper in Guangdong, reported a rape by an older male journalist with whom she worked.[24] The mainstream media refused to report the case, casting it to the shadows of social media, where much of the discussion targeted the young woman, criticizing her tattoo, inquiring why she hadn't protected herself, or assuming she'd invited the attack.

Sophia Huang Xueqin, an independent journalist, was outraged by the posts on this story amassing in her WeChat account. The next day, she decided to share her own story of being sexually harassed by an established journalist five years earlier, when she had been a cub reporter in Guangzhou, the capital of Guangdong province. Though she had repeatedly tried to deflect his physical advances, her rejection did not stop him. The experience had changed the trajectory of her entire career: devastated by the mistreatment at the hands of a colleague she'd revered, and feeling uneasy seeing him in the workplace, she left her promising job only a month after the harassment began. "I didn't say anything when I resigned," she said in an interview, "and the girls who came after me, they suffered too." But witnessing the online castigation of the *Nanfang Daily* journalist shook her out of her silence. "It is very common logic to blame the victim," she noted. "But why should I be ashamed?" Sophia posted her story, urging a reexamination of assumptions that those attacked must have invited the behavior—but she did so on her private account, not daring to risk provocation of the authorities.[25]

Then, in 2017, when the #MeToo hashtag exploded in the United States and filtered out to other countries, Sophia found the courage to speak—not about her own experience, but about the scourge of sexual harassment in the workplace. Sophia began covering the issue, evading censors by launching her own online platform for survivors to share their stories of harassment and abuse, and creating a survey to measure sexual harassment in the media industry. "I decided to investigate how serious the situation is," she remembered, "and what keeps us from speaking out."[26] Within one week, over two hundred women had completed Sophia's survey, many anonymously sharing personal stories, notwithstanding concerns about government monitoring and pressure from employers to remain silent.

It was in this context that Luo Xixi, the Cisco employee and former Beihang University student, similarly inspired by the rise in women's voices triggered by the global #MeToo movement, decided to reach out to Sophia, sharing the harrowing attack she'd faced at the hands of Professor Chen back in 2004. Luo's courageous decision in January 2018 to become the first Chinese woman to use her name publicly—and to name her powerful attacker in her post on Weibo—helped her story break through.[27] This, coupled with the media savvy of a trained journalist like Sophia, who began to cover Luo's story, opened the way for other Chinese women to come forward.

Young Chinese feminist activists—those remaining in China as well as those working from new environs, including the United States, since the 2015 crackdown on the Feminist Five—seized on Luo's case, bolstered by the #MeToo movement sweeping the globe. Although the repressive climate of government censorship and the collapse of the NGO sector posed communications challenges, years of operating in a difficult environment had taught feminist organizers how to evade government oppression. "Under the harsh conditions in China, feminist activists have to be very creative," Lu Pin, who helped fan the flames from her exile in New York, said with a smile. "The creativity we have is very good—something the rest of the world can learn from."

Feminist organizers began circulating a petition to Beihang University, calling for an investigation into Luo's allegations against Professor Chen and a permanent mechanism to address sexual harassment at the school. Recognizing the risks faced by current students, who relied on the support of professors and university administrators to obtain degrees, organizers cleverly enlisted signatures from alumni, who had moved on from the school and were liberated to sign. The petitions traveled around the internet at record speed, attracting large numbers of participants. In the past, allegations against prominent professors had been concealed or dismissed. But in the face of a growing outcry from alumni, Beihang University acted immediately, conducting an investigation and firing Professor Chen from his teaching position after just ten days. Seventy-two hours later, the Chinese Ministry of Education stripped him of a prestigious award.[28] The unthinkable had happened: women had faced down the censors to organize and had won accountability. And they were inspired to do more.

Organizers converted the Beihang University petition into a template, sharing their strategy with alumni from other Chinese universities around the country and across the globe. Only a few months after Luo's Weibo post had outed Professor Chen, petitions were submitted to Chinese administrators on over ninety campuses, signed by tens of thousands of alumni.[29] Activists made a point of targeting Peking University, one of the most revered educational institutions in China, to send a clear message that no one was immune. Students even began to hold protests, prompting several universities to investigate allegations and impose consequences for the first time. The government tried to quash women's activism as it had before, with state-run media ignoring the deluge of accusations, and censors deleting posts on Weibo and other platforms within minutes. But because the movement had gone viral, the government's censorship failed. There was no way for it to keep up.

Using social media, organizers helped the movement spread around the country. Activists whose written posts were deleted—censors could easily pick up Chinese characters—learned to convert their messages to pictures, taking screen shots of stories shared by women and reposting the images as soon as text posts were taken down. After the phrase "MeToo" was banned, women replaced the Chinese characters for #MeToo with homophones and images, using an emoji version made up of pictures of a bowl of rice (pronounced "mi") and a bunny ("tu"). Feminists even figured out how to embed posts using blockchain technology so they couldn't be taken down.[30] Given the sheer number of women on social media, these techniques often worked. Historically, censors could control activism by small groups by deleting their posts instantly, but with the widespread participation of women, that same post would be reposted again and again, exhausting and eluding the censors. "We win by having more people," Lu Pin said with steely re-serve. "We can avoid censorship when we mobilize."

By the summer of 2018, despite the government's crackdown, the Chi-nese #MeToo movement had spread well beyond the ivory tower, reaching some of China's most prominent leaders in journalism, philanthropy, and the arts. In one week alone, women lodged complaints against Zhu Jun, a star on the major Chinese television station CCTV; Zhang Wen, a veteran journalist and the founder of *New Weekly* magazine; and Sun Mian, the chairman of the Chinese Buddhism Association.[31] Allegations against Zhou Fei, a top leader at the China branch of the World Wildlife Fund, were also widely shared online. Many of the accused swiftly resigned, suggesting that public opinion on sexual harassment was rapidly shifting.

Although the Chinese #MeToo campaign was concentrated among urban, well-educated women, leaving out millions of rural women who remained unconnected to the internet, some feminists took steps to broaden the reach of the movement beyond the upper classes. The campaign began to focus on poorer women and factory workers, who faced even greater challenges—and higher costs for speaking out. Organizers of a Weibo platform for female factory employees encouraged women in China's tech industry to share sto-ries of sexual harassment. One courageous student activist named Yue Xin, who ignited the #MeToo campaign at the elite Peking University, decided to travel to southern China to help unionize female workers.[32]

Although government censorship chilled the extent of public debate and made online communication exceedingly difficult, widespread access to the internet and social media created an avenue for dialogue and dissent that hadn't existed in earlier waves of the women's movement in China, amplify-ing voices that otherwise would have been silenced. "Even with censorship, the government can't entirely block the space created by technology," Lu Pin declared, "because it can't turn off the internet. As long as the internet is op-erational, we have the space to speak." The online activism created a level of awareness about problems like gender discrimination and sexual abuse that was unprecedented in China—and unlikely to be reversed.

But this achievement has been borne on the backs of activists who have faced intimidation, exile, and imprisonment—or have disappeared entirely. While government censors may find online communication impossible to contain, the opposite is true when it comes to the freedom of women's activists, those whose daring work inspired the Chinese #MeToo movement in the first place. As long as these women are at risk, the long-term success of the movement remains endangered.

....

Two years after #MeToo swept across China, many feminist activists—those still within the country, as well as those who were part of the post-2015 diaspora—were able to declare a victory. They applauded shifts in accountability and highlighted the termination or resignation of rafts of prominent Chinese men who previously would have weathered or been shielded from accusations of sexual harassment. "Because of the #MeToo movement, 2018 marked a permanent shift in recognizing and acknowledging how common sexual harassment is and how many women were oppressed," wrote Sophia Huang Xueqin, the journalist who helped Luo Xixi's Weibo post go viral, in an email to us. "You can see that women's consciousness of their rights is awakening, and the shame of being sexually harassed is going away. That awakening is the biggest achievement of #MeToo in China."

The Chinese government has also taken steps to reform policy in recognition of the growing power of women's voices. In November 2018, China announced proposed changes to its civil code that, for the first time, defined and prohibited sexual harassment in the workplace. That same month, the Ministry of Education issued new guidelines for teachers and professors, with harsh consequences for sexual harassment. In December 2018, the People's Supreme Court recognized a right to sue for equal employment rights, including to redress harm from sexual harassment. In February 2019, the government issued a directive prohibiting employers from advertising positions for "men only" or asking female job applicants about their marriage and family plans or requiring pregnancy tests. And in October 2019, a Shanghai court issued the first ruling in China regarding sexual abuse on public transit, sentencing a man to six months in prison for groping a woman and an underage girl.[33]

But transformative legal changes have been elusive, with gender discrimination laws still largely unenforced or undefined. And a growing number of accused men have pushed back, bringing lawsuits against their accusers. In 2019 alone, six prominent men sued their accusers for defamation, and the outcome of such cases could affect whether women continue to speak out. Already, one of those men—Zhou Fei, the World Wildlife Fund official who allegedly harassed Wang Qi, a young employee—prevailed in court, with the judge ordering his accuser to provide an apology and erase her online account of the incident.[34]

The Chinese government also persists in its attacks against online feminist activism in an attempt to slow its spread. Technological tools have become a double-edged sword—indispensable to activists but also to the government, which has created social media accounts to disseminate disinformation about feminism, a technique used by authoritarian governments around the world. "For the past few years, we've really had to struggle," Lu Pin said from New York. "We've had a big antifeminist wave online." On International Women's Day in March 2018, the Weibo account for Feminist Voices—the site Lu had founded—disappeared, thereby silencing Lu's voice in her home country. "We can debate them if we can speak freely," Lu said of her opponents. "But there's not enough freedom of expression. That's our biggest problem." Activists also worry about the broader effect of the government's growing censorship campaign. "In China, everyone is self-censoring now," lamented Li Maizi, one of the Feminist Five, who remains in mainland China and stands out for refusing to rein in her activism.

Today, for feminists like Li still within China, the specter of censorship has been dwarfed by fears over whether they will survive. The attacks have been swift—and more severe than ever. In July 2018, Yue Xin, who sparked the #MeToo campaign at Peking University and then led an effort to help combat sexual harassment against factory workers, saw her Weibo platform shut down by the government; by August, the police had raided the apartment where she and her colleagues were living, and she has not been heard from since. Sophia Huang Xueqin lost her job writing for mainstream media publications; in late 2019, she was jailed for three months, on the same vague charge of "picking quarrels and provoking trouble," and upon release was denied her passport, computer, and mobile phone.[35]

Notwithstanding the growing government backlash, activists celebrate a revolution in popular perceptions of gender equality, which has paved the way for institutional reforms. "Public attitudes have changed a lot," Lu Pin observed. "Young women are sure of their own power. They can talk, they can speak for themselves, they can change society. That is the most important thing—the empowerment of women." Leta Hong Fincher, the New York–based China scholar, agreed, noting that the harsh backlash against the feminist movement in China is a testament to its power. "It's going to be very hard for the government to squash this," she said in a roundtable discussion at the Council on Foreign Relations. "They can't imprison half the population. That's why I believe the feminist movement is potentially the most transformative social movement in China, at least since 1989." Despite the resistance, to Hong Fincher, "this cannot possibly be the end. It is, if anything, the beginning."[36]

The viral spread of the #MeToo movement in China, while now slowed, is also a warning sign to other autocratic governments that women's voices have the power to vanquish government repression. "The strength of women recognizing the commonality of their oppression, coming together, and acting collectively—even the most formidable authoritarian government in the world is really struggling against it," Fincher observed. "How do they counter this rise of women? Because there are so many of us." To Lu Pin—who is grappling with how to continue propelling the movement now that her Feminist Voices publication has been banned—the potential of women's collective action can trump censorship. "The government can block our platform," she said in a Council on Foreign Relations dialogue. "But it cannot stop people from pursuing feminist thought. Women in China have now awakened, especially young women. And I don't think the government can stop our movement, because our community won't give up."[37]

Chinese feminist activists believe that women's movements have the potential to undermine authoritarian governments everywhere—not only in China, but also in other countries where authoritarianism and attacks on women's rights go hand in hand, including Egypt, Iran, the Philippines, Russia, and Turkey—and that democratic governments like the United States ought to be doing more to support feminist movements as a way to advance democratic governance. "There is something about women's rights activists," Fincher said, "that really challenges the core of authoritarian governments everywhere, because feminism is completely incompatible with authoritarian repression."

Even in the face of rising censorship and repression in China, the global power and reach of the #MeToo campaign help sustain the movement there. Today, a Chinese feminist diaspora thrives in New York, where activists continue to press for change in their home country, hosting educational seminars, transmitting information back home, and calling on like-minded leaders in other countries to join forces and support their efforts. "The movement is global, because women around the world are confronting patriarchy," Leta Hong Fincher said. "And thanks to global connectivity, even though China has a great firewall, it's not able to completely seal Chinese citizens off." Liang Xiaowen, the young university activist who remains in exile in the United States, echoed this sentiment. "There is a #MeToo movement in every country, inside and outside of China," she said. "And every country's own #MeToo movement is a protection and encouragement of the #MeToo movement of another country."

These ties between activists, which cross borders and traverse cyberspace—and that propelled the Chinese #MeToo movement in the first place—promise to keep the flame alive. "Feminist fires are scattered around the world," said the journalist Liwen Qin. "Ultimately, what I hope is that because the weather is warm and dry, in the end these small fires will burn down the whole field."

Luo Xixi, whose post about Professor Chen ignited the Chinese #MeToo movement, concedes a hard road ahead, acknowledging the delay in implementing promised reforms and the risks that women face for coming forward and speaking out. When Chen was punished after being exposed, many friends of Luo's parents blamed her for ruining his future, ignoring how his harassment had forever altered hers. Luo still fears for her parents' safety in China and has not returned to the country since going public. But she believes success can be measured in part by the growing number of women who have been willing to come forward despite the risks. "The #MeToo movement has shown people that we are not alone," Luo insisted. "And when you see you are not alone, you have the courage to come forward." Progress is also reflected by the change in the way many parents are raising the next generation. "I have a lot of hopes for my daughter," Luo told us in 2020, following the birth of her child while she was on parental leave from her new job at Google. "I am finally overcoming what happened several years ago, and I have become stronger and tougher—but I will tell her my story. She will become the fire."

Protesters convene in front of Tunisia's parliament on December 14, 2019, performing the Chilean protest anthem "A Rapist in Your Path" that went viral on social media globally the previous month. The inclusive feminist collective Falgatna ("we're fed up" in Tunisian Arabic) organized the demonstration in Tunis. Credit: Ala Zemzmi

Chapter Three

EGYPT AND TUNISIA: TWO REVOLUTIONS

#EnaZeda

#أنا_كمان

#AnaKaman

The sexual harasser does not legislate.

—*Falgatna protestors*

Inciting and calling for the irresponsible liberation of women.

—*Case 173/2011 charge against Mozn Hassan*

To this day, we don't know her name. Here is what we do know.

On October 10, 2019, a nineteen-year-old student in the coastal Tunisian town of Nabeul was walking back to her high school from her lunch break when she became aware of a car behind her. As the vehicle drew closer, she panicked. Would she be harassed? Attacked? Abducted? She decided to take pictures of the license plate. When she turned, she saw a man inside the car watching her, pants down, hands moving. She realized he was masturbating.[1]

She hit the photo-burst button on her smartphone, then ran as fast as she could. At home, shaken, she asked the administrator of a local private Facebook group to post the photos. She could warn other young women in Nabeul: Look out for this guy. Does anyone know who this is? People did recognize him; he was Zouheir Makhlouf, a human rights advocate who had just been elected to Tunisia's parliament.

The student became afraid, unsure if anyone would support her. But soon, news of the photos spread. Outrage and disgust rose. The public prosecutor in Nabeul opened an investigation, without a complaint being filed. But Makhlouf, confronted with the photos, claimed he'd done nothing wrong. It was all a misunderstanding, he said. He was diabetic. He'd been relieving himself into a bottle. The moisturizer? For a medical condition.

New members of parliament would take their seats within weeks. And despite the outcry against Makhlouf, it looked as if he might be shielded from prosecution, thanks to a Tunisian law giving members of parliament immunity. This would hardly have been the first time a Tunisian woman had been denied justice in the face of harassment. On women's rights, Tunisia has long been hailed as one of the most progressive Arab countries, and in 2017 it passed landmark legislation to combat violence against women. Yet a report released that same year found that in 97 percent of sexual harassment cases, either victims didn't file complaints or perpetrators received no fine or sentence.[2]

This time, however, women started organizing, determined to accomplish what the legal system would not. Although the student remained anonymous, a Tunisian women's rights organization, Aswat Nissa—"Women's Voices," in Arabic—managed to meet with her confidentially, to see if she needed a lawyer or protection. The group wanted to "show solidarity," said Ikram Ben Said, Aswat Nissa's founder, "that she is not alone, and it's not happening only to you." The group started a private Facebook group with the name and hashtag #EnaZeda, Tunisian dialect for #MeToo, and invited other survivors to share their stories of sexual harassment and assault. The phrase had been used before, at a protest to mark the 2014 death of a thirteen-year-old girl who had been attacked and killed by her father. A lone feminist protester had carried a sign reading "Ena Zeda"—meaning she too had been victimized by her father.[3]

This time, the phrase and hashtag went viral. Women of all ages, in cities and rural areas—and even some men—came forward. At their schools and workplaces, at the hands of family members, the military, the police, and the media, thousands of people reported having been subjected to childhood abuse, marital rape, and all manner of sexual harassment and violence.[4] "It's something that's shared by all women and all girls, whatever your social class, your age," Ikram said. "I don't think one woman has not been sexually harassed in her life."

Aswat Nissa became overwhelmed with thousands of requests to join the private #EnaZeda group.[5] Lawyers started posting that they would donate their services to represent victims. "I was in shock," Ikram recalled. "I panicked. I said, 'We cannot manage this.'" She worried about the safety and anonymity of all these survivors.

But soon, Tunisian women from around the country and world stepped up to volunteer. One was Rania Said, a thirty-three-year-old PhD student based in New York, who became a moderator for the #EnaZeda Facebook page. Rania's graduate work was focused on women's testimonies from the 2011 uprisings in Tunisia, Syria, and Egypt, and although she wasn't a professional organizer, she felt called to join the digital campaign.[6] "I became involved with a vengeance," she said when we spoke in January 2020, her voice still full of tired excitement. Rania began volunteering hundreds of hours to sift through the thousands of harrowing accounts of sexual harassment and assault. Within days, the network numbered about two thousand members—and it was still growing. Rania contributed original content and made infographics about rape culture. When the testimonies became too much to bear, she would deactivate Facebook on her devices, but then she'd be drawn back in. "It was crazy," she said. "I was not sleeping, they were not sleeping, reading all the stories we were receiving."

. . . .

Another story started to catch fire in the #EnaZeda Facebook group, this one driven by students at the École Normale Supérieure (ENS), one of Tunisia's most exclusive universities. It was an open secret among current students and alumni that a professor on campus had for years preyed on female students, inviting them to his office under the guise of giving them books or tutoring support, only to sexually harass or assault them. Student complaints to three different principals had been ignored. Out of options, a whistleblower turned to the #EnaZeda Facebook group and named the teacher: Aymen Hacen, a professor of French.[7]

One of Hacen's victims was Salma Ben Amour, a 2019 alum, who alleges she'd been targeted by Hacen as a twenty-three-year-old student. Confident and forthright, Salma began organizing students and alumni to stop sexual harassment on campus. When we met in a Tunis café, she recounted how she'd accepted Hacen's Facebook request to be friends, and he started grooming her by liking and commenting on her photos. "He was very selective," Salma said. Starting in a woman's first year at the school, he would pinpoint her weaknesses and strengths, in an attempt to "manipulate the victim," Salma said.

In 2016, Salma said, Hacen asked her to his office, sat close to her, and started asking questions: "Do you have a boyfriend? Are you a virgin?" Salma escaped with a polite excuse, but Hacen demanded that she return the following week so he could give her a book he insisted she use for a finals paper. When she attempted to leave, Hacen tried to hug her and touched her body without consent. Salma reported the harassment to the head of the department. But instead of opening an investigation, the school official shifted her paper assignment to another instructor. "If I had failed," Salma said, "I would have been fired from the school."

Students travel from all over Tunisia for a free, state-sponsored education at ENS, one of the country's few elite schools with a coed student body. "All families dream of sending their children to the school because you get a job directly after you graduate," Salma said. Hacen knew that his students' futures depended on their performance, and he exploited this fact to great effect. Salma recounted the story of another young woman: "He put her in front of a mirror and asked her to say, 'I'm beautiful, I'm beautiful,' then tried to kiss her." When she rejected him, Salma said, the girl got bad grades.

For some students, especially those from more conservative parts of the country, the stakes and potential consequences were even graver. Tunis may have the feel of a cosmopolitan global city, but women in rural Tunisia still face hard-line religious norms. As Salma explained, "If a girl from Kasserine"—an agricultural outpost in west-central Tunisia—"tells her family that she was sexually assaulted, she would get killed."

But as in the campaign against Zouheir Makhlouf, technology changed the calculus in the Hacen case. Not only did it bring long-overdue attention to the ENS students' grievances; it also allowed them to connect, organize, and keep up a drumbeat when the authorities lagged. The students' campaign escalated quickly. Organizers from #EnaZeda taught students the Chilean protest song "A Rapist in Your Path," and they performed it inside the school. Students were asked to appear anonymously on *Les 4 Verites* (The Four Truths), one of Tunisia's most famous TV programs.

More women came forward online. Student organizers discovered that Hacen had been accused of raping a student at his previous school posting, in Lyon, France.[8] Alumni there added their voices in support of the ENS #EnaZeda group.

Hacen fought back. He filed a defamation lawsuit, launched a media campaign, and tried to gather a small group of colleagues to sign a petition asserting his innocence. Undeterred, the ENS students doubled down. They created symbolic photo content reenacting crimes that had happened behind closed doors, and posted it online, to "concretize the assaults that took place," Salma said. In the café during our interview, she scrolled through her phone, showing us photos. "The signs say, 'Sexual harassment is a crime,'" she explained. "This is a victim hiding herself." Students also posted screenshots of text messages they'd received from Hacen. One read, "I developed a theory of analyzing one's character by analyzing the morphology/language of their feet. This is serious, and I have determined a few interesting results. Could you take two or three photos of your feet, with toes and soles, and send them to me?"

. . . .

By November 2019, the #EnaZeda group had over seventy thousand posts and comments and over seventeen thousand members. On November 13, Aswat Nissa gathered women wearing #EnaZeda T-shirts outside the Tunisian parliament building to protest the induction of Zouheir Makhlouf. He was sworn in anyway.[9]

It seemed a setback for the movement. But the women's work wasn't over.

In December 2019, ENS students made a formal complaint about Aymen Hacen to the Ministry of Education. Although the ministry was set to hold a hearing, the students were told they couldn't attend, Salma said, because this was a professional, not a judicial, board. Shut out of the formal process, the students continued their own investigation online, sharing legal documents and case updates on Facebook. They saw that when students posted testimonies and evidence online, others—lawyers, the media, unexpected allies—started picking up the investigation to help.

It worked. In December 2019, Hacen was suspended from teaching. Two months later, he was tried before a Ministry of Education inspection panel, and his case was later referred by the ministry to the Commission for Combating Violence Against Women.

Also in December, protests against Zouheir Makhlouf continued. Aswat Nissa called a press conference with lawyers for the Nabeul student who'd originally outed him, and who remained anonymous.[10] "She was depressed because she was seeing this man who sexually harassed her sitting in one of the most powerful institutions in the country," said Sonia Ben Miled, an Aswat Nissa spokeswoman who met with us in a Tunis office packed with protest signs in the shape of women and tall piles of campaign flyers. "We wanted to remind people, the media, the parliament, everyone, that this case was not closed."

At the event, a mysterious representative showed up on behalf of Makhlouf, brandishing dubious legal paperwork. When Sonia continued the press conference, another man showed up, threatening the journalists in attendance and confronting the organizers.[11] Aswat Nissa livestreamed the interaction until members of the security staff forced the man to leave. The incident told the Aswat Nissa team one thing: they were getting to Makhlouf.

. . . .

Although the #EnaZeda campaign sparked by brave students in Nabeul and Tunis brought the global #MeToo Movement to Tunisia, it didn't come out of nowhere. Without the popular uprising in the country eight years earlier, which had brought women activists out into the streets, demanding to be heard, #EnaZeda might not have been possible at all.

Ikram Ben Said, the founder of Aswat Nissa, spoke to us in February 2020, from Jordan, where she now works to mobilize youth and civil society. She vividly remembered the moment she decided to publicly join the fight for women's rights. On a rainy day in December 2010, Ikram was in her classroom at a Tunis college, teaching international marketing. At the time, she was thirty years old, volunteering at an organization called Amal ("hope," in Arabic) that provided economic and psychological support to single mothers. She was a self-described "angry young woman," frustrated by her nation's lack of freedom under the autocratic rule of President Zine al-Abidine Ben Ali. She also knew that charity was not enough to improve women's lives, that any meaningful reform required a change in society itself.

Standing at the front of her classroom, Ikram began to realize she was not meant to be at the chalkboard that day. Street demonstrations had been raging in Tunisia, incited by the callous treatment of a fruit vendor named Tarek al-Tayeb Mohamed Bouazizi. On December 17, Bouazizi had been confronted by inspectors in a marketplace in Sidi Bouzid, in the center of the country. According to witnesses, one of the inspectors, a woman, mocked and spat on him as she confiscated his wares and scales, her gender adding to his humiliation. Bouazizi, furious over his inability to earn and broken down by a lifetime of toil under the corrupt and neglectful Ben Ali regime, later went to a government office to complain, but was denied an audience.[12] In response, he set himself on fire. Bouazizi soon died from his injuries.

"My gut feeling told me, 'You have to go to the streets,'" Ikram said. "I looked at my students and I said, 'Listen, I think you have heard what is happening now in the country, and I believe that my place today is not here.'" Then she left. "I think since that moment, I didn't come back mentally, physically," Ikram said resolutely, almost as if she were speaking about a different person, now long gone. "I was in that public space."

For the twenty-eight days of the Tunisian revolution, Ikram braved confrontations with the police to march in the streets, one of thousands of Tunisians demanding democracy. By January 14, Ben Ali's government had been toppled, and he'd fled Tunisia for safe haven in Saudi Arabia.[13] Meanwhile other leaders from across the Middle East watched nervously as people began filling the streets, demanding an end to autocratic rule in their countries.

As of January 25, the uprisings had reached Egypt, with reports of close to fifty thousand people streaming into Tahrir Square. After just eighteen days, President Muhammad Hosni al-Sayed Mubarak, who had been in power for nearly thirty years, stepped down.[14]

As Tunisia and Egypt grappled with what would come next, women in both countries knew that this could be their moment. They wanted to ensure that women's equity would be enshrined in the new governments and laws to be created—that this time, promises made would be kept, and would lead to meaningful change.

This wasn't the first time Egyptian and Tunisian women had demanded their rights. In fact, they'd been agitating for a century, since before their nations' independence from colonial occupation, which Egypt achieved fully from the United Kingdom in 1952 and Tunisia from France in 1956.

In Egypt, one early feminist leader was Huda Sha'arawi, who during the Revolution of 1919 helped lead women's protests against British colonization and gathered women for lectures in public spaces—an activity then considered taboo—advocating for their welfare and suffrage. Just two years after the Nineteenth Amendment became part of the US Constitution, Sha'arawi attended the 1922 International Woman Suffrage Alliance Congress in Rome. She led a delegation of women's activists in picketing the Egyptian parliament in 1924, and after their list of feminist demands was ignored by the nominal Egyptian Wafdist government, which she'd fought for and supported, she left the party entirely. In 1923 she founded the Egyptian Feminist Union, building transnational links with other women's groups across the Arab world and challenging Western hegemony in the international women's movement. Against the backdrop of a vibrant women's press in Cairo and Alexandria, she continued to fight for women's liberation until her death, in 1947.[15]

In neighboring Tunisia, women were standing up to colonialism and demanding inclusion in education and public life. One of the country's earliest feminist activists, Manoubia Ouertani, caused an uproar by removing her veil during a public lecture on feminism in 1924, kicking off a flurry of articles in the Tunisian press debating practices of veiling and seclusion. In 1936, building on Ouertani's work, Bchira Ben Mrad founded the first legally recognized Tunisian women's organization, the Muslim Union of Tunisian Women, to ensure that women had roles in the nationalist struggle. The 1930s saw the creation of new women's magazines, and Tunisian women participated actively in the independence movement, leading resistance protests in every part of the country. Though participation in these groups was largely restricted to upper-class, educated women, the activists' pioneering work helped lead Tunisia's new prime minister, Habib Bourguiba, to pass groundbreaking laws in 1956 that Tunisian feminists had fought for over decades, permitting women to choose their husbands, banning polygamy, and even allowing abortions. Bourguiba also famously banned headscarves—never mind whether women wanted to wear them—going so far as to remove hijabs from women's heads himself, with a paternalistic pat on the cheek.[16]

Yet after independence, both countries' governments began to co-opt the women's movement. State-sponsored groups subsumed existing independent women's organizations, alongside growing intolerance of women's organizing. Radhia Haddad, Bourguiba's niece and the chairperson of the state-sponsored National Union of Women of Tunisia, in the 1970s became the country's first-ever female member of parliament, tirelessly fighting for women's rights, education, and economic inclusion. But when she pushed for even more progressive laws for women and left her uncle's political party in protest when he resisted, she was prosecuted by the state, and her passport was confiscated.[17]

Before the uprisings of 2011, both Egypt's and Tunisia's leaders had positioned their governments as champions of feminism and secular modernity. When foreign governments, flush with aid, pressed them on human rights, they often held up their empowerment of women as cover. In Tunisia, Ben Ali had continued to support Bourguiba's progressive laws and rights for women, and in Egypt, Mubarak had supported divorce rights and quotas for women's parliamentary participation. But much of this was window dressing. Women remained second-class citizens in the eyes of the law and tradition. Even worse, both regimes mercilessly targeted and tortured female (and male) human rights activists and political opponents, whose organizing threatened their authoritarian control.[18]

During the 2011 revolution and in the years that followed, sexual assault was a favored tool of Egyptian security thugs trying to suppress dissent. Women were beaten, stripped, raped, and subject to "virginity tests," all efforts to deter them from participating in demonstrations. Instead, the tactics led to a surge in activism, with Egyptian women mobilizing to prevent the kind of sexual violence endemic in Tahrir Square. Among them was the longtime feminist campaigner Nawal El Saadawi—a survivor of female genital mutilation, author of the groundbreaking 1972 book *Women and Sex*, and founder of the Arab Women's Solidarity Association—who stood shoulder to shoulder with the younger generation of activists. Women donned fluorescent-green vests with "Combating Harassment" written on the back, formed human chains, and hit back at harassers with stun guns and spray paint.[19] Armed with cell phones and aided by social media, they boldly occupied the public sphere—and refused to leave.

Activists in Tunisia were watching. "Even though Egypt followed Tunisia chronologically, we were all looking up to Egypt and its potential," Ikram said. "We felt that ten years ago, when Egypt became a democracy, then the entire Arab world would follow suit." That democratization, she and others hoped, would lead to meaningful changes in women's rights.

But as Tunisia began the work of casting off decades of dictatorship and refashioning itself as one of the few democracies in the Middle East, it looked as if women would yet again be pushed to the sidelines. "From day one, we were really marching alongside our brothers and husbands and comrades and partners," Ikram said. "But the first decisions they made, they were made against us and our bodies. . . . Yes, Ben Ali went, but the system is still here."

Ikram knew that for women to be included in legal and policy decisions, and for economic policy to be more responsive to women's needs, women had to be involved at the highest levels: they needed to be elected. That's why in March 2011 she founded Aswat Nissa, whose mission would be to fight for women's rights and raise their voices. She would take what she'd learned from the 2011 protests and apply it to women's organizing.

In Egypt, too, women stepped forward to lead, joining constitutional commissions and taking to the streets when they saw their efforts being threatened. One of those women was Mozn Hassan, who founded the grassroots organization Nazra for Feminist Studies and helped coordinate legal, medical, and psychological aid for women who'd been sexually assaulted during the 2011 uprisings and the difficult years afterward. "Honestly, it changed me as a person," said Mozn, who admitted that she was still shaken by the trauma of that time.[20] "I have been totally changed working with women who have been raped while people are talking about revolution or changing the government—and seeing all those people not caring."

After the uprisings, just as Ikram and Aswat Nissa did in Tunisia, Mozn and her organization turned their attention to campaigning for legal changes that would protect women, enshrine gender equity, and advance women's political participation. And for a time, it looked as if their efforts would pay off.

Nazra fought to ensure that women's rights were included in Egypt's 2014 constitution, winning the inclusion of fourteen articles that "are not only on what people think are mainstream women's issues, like violence," said Mozn, but "how to genderize a constitution. What is the right of women in health, in education, in the economy." Mozn joined a coalition of women's groups to change Egypt's penal code and successfully helped lobby for the first law ever to allow Egyptian women to charge their harassers and face them in court.[21]

But today, while women in Tunisia continue to make strides ensuring that legal protections against sexual harassment and violence are enforced, activists in Egypt, like Mozn, have faced a much harder road, with #MeToo organizers finding themselves labeled an existential threat to the very country they'd hoped to remake.[22] In Tunisia, after the fall of the Ben Ali regime, a quickly installed civilian caretaker government managed to navigate a perilous transition to democracy. But in Egypt, the transition has been much rockier. The military's Supreme Council of the Armed Forces took control in January 2011, followed by years of turmoil that were punctuated by brutal crackdowns against protests, power grabs, and the rise of Islamist parties in fraught elections. Two and a half years later, General Abdel Fattah al-Sisi, then the minister of defense, led a coup d'état against the ruling party, the Muslim Brotherhood. After more political chaos and attacks on democratic norms, in 2014 al-Sisi was sworn in as president. Egypt has become only more draconian under the strongman.

At first, some women's activists hoped that al-Sisi could be a supporter of women's rights. On his third day in office, after a woman was sexually assaulted in Tahrir Square by a mob celebrating his inauguration, al-Sisi's office issued statements condemning the attack. It was an assault that might have gone unnoticed. But a gruesome mobile-phone video—showing the woman raped, stripped, and beaten—had been posted on YouTube and quickly gone viral.[23]

Al-Sisi took the unprecedented step of visiting the woman in the hospital as she recovered—striking a new tone for a man who, as director of Egypt's military intelligence, had in 2011 defended the military's subjection of women to "virginity tests," and whose own security forces had been per-petrators of mass sexual assaults. "I have come to tell you that I am sorry," al-Sisi told the survivor, delivering flowers as state television cameras trailed him. "I am apologizing to every Egyptian woman. We as a nation will not allow this to happen again." He promised to form a committee to develop a national strategy to address sexual assault, made up of leaders from the gov-ernment, civil society, and Muslim and Christian groups.[24]

Yet since then, human rights in Egypt have rapidly eroded.[25] And to-day, one of the greatest threats to women asserting their rights is violence—not only within their homes or their communities, but at the hands of the state.

· · · · · · · · · · · · · · · · ·

In August 2017, Rania Fahmy, who lived in a provincial city in Upper Egypt, was groped on her way to the market.[26] This was not an unusual occurrence in a country where 99 percent of women say they've been subjected to street harassment. But on this day, Rania decided to fight back. She bashed her attacker over the head with her purse, then chased him down the street, undeterred by her abaya. Video footage from a security camera quickly went viral on Egyptian social media, with women expressing solidarity using the hashtags #AnaKaman (#MeToo) and #TimesUp.

Emboldened by the online support, Rania then did something even more unusual: she took her attacker to court. It was one of the first and most high-profile attempts to use the 2014 law Mozn Hassan and other women's rights activists had fought to pass—a law that, in the years following, had rarely been enforced. Despite attempts by the defendant to bribe Rania's lawyer, Rania persisted, and in February 2018 she became one of the first women to win a ruling against her harasser. Her assailant was sentenced to three years in prison. She received an award from Egypt's state-funded Na-tional Council for Women and was hailed across Egypt and internationally as a #MeToo hero.

But the euphoria over Rania Fahmy's case, and the seeming momen-tum her victory lent the #AnaKaman movement, was to be short-lived. Three months later, another woman, Amal Fathy—a longtime activist who'd weathered the 2011 revolution—uploaded a twelve-minute video to

Facebook documenting her harassment at a local state-run bank.[27] A taxi driver had groped her on the way to the bank, where a guard directed lewd comments at her while grabbing his crotch. Two days after Amal posted her video, masked and heavily armed police appeared at her home. They arrested Amal and, for good measure, took her husband and three-year-old son into custody as well. Her family was released, but Amal found herself in jail, forcing a smile behind security glass as she lied to her son that she was there getting medical treatment. Held for almost eight months, she was finally tried and convicted of charges she could hardly believe: threatening national security and spreading "fake news."

Amal was placed under house arrest until March 2020. She fought panic attacks and made near-daily visits to the police station to meet the unclear terms of her probation. She has been branded an extremist—all for documenting sexual harassment at a state-run institution, or, according to the Egyptian government, "spreading false news and rumours to disrupt public security and harm national interests."

The stakes for speaking out in Egypt were already high for women. Before and after the 2011 uprisings, women reporting harassment or assault risked their career opportunities, reputations, and safety. But in recent years the government crackdown on public dissent—including dissent voiced by leading women's activists—has become even more unsparing.

Mozn Hassan, the Nazra founder, is now also largely confined to her apartment. For speaking out about women's rights, she has been met with the full range of tricks of a dystopian regime: both her and Nazra's bank accounts were frozen in 2017, and she is banned from traveling outside Egypt. Mozn and other leading activists had their offices raided and have been targeted through the infamous antiterrorism "Case 173," which accuses Egyptian human rights defenders of receiving foreign funding for illegal purposes. Yet even after Nazra was forced to close its doors, and Mozn was formally charged with "inciting and calling for the irresponsible liberation of women," she still continued to raise the alarm with international media. "Criticism of Egypt, the society, or what women face here is being turned into a matter of national security that the government believes should not be a subject of public discussion," she defiantly told the *Wall Street Journal* in the fall of 2018.[28]

Mozn spoke to us in March 2020, on a Zoom call from Cairo that kept failing, due to a bad connection or, perhaps, interference from surveillance. She is smart and forceful, but her voice that day held a weariness born of carrying on a righteous but unfair fight. During our conversation, she said she saw #AnaKaman and Egyptian women's modern-day campaign for justice as part of a long "historical struggle," citing in particular the heroic example of Doria Shafik, the twentieth-century feminist activist who'd suffered eighteen years under house arrest. Mozn drew a direct line from Doria's work to today's feminist organizing and the government's punishment of movement and #MeToo leaders. "Doria Shafik paid her life as a price to women's rights," she said on our call. Although Mozn, too, has paid a high personal cost for speaking out, she still believes in the power of digital organizing to help Egyptian women find their courage, continue speaking out about harassment, and demand justice. "The power of #MeToo as an international movement was we got this solidarity," she said. She and other women have continued using digital networks to publicize survivors' #MeToo stories—accounts like that of May al-Shamy, one of the first Egyptian women to file a police report against a workplace supervisor for sexual harassment.[29]

. . . .

May, a former fashion editor, worked for over six years at *al-Youm al-Sabaa*, an influential Cairo newspaper aligned with the state government. In August 2018, she was at her desk late one day in the paper's open newsroom when her manager approached. May alleges that rather than discussing work as usual, he came to her with a question: he wanted to ask if she was divorced from her husband yet, so he could pursue a physical relationship with her. When May objected, her manager aggressively groped her. She told him he couldn't touch her, burst into tears, called her husband, and left the office.[30]

Emboldened by the #AnaKaman campaign, on August 31, 2018, May decided she would share her experience of sexual harassment on Facebook—because this wasn't the first time her manager had approached her or been abusive. Her story went viral on social media, and colleagues launched an online campaign of support, using hashtags like #SupportMayElShamy. But the backlash started almost immediately.

May shared her story with us in an interview from her home in May 2020. She'd been without work for two years. Her husband, Yehia Soliman, sat by her side as their toddler crawled over both their laps. In a departure from many families, who tend to silence women who speak out about sexual harassment and assault due to social taboos or shame, Yehia had stood by his wife throughout her ordeal.

After the assault by her manager, May took up the incident with the newspaper internally but got nowhere. The paper claimed she'd performed poorly in her job and was making allegations only to get a promotion. When May asked for footage of the incident from the paper's security cameras, she was told video was erased after fourteen days to free up storage, so there was no record. "When I asked the IT engineer to give witness testimony or to give me the video," May said, "he refused and explained that he can't do that because he might get fired."

In retaliation for her complaints, May was fired in early October 2018. So she and Yehia decided to pursue a legal case—even though precedent suggested that their odds of success were slim. In a previous episode involving a journalist's complaint of harassment, a woman working at *Rose al-Yusuf*—a newspaper named after a famous reporter and activist who wrote about women's rights in the 1930s and 1940s—filed a police report, only to have the courts take no real action. Like May, she was fired. And indeed, in late October 2018, the public prosecutor did as the *al-Yusuf* journalist's experience portended: rejected May's case, citing lack of evidence. Witnesses to the groping had refused to testify out of fear of retribution. Some said May's manager had been "acting like a kind of father checking on his girls," or like an older brother, and said it was fine for him to have groped her. This enraged Yehia. "I told the court representative that the victim is the one who identifies whether this is an appropriate touch or an inappropriate touch," he said.

May next filed an employment-rights case, seeking compensation for illegal termination. In December 2019, the newspaper was fined, and she was awarded a paltry sum—fifty thousand Egyptian pounds, a little over US$3,000—though it came on condition that she drop any harassment complaint. As of May 2020, she still hadn't received the money.

Instead, very quickly, May and Yehia became targets of the al-Sisi regime. A campaign falsely linked May to the banned Muslim Brotherhood party—a contention repeated by famous TV presenters and one that could have landed May and Yehia in jail. May turned again to Facebook to deny the allegations, saying, "My case has no political tendencies nor dimensions at all. . . . My case has to do with sexual harassment only," and closed the post with the hashtags #MeToo and #SafeWorkingSpaceforWomen.

Yehia's job as a pediatric surgeon was threatened. Whispers and social media posts attempted to sully his reputation. People suggested that the couple's marriage didn't follow the "Egyptian lifestyle," and that because May didn't wear a headscarf, it had been acceptable for her manager to grope her. *Al-Youm al-Sabaa* is part of "the strongest media company in Egypt," Yehia said, "and it is well known that they are controlled by the secret intelligence. We were fighting our own government."

Out of options and fearful over her family's future, May stopped talking publicly about her case or #MeToo. Yet because her attacker was politically connected within the regime, word went out across Egyptian media: May al-Shamy would never work in journalism again.

Although speaking out cost May her job and her reputation, she still fiercely believes in the #AnaKaman movement, and indeed wishes it would go even further. "I feel proud," she said, "even though I've been through hard times." May also underscored the importance of men's engagement with the movement, to ensure that women have the critical support and protection they need to feel safe to make complaints. "If I didn't have Yehia's support—and I have Yehia's support—I wouldn't be able to supply food or live," she said. "Any independent woman who has been through a harassment experience couldn't speak about it unless she had a husband or a family providing her material and moral support."

The couple emphasized the need for women to feel safe to serve as witnesses as well, lest they decline to testify out of concern for retribution, as May's colleagues did. "Women will always remember the May al-Shamy case," Yehia said, "because it made them frightened to speak. Her story, here in Egypt, it's not a happy-ending story. It's a nightmare story. . . . So women need more support when they do something like this, they need more legal support."

Today, May dreams of pursuing a master's degree, of studying digital media and feminist organizing, yet she believes the only way to move on and escape the government blacklisting is to leave Egypt. Even so, she said, she has no regrets: "If I could turn back time, I would do the same thing."

. . . .

Under a regime that strives to silence all forms of dissent—and that has painted #MeToo as a form of sedition—refusing to stop speaking is the most powerful form of resistance. The question is, are the right people listening?

In ideal circumstances, the United States would be one of the biggest potential allies in the fight for Egyptian feminist activists' free speech and free assembly. In 2019, Egypt received $1.4 billion in security assistance from America, which should give the US real influence in accelerating change for Egyptian women. But instead of calling for the release of women activists, the administration of Donald Trump publicly praised al-Sisi for initiatives that supposedly benefited women. During the Egyptian president's 2019 visit to Washington, DC, Ivanka Trump declared on Twitter, "Egyptian President Al Sisi delivered an important speech last weekend calling for major reforms aimed at empowering Egyptian women. We encourage & support these reforms, & look forward to working w/ the Egyptian government to advance these efforts. @AlsisiOfficial."[31] While Ivanka tweeted, women activists languished in Egyptian prisons.

In addition, the US Agency for International Development (USAID) has spent nearly $30 billion on development assistance in Egypt since 1978, focused on helping women lead "healthy, productive lives."[32] But traditional aid programs from the United States and other donors have not effectively supported Egyptian women's movements to achieve equity and safety—one reason that Mozn Hassan was moved to found Nazra, in 2011. "Our region has lots of money coming to women, but at the same time it is not coming for women, or feminist agendas or this holistic approach," she said pointedly. "No one is saying that economic empowerment is not important, but *only* economic empowerment is not helping women." She argued that while women may receive microloans or job training, those are not enough in a regime where women are arrested for speaking out and attempting to reform the political and legal system—where real power is held. Mozn has tried to build an Egyptian movement because she believes that feminism and gender equality are inextricable from freedom and development. "It's so problematic, because people are saying women's rights and the gender part of human rights are not a priority," Mozn said flatly. "We are the only region which doesn't have a regional feminist fund." After we spoke, Mozn filled this gap herself, founding the Doria Feminist Fund, named in honor of activist Doria Shafik.

As America fails to use the soft power its billions of dollars of aid might offer, US allies of women human rights defenders have turned to innovative use of existing laws. In 2017, dozens of American NGOs recommended using the Global Magnitsky Human Rights Accountability Act against rights abusers in Egypt. The law, which has inspired passage or consideration of similar legislation in the United Kingdom, Canada, and the European Union, provides tools to sanction repressive regimes, such as freezing the assets of human rights violators and banning their entry to America. The NGOs assembled compelling evidence for using the Magnitsky Act and delivered it directly to the doorstep of the US secretary of state. But instead of enacting sanctions, demanding the release of imprisoned activists, or pressing for legal change, the United States armed al-Sisi's authoritarian regime. Despite proposed cuts to foreign aid overall, in July 2018 the Trump administration unfroze close to $200 million in foreign military assistance to Egypt, financing previously withheld due to concerns about human rights and bad governance. The intention of these funds: to aid Egypt's purchase of American-made military equipment.[33]

In May 2019, al-Sisi won an illegitimate referendum to amend the Egyptian constitution so he could remain president until 2030. But even in the face of continued threats of house arrest, exile, or prison, the most vocal Egyptian advocates against sexual harassment and violence refuse to be scared into silence.

"Being a feminist activist, in Egypt or in this region, you know that you aren't doing feminism in Sweden. It's really hard," said Mozn, tired but determined. When we asked if she regretted speaking out, she said no. "I did the right thing, because being a feminist activist and leading a movement, you have to pay the price."

. . . .

Bochra Belhaj Hmida, a veteran activist and member of the Tunisian parliament, understands well the pressures Mozn and other Egyptian feminist organizers face today. "Sisi is a dangerous man that will finally destroy all his opponents," Bochra said to us, shaking her head during an interview over coffee at a Tunis café.[34] "I know many of the people who were arrested, children of my friends. He would never be so oppressive toward every voice without the approval or at least the compliance of the biggest countries."

Bochra is warm, wise, and battle tested, part of the generation of Tunisian feminist leaders who dealt with constant harassment and surveillance, and often imprisonment, under their country's authoritarian government— and still kept fighting. "Women have learnt," Bochra said, "the more they oppress you, the more they humiliate you, the more powerful you become. It's like the fear decreases." A force to be reckoned with, she unapologetically exhales smoke from her cigarette.

In 1989, Bochra cofounded the Tunisian Association of Democratic Women (ATFD), and she served as president from 1994 to 1998, during the Ben Ali regime. ATFD opened shelters for women survivors of violence, provided legal support for victims, worked with other women human rights defenders, and lobbied for legal reforms like a 2004 amendment to Tunisia's penal code to criminalize sexual harassment.[35] The amendment was imperfect progress: it did not go far enough to protect victims. The Tunisian government would allow women advocates to push only so far, keeping a tight rein on their activities. "We had some space to work," Bochra recalled, but "when we wanted to speak up about women's issues and inequality issues in general, all the doors were closed to us."

When the 2011 revolution came, ATFD and other feminist groups were ready to enshrine women's safety and equality in the nation's new laws— they were finally free to realize the vision Egyptian women still today have not, due to threat of state violence. But as the country began to build a new government, some activists grew concerned that women's rights would be blocked by the rise of Islamist political groups and their battle to codify "complementarianism" in Tunisia's constitution.[36] A theological position not only in Islam but also in some branches of Christianity and Judaism, complementarianism maintains that men and women hold "complementary roles" in marriage, religious practice, and public life. But in reality, this is code for women's "submission."

What first seemed like a threat was overcome, however, through organizing and widespread street protests. Women activists thus achieved historic victories in Tunisia's 2014 constitution, which promises that "the state commits to protect women's established rights and works to strengthen and develop those rights," and guarantees "equality of opportunities between women and men to have access to all levels of responsibility and in all domains." Tunisia also became one of only a few countries in North Africa and the Middle East to commit to legislative equality, with the constitution's assertion that "the state works to attain parity between women and men in elected Assemblies."[37]

In April 2014, Tunisia also fully accepted all provisions of the United Nations General Assembly's 1979 Convention on the Elimination of All Forms of Discrimination Against Women (CEDAW).[38] "We were able to obtain the equality between male and female citizens before the law," Bochra said, still proud. "The revolution that was seen as a threat became an opportunity to obtain more rights and more acquisitions for women and for the society in general."

After the constitutional victory, Bochra came to believe that to best help change laws to secure equality for women, and to combat sexual harassment and assault, she needed to run for office herself. "After the revolution," she said, "I wanted to do politics, because I believe that our chances to make a change when we are inside the system are bigger than when we are outside the system." In October 2014, she was elected to Tunisia's new legislative branch of government, the Assembly of the Representatives of the People, to represent Tunis.[39]

Bochra immediately got to work fighting for women's rights. In 2015, she helped pass a law that did not exist in any other Arab country at the time, the right of a mother to travel freely with her children. In June 2016, she helped pass a new amendment to Tunisia's electoral law, guaranteeing full gender parity in municipal and regional elections. In 2017, she helped strike down a prohibition on Muslim Tunisians marrying non-Muslims.[40]

And in July 2017, Bochra helped ensure a breathtaking victory in Tunisian women's fight against sexual harassment and assault: passage of the historic Violence Against Women law. The legislation was desperately needed. A national survey released in 2010 had found that almost 50 percent of Tunisian women experienced violence in their lifetime.[41] Decades in the making, the new law prohibits physical, sexual, political, economic, and psychological abuse; forbids harassment in public spaces; and rejects a former penal-code loophole that granted amnesty to rapists who married their underage victims. It also helps survivors with legal and psychological support.

Other members of the Tunisian parliament took to calling the legislation "Bochra's law," as she fought so hard for it. "They came to me on the day of elections to beg me to make some amendments," Bochra said. "I was like, I don't want to make any changes. I was so proud that we got to this point; I won't change anything." Fellow activists, watching from the parliament balcony, cried during the vote for the law's passage.

"We were able to obtain an exemplary law, one of the best in the world on violence against women," Bochra said. "There were actually some women from the Islamists that supported me against their own party. So that was an experience that teaches us how to win battles."

After leaving the political arena men had dominated for decades, Bochra was in 2017 appointed as president of the Individual Freedom and Equality Commission (COLIBE), by Tunisian president Béji Caïd Essebsi.[42] In accordance with the 2014 constitution and with international human rights frameworks, the commission is tasked with reporting on reforms needed to ensure equality and individual rights, particularly those between women and men. It completes the unfinished work of aligning the principles of the new constitution with old codes from the former dictatorship—stretching back to Tunisia's status as a French protectorate—and continuing the work of trailblazing Tunisian feminists.

. . . .

Without groundbreakers like Bochra, a movement like #EnaZeda and organizations like Aswat Nissa would not have been possible in Tunisia. "I want to say that this didn't happen in a vacuum," Aswat Nissa's Ikram Ben Said told us. "This is the result of at least twenty, thirty years of the older generation of feminists who were really talking about gender-based violence and sexual harassment in public space, in private space."

And today's leaders are ready to push even further. Next-generation Tunisian feminists want to see full implementation of the 2017 Violence Against Women law and other progressive legislation, insisting that words on paper are not enough without robust application and enforcement. They also want the Tunisian government to make good on promises for equal political power for women. Indeed, the week we met the Aswat Nissa team in February 2020, the Tunisian prime minister's cabinet was announced—with only six of thirty positions held by women, despite the constitutional call for parity.[43]

"Our fight to liberate ourselves also goes through social-economic equality and rights and democracy, and not only the quota and having more women in the parliament," Ikram said. She believes that women serving in parliament cannot alone solve the problems of entrenched patriarchy, as women in positions of power don't necessarily further women's rights and gender equality. To that end, in 2012, Aswat Nissa launched a Women's Political Academy, attended by over two hundred young women from different political parties and regions, fifteen of whom have become elected officials. "We've trained them in order for them to become leaders in women's rights and gender equality within their municipality or in the parliament or their political parties," Aswat Nissa spokeswoman Sonia Ben Miled said. The organization wants these leaders not only to help eradicate sexual and physical violence but also to ensure economic agency for all Tunisian women.

With limited resources, Tunisia's new organizations and movements will keep using every digital tool available. "For millennials, this is their way to advocate, to organize, to speak," Ikram said. Rania Said, the #EnaZeda Facebook moderator based in New York, agreed. As with much open-source organizing among young people around the world, these new activists may never even meet in person—and it doesn't matter. "Tunisia is very much a Facebook nation," Rania said. "I was twenty-three when the Tunisian uprising started, and we could not talk before, and now we have these tools that allow us to tell our stories."

Salma Ben Amour, the organizer against sexual harassment at the École Normale Supérieure, said she believed that the digital solidarity of the transnational #MeToo movement helped power Tunisia's #EnaZeda campaign. "We're all sharing the same cause," she said. "We have different traditions, but we face the same things. Because if in Pakistan people can speak out, then why not us?" Now that she's seen the potential of women's collective organizing, she told us, she's eager to ensure that Tunisia's laws upholding women's rights are enforced.

. . . .

How can donor countries like the United States and foundations best accelerate this kind of work? Unlike in Egypt, where the authoritarian government forcibly suppresses feminist activism, Tunisia has seen a flourishing of progressive feminist organizations in the ten years since its revolution. This generation of Tunisian feminists sees support for LGBTQ inclusion, ethnic minorities, and reproductive rights as crucial to their own advances. It is time US foreign aid reflected that—by reallocating aid to align with locally determined gender priorities.

These groups do critical advocacy work, and they do it despite small budgets and, from the donors' side, an enormous amount of red tape. "By definition, bureaucracy is the contrary of change," said Ikram, who rightly insisted on more local ownership of development projects. "Our work deserves creativity and innovation and to be radical." She agreed that donors ought to evaluate grantees for effectiveness, but not at the cost of hindering their potential impact. "Keeping civil society accountable, transparency, and policies against fraud, we agree on all this. But focus on the most important thing; focus on the ground, on mobilizing, organizing. Because by burdening us with all this bureaucracy, you are really killing the spirit of activism. And this is really very dangerous, especially in our region."

Constantly shifting donor priorities, often based on anything other than local needs, also impede progress. "Today the agenda is this, tomorrow it's women in terrorism," Ikram said, exasperated. She'd like to see donor models evolve and change the power dynamic. "Many are afraid to have this conversation with donor governments. And I think we need to be brave enough and say, 'Listen, this is the way things work. This is how we see it,' and not be donor driven." She said Aswat Nissa has adjusted by operating with smaller budgets and ensuring it doesn't have a large staff to pay, so the organization can maintain the integrity of its mission and approach. But this seems like an unfortunate solution for a successful local movement, when instead donors could and should change their investment approach.

Until then, the movement will continue to thrive on creativity, organizing, and raw hustle. #EnaZeda is just one part of today's broader feminist moment in Tunisia, in which activists have used everything from social media to art to politics to advance their cause. It is also a moment of unprecedented intersectionality. Amal Bint Nadia, a thirty-one-year-old activist, is an organizer for Falgatna ("fed up," in Tunisian dialect). She works with Chouf, an organization that advocates for women, including lesbian, bisexual, and trans women, and she founded the Chaml Collective, which uses literature to advocate for women's rights. "We can talk about it, here in this café, which is something we couldn't do before the revolution," Amal said when we met in downtown Tunis. "Well, maybe we could do it, but it wouldn't be very safe."[44] Now, acknowledging there was still much work to do, she said she wanted to see continued debate on women's rights. "We cannot make a revolution in ten years."

Amal recounted a story. The month after #EnaZeda caught fire, in 2019, Tunisian organizers saw how the Chilean anthem "A Rapist in Your Path" was spreading on social media internationally. "When we saw the Chileans' video," she said, "we thought maybe if we translate it to the Tunisian dialect and adapt it to our reality, it will be a demonstration where we can show that we are really mad." She and other next-generation activists were fed up with incremental changes and thought they could come together outside traditional structures like organizations or political parties "to be just citizens and feminists."

The activists knew what to do: organize. "Some people started to translate it; others suggested that we do the rehearsals at their place, and that they can provide a cup of tea," Amal said. "So we started spontaneously to get organized as a collective." The group decided that unlike traditional organizations, theirs would have no hierarchy; everyone would have a voice in decisions for the demonstration. They would also openly welcome anyone who identified as a woman—including lesbian, queer, transgender, and nonbinary participants.

On December 14, 2019, about one hundred women gathered in Tunis, in a plaza outside the prime ministry, to protest sexual abuse, harassment, and violence. For many of the activists, this was their first time meeting in person. Blindfolded and pointing their fingers toward the prime ministry, they added a special line to the Chilean song, aimed at Zouheir Makhlouf: "The sexual harasser does not legislate."[45] Their point: new laws were not worth the paper they were printed on if the system continued to grant impunity to sex offenders, and especially to elected officials.

In May 2020, Tunisia's political leaders could no longer deny the movement's demands for justice for the anonymous young student who'd been brave enough to speak up. Makhlouf announced his resignation from parliament.

#EnaZeda had won.

An anonymous survivor in the BBC's *Sex for Grades* documentary speaks about her trauma following the sexual abuse she experienced while a student at the University of Lagos in Nigeria in 2019. Journalist Kiki Mordi helped design special masks to both protect the identity of her sources and represent their strength and power. Credit: Getty Images

Chapter Four

NIGERIA: FAITHFUL FEMINISM

#ArewaMeToo

These people, these men making all of these laws and policies, do not understand what women go through.
—Fakhrriyyah Hashim

In February 2019, in Nigeria's cosmopolitan capital, Abuja, a twenty-seven-year-old entrepreneur and activist named Fakhrriyyah Hashim was scrolling through Twitter and saw an unusual tweet come up in her feed: a woman in northern Nigeria had bravely broken with taboo and named the man who had sexually and physically assaulted her.

The woman was Khadijah Adamo, a pharmacist based in Kaduna State, three hundred miles away. Two years earlier, Khadijah's boyfriend had threatened to "kill and bury her body"—and came dangerously close to succeeding when he attacked and choked her. "I used to say if any man laid his hands on me, I would make him regret it. But that day, I was crying and begging for my life," Khadijah had blogged.[1] "One thing is for sure, I'm never going to let that happen to me again. It shouldn't have to happen to anyone."

Fakhrriyyah had never met Khadijah, but she was also from northern Nigeria. And as a sexual abuse survivor herself, she knew it was unlikely that a tweet would lead to justice in Kaduna. Nigeria's northern region is the most repressive for the country's women. Girls can be forced to marry as young as twelve or thirteen, bought like chattel for a "bride price." Local religious leaders mandate silence and submission for girls, instead of school. The police rarely enforce sexual or domestic abuse laws, and Sharia law is widely observed. Communities also regularly face violence. The terror group Boko Haram has been responsible for more than twenty thousand deaths and the displacement of over two million people.[2] And just a week after Khadijah's post on Twitter, intercommunal ethnic violence killed 141 people.

The north is not the only place where Nigerian women face rampant discrimination and sexual assault. President Muhammadu Buhari made clear to all Nigerian women how he viewed them when he proclaimed in a 2016 press conference that his wife, Aisha, "belongs to my kitchen." The country has one of the worst economic gender gaps in the world, according to the World Economic Forum. And a quarter of all Nigerian girls experience sexual violence by the time they turn twenty.[3] In 2014, when 276 Nigerian schoolgirls were kidnapped in Chibok by Boko Haram, a viral Twitter campaign called #BringBackOurGirls helped raise attention to violence against girls and women—but when the #MeToo movement swept the globe in 2017, it seemed to miss Nigeria.

It was easy to believe that in such an environment, Khadijah's #MeToo tweet wouldn't make a ripple. But Fakhrriyyah decided to add her voice in solidarity anyway. "I am here for Hausa women out saying [calling out] their abusers," she said in 2020, in an interview from her graduate-school dorm room.[4] She posted her tweet with the hashtag #ArewaMeToo, adding the Hausa word for the northern region.

Fakhrriyyah didn't think much of it after she tweeted. But the next day, she noticed something unexpected on her timeline. "So many people, especially women, started relaying their own experiences and using the hashtag," she said. Defying the constraints of tradition—"Normally, women would keep quiet," Fakhrriyyah said—hundreds of women began posting on social media, sharing their own stories of sexual abuse and harassment. In response, unheard-of demonstrations broke out in northern cities, where protestors carried signs reading, "Consent Is Key" and "End Rape." Lawyers, media personalities, and women across the country joined the movement. The Kaduna protests inspired Twitter hashtag campaigns in other regions, including majority-Christian communities where women faced similar abuse and discrimination. The local movement's rapid, decentralized spread, with women organizing independently online and in person across the country, surprised even its founders. Within two weeks, Khadijah's attacker—a man named Lawal Abubakar—apologized, admitted guilt, and said he took "full responsibility" for his actions.[5]

Over the course of the next nine months, a group of unlikely allies—women who persevered even with paltry funding and in the face of backlash from religious conservatives, the police, and their own families—would continue to force #MeToo into the national spotlight. Inspired by the global #MeToo movement, Fakhrriyyah and other activists set about making the #ArewaMeToo campaign their own, taking aim at educational, faith, and legal barriers that allowed sexual harassment and abuse to go unchecked. The #MeToo movement "prepared the land," Fakhrriyyah said. "So that moment in February 2019 was when those seeds began to sprout."

What started with a single tweet turned Fakhrriyyah into an unexpected leader offline. For #ArewaMeToo to have lasting impact in a country where less than half the population has internet access, she realized, any online outcry would need to be translated into real-life action. So activists moved offline, starting local chapters in five northern Nigerian states within months.[6] Community leaders began to investigate reports of sexual misconduct, connecting survivors to local NGOs and legal clinics in their growing network so the women could learn about their rights—and press charges. WhatsApp quickly became an important platform for activists organizing in the north, enabling them to digitally connect women across the region who could then meet locally.

One of those organizers was Hassana Maina, a university student in Borno, in northeast Nigeria. Hassana had also become active after reading Khadijah's taboo-defying story. "That empowered people," she said in an interview from her home in Borno.[7] "I mean these are our conservative, shy, northern women, but they were coming out to talk" about sexual violence. Even though Hassana was finishing her university studies, she decided to start an #ArewaMeToo chapter in Maiduguri, Borno's capital. "Seeing those messages, I just felt like something has to be done," she said. "And when you say something has to be done, most of the time we forget that someone has to do it."

Despite the risk, she would be that someone. After working on consent education in schools, Hassana had come to believe that in the absence of legislation or enforcement, social media shaming of perpetrators could help deter sexual harassment and assault. "I believe, personally, that it is our silence that emboldens predators to do it to other people," she said. If the law or the police wouldn't stand up for women in the north, it was time to name names. Hassana took to Twitter and quickly brought women together, tweeting that if anyone in Maiduguri wanted to help take the #ArewaMeToo message to the streets, they should "DM" her, or message her directly. Her Twitter page is a record of the movement in its early days, when seemingly solitary women found they weren't the only ones ready to take action in their communities. "I had a lot of messages from young, vibrant, enthusiastic youths," Hassana said. "I had never met them. I don't know who they are."

Online advocacy made offline organizing feel safer by uniting women who'd had no way of knowing they weren't alone. "Many people are not able to open up to people in their immediate environment because it can be dangerous," Fakhrriyyah said. "Without technology, I don't think we would have had a voice."

Even so, the women soon learned that social media could not protect #ArewaMeToo activists from all retaliation.

. . . .

Fakhrriyyah and her fellow #ArewaMeToo leader Maryam Awaisu, a novelist and sexual assault survivor based in Kaduna, learned through a WhatsApp group in February that Abubakar Sadiq Aruwa, an aide to the Nigerian minister of finance and a former staffer for the governor of Kaduna State, had been accused of sexually assaulting minors at a local secondary school. When Fakhrriyyah directed a "tweet storm," or barrage of Twitter posts, at the minister, demanding that she at least suspend Aruwa so that the allegations could be investigated, the official's office reached out quietly and asked the movement to pipe down. The women refused. "When we look at sexual violence, it's a power struggle," Fakhrriyyah said, and a man like Aruwa "gets his power from the political class he's very much connected to. So as a strategy, it's imperative that we target where he gets his power from." Whether true or false, serious allegations had been made and he should not be immune from investigation. Aruwa denied wrongdoing but was forced to resign amid the online pressure, in what looked like another win for the burgeoning movement.[8]

But then Aruwa retaliated. He released a statement through his attorneys listing seven Twitter handles that he alleged were making "defamatory commentary" and "spurious and unsubstantiated allegations of rape." On February 19, Maryam was arrested at her office, in an overwhelming show of force by Nigeria's infamous Special Anti-Robbery Squad, a police unit so brutal that October 2020 street protests and global outcry led to a government pledge to disband it.[9] Although the unit had no authority to make an arrest for alleged defamation, they confiscated Maryam's laptop and phone and took her to another city to be questioned. Panicked, her movement colleagues went to the best place they knew to draw attention to her case: Twitter.

Amnesty International's Nigeria office joined the call for Maryam's release—saying in a press statement that she and other human rights defenders who were part of Nigeria's #MeToo movement "must not be silenced or punished for the vital work they do." Maryam was thankfully let go within hours.[10] Yet the message was undeniable: #ArewaMeToo activism was dangerous work. The women behind the movement would pay a steep price for speaking out.

Yet the backlash to #ArewaMeToo wasn't over. The religious community was the next to come to Aruwa's defense. In a tactic repeated around the world to attack feminist organizers, conservative religious critics alleged that women's rights threatened local religious norms. A young Islamic cleric, a friend of Aruwa's with a popular online following, began labeling the #ArewaMeToo organizers lesbians and demanded that they start a new hashtag campaign to defend traditional northern values.

Fakhrriyyah and other Muslim Nigerian women have pushed back on such attacks, attempting to reclaim and reframe what their faith says about women and abuse. When sexual assault happens in some conservative Muslim societies, religious leaders often want matters settled quietly, out of the public eye, lest accusations bring shame to their faith and community. That tradition has silenced survivors—something Fakhrriyyah and others have fought to change. When we spoke in June 2020, Fakhrriyyah shook her hijab-covered head in bewilderment, rejecting the idea that she and other feminist activists were "being influenced by the West to abandon traditions, that we're telling women that they shouldn't be homemakers."

She continued, "This religious scholar gained a lot of attention, because the one thing you can use to condemn anything in northern Nigeria is to say that it is homosexual." Such an assertion "can literally have someone killed." Fakhrriyyah and Maryam decided they wouldn't acquiesce, and they refused to condemn the LGBTQ community, who were also victims of sexual violence. Fakhrriyyah said, "I've realized over the past few years of being out-spoken about human rights issues, one of the worst things you can do while trying to address one social scourge is putting another group under the bus."

The Aruwa case wasn't the first time #ArewaMeToo organizers had been thrown into conflict with their religious community. Fakhrriyyah was moved to take on this work in part because of the prevalence of sexual abuse against children at schools and at home by Islamic teachers. Maryam, her fellow organizer, was herself a survivor of sexual assault by an Islamic scholar.[11]

Hassana, the university student in Borno, told us that she, too, had been sexually harassed in school, when one of her university lecturers invited her to his office during her final year. "He had his hands on my hips, and he commented that I was getting fat," she said. "So I sat down and I calmly told him that I go to schools and I talk to young people about sexual assault and sexual violence." That stopped him, but Hassana knew that not every student could be so brave—or so lucky. And individual experiences added up to a systemic problem, with sexual harassment keeping girls out of the classrooms they needed to be in for economic advancement and personal agency. "There's this whole ideology of why am I going to send my daughters to a school for male lecturers or male teachers to harass," Hassana said.

What was meant to break #ArewaMeToo only made the women more de-termined. Building on their social media momentum, they started speaking to members of the media locally and far beyond northern Nigeria—to Al Jazeera, *The Guardian*, and international Muslim community outlets. "A lot of people are actually uncomfortable, and to a certain degree annoyed, by the fact that we're talking about these things, as if we're opening our pants to the world," Fakhrriyyah said in an interview with the Muslim women's website Amaliah .com.[12] "We have to change the societal perception of a woman's dignity."

Fakhrriyyah and the #ArewaMeToo chapters increased their outreach to Muslim religious leaders, visiting houses of worship and Islamic schools. Their aim was to bring these groups into the conversation on sexual harass-ment and assault, and to dispel misconceptions around Islam's teachings. "If we wanted to have the public's ears," Fakhrriyyah said, the women had to "speak to religious scholars, see how we can translate what we're doing in a way that people welcome it."

In Borno, where Boko Haram remains active, Hassana braved danger to speak at schools about consent. "I go to Islamic schools, we go to diploma congressional schools, to talk to young people about sexual violence and about the culture of shame and silence," she told us. She was going to do the work no matter what. "There's this poem I wrote about women being the embodiment of sin. I think that's the general presumption here. And so little by little, with diplomacy, with the right amount of arrogance, we're trying to see how we can dismantle the patriarchy. Because I think at the end of the day, that's what fuels all of this—the rape culture, victim blaming, and all of that. All of this has to be children of the patriarchy."

Because a culture of sexual harassment and assault thrives on control and power, it can take hold in any congregation, in any faith—as was soon demonstrated in Lagos, where one woman's battle helped ignite the #MeToo movement in Nigeria's Christian south.

· · · · · · · · · · · · · · · · · ·

Busola Dakolo seemed to be living the perfect life. She was a successful photographer based in Abuja and was married to a well-known Nigerian musician. But that all changed when she made allegations about a sexual assault that happened when she was a teenager. The man she accused was the prosperity-gospel preacher Biodun Fatoyinbo. A Pentecostal pastor often seen driving around the capital in his Porsche, he was head of one the largest, fastest-growing churches in the country, the Commonwealth of Zion Assembly. Fatoyinbo appeared often in the media, preaching the word of God to thousands on Sundays across the church's multiple locations.[13]

Busola had no reason to speak out. She knew she wouldn't be celebrated for making allegations about a holy man. Going public with accusations of sexual harassment and assault broke with expectations that Christian women should simply pray, forgive, and leave matters to God. But when Busola looked at her three daughters, she felt she had to say something—for their future, and, she says, to protect other girls and women in his flock. "We want our environment to be safe for the children," Busola said in a June 2020 interview from her photography studio.[14] "I was just thinking, that could be my daughter."

In Nigeria, as in the United States, Christian pastors hold tremendous social and political capital. The country's vice president is a pastor at the Redeemed Christian Church of God, and political candidates often pay courtesy calls to pastors at megachurches.[15] The trope that women are the embodiment of sin spreads far beyond the conservative Muslim north to all kinds of houses of worship—including conservative Christian churches, where women's bodies or their simple presence can be considered a temptation, and if men "fall from grace" and harass or attack a woman sexually, it's the victim's fault. The culture of silence and victim blaming is so pervasive in religious communities—not only in Nigeria but globally—that it has triggered its own version of #MeToo: "Church Too," with female parishioners sharing stories online of sexual assault and abuse at the hands of their alleged spiritual leaders.

Busola knew she'd face overpowering doubt and criticism if she came forward with her claims about Fatoyinbo. But she says she was done with shame. Just as well-known women in the United States had turned to social media, Busola leveraged her social following to plead her case. Even if her efforts did nothing to bring Fatoyinbo to justice, she thought perhaps her words would inspire other women to come forward, or would sound a note of caution, and thus protection.

In June 2019, Busola met with the journalist Chude Jideonwo, of the Nigerian news website YNaija, in the sanctuary of a church. She alleged that the pastor she'd seen "as a father" had raped her twice when she was his sixteen-year-old parishioner.[16] The interview is devastating to watch. Busola's voice shakes as she says that Fatoyinbo "covered my mouth," and that she bled on her living room floor after one assault. Her parents had no suspicions: they believed the pastor's visits were for their daughter's spiritual development. Instead, Busola alleges that Fatoyinbo assaulted her first at her home, then on the hood of his car on an abandoned road. Busola says she told no one, afraid she wouldn't be believed. Who was she next to this glamorous figure?

But now she was grown up, a glamorous woman in her own right. She felt it was time to tell her truth.

Her interview with Jideonwo went viral on YouTube and triggered widespread condemnation of Fatoyinbo on social media. He immediately responded, denouncing the allegations as "fallacious, non-existent and which are all denied in every measure," saying, "I have never in my life raped anybody even as an unbeliever and I am absolutely innocent of this." Within days, though he denied the allegations, Fatoyinbo stepped down. He turned to social media in response, posting a statement on Instagram that received over thirty-three thousand likes, in a seeming show of belief in his innocence: "I have decided to take a leave of absence from the pulpit." The Pentecostal Fellowship of Nigeria and the Christian Association of Nigeria opened investigations. Other women reported stories of abuse at the hands of other religious leaders.[17]

But the reckoning incited backlash. Almost immediately, Fatoyinbo's supporters mounted a coordinated social media campaign in defense of him. Christian bloggers and Instagrammers quoted scripture and accused Busola of lying. Members of the megachurch started their own hashtag campaign, #IStandWithBiodunFatoyinbo. "I've been bruised by media," Busola said matter-of-factly. But now that she'd broken her silence, she was determined to fight. Defying Nigerian religious taboos, she started sharing her claims in the international press. "Our culture doesn't allow speaking of these sorts of things against anointed men of God," Dakolo told *The Guardian*. "They'd rather hide it, and the party that is being victimized tends to live with that self-blame. . . . The society, the church, keeps sweeping things under the carpet."[18]

With her husband's support, Busola filed a police report in July 2019. But three weeks later, the couple were the ones targeted for investigation. As Busola drove home alone one night in Lagos, she noticed an unmarked minivan following her. It then drove in front of her, blocking her path. Three men got out of the vehicle and demanded that she board the van. Afraid, she refused. An armed officer from the Abuja police's inspector general's office then served her with a letter, alleging "criminal conspiracy, falsehood, mischief, and threat to life"—not by Fatoyinbo, but by Busola and her husband.[19]

Only a month later, Fatoyinbo was back in the pulpit. He claimed the allegations were evidence of his ministry's strength. "As a Christian, you must face opposition," he preached. "If God, who is holy and faithful, has enemies, you are sure going to."[20]

In September 2019, Busola filed a civil lawsuit against Fatoyinbo, for "intentionally inflicting and causing continuous emotional distress." He filed a countersuit, alleging that her accusations were "frivolous," "grossly incompetent," and "statute-barred," due to Nigeria's statute of limitations for sexual assault—a mere two months.[21] Her case looked hopeless, but Busola refused to give up. "Why am I doing all this?" she said in our interview. "Because we're used to being in a society where the system doesn't work, and then we just keep quiet."

In response to Busola's allegations, over the summer of 2019 survivors took to the streets in protest. Angry, emotional crowds gathered in Lagos to demand justice, holding signs saying, "You should be praying for us, not raping us" and "Thou Shalt Not Rape. #ChurchToo."[22] These scenes were captured by a twenty-eight-year-old freelance journalist, Kiki Mordi, who stood on the sidelines, filming it all for a secret, bombshell documentary for BBC Africa.

. . . .

"Busola Dakolo started a conversation," Kiki said, when we spoke to her in Lagos, close to a year after the protest.[23] "It's a fight that doesn't promise a lot for her. She's getting all the trauma and the challenge with very little upside personally, but she's doing it for other women." Kiki turned quiet for a moment. "I cried the day I watched that video and didn't even watch it to the end. Because I knew exactly what she was talking about."

Women journalists around the world have fought to tell stories of sexual violence, only to be discouraged by lack of support from male editors. But Kiki managed to succeed where so many others have been silenced, persuading the team at the BBC's Africa Eye investigative division to recognize that sexual harassment and assault were a priority topic for coverage in Africa. Their collaboration eventually resulted in the 2019 film *Sex for Grades*, a devastating portrayal of the culture of sexual harassment at some of Nigeria's top universities.

Kiki's case to her editors was perhaps more persuasive because she is a survivor herself. For the documentary, she shared emotionally on camera how eight years before, she'd been sexually harassed at Nigeria's elite University of Lagos (UNILAG). Kiki had dreamed of becoming a doctor, a plan thwarted when she refused to have sex with her professor—a "sex-for-grades" negotiation that's not uncommon in Nigeria.[24] Her lecturer retaliated by withholding her exam grades for two semesters. When Kiki reported the professor, UNILAG failed to act. Devasted, she dropped out of university entirely.

Kiki became determined to share her story so that other young women wouldn't be victimized, even if speaking about her own experience was painful. "It happened to me, and I can't allow this to happen to someone else again," she told us.

As they were putting together the documentary, the BBC's editors learned that Kiki's experience was far from rare. In Nigeria's south, it was an open secret that university professors preyed on their students. "We genuinely did not need to go that far to find evidence," Kiki said. "The case was strong on arrival." Quickly, countless female students sent in anonymous screenshots, recordings, and direct messages on social media, naming specific lecturers. But women were still hesitant to speak on camera, fearful of university retribution and online backlash. So Kiki came up with an ingenious plan: for the first time ever, young women journalists posing as students would go undercover at UNILAG and the University of Ghana, another leading West African institution. And student survivors would conduct interviews on camera wearing artist-designed masks that would convey their strength and protect their privacy.

One undercover student from *Sex for Grades* agreed to speak to us about her experience, though she asked to remain anonymous, fearing retribution against family members who still attended the school. "It feels like it's a standard practice," she said. "If you're a lecturer in UNILAG and you don't sexually harass women, you're the unicorn. I'm not joking. They all do it. Everybody, all departments, philosophy, law, social sciences, French, everywhere."[25]

She decided to participate in the BBC documentary because the university had been unresponsive to female students' complaints about their lecturers. "It could hold me back from graduating," she said. "They could expel me, because if I did not have concrete proof, they will say I'm making up stories involving their lecturers harassing me." Like other women who've reported sexual harassment only to be stonewalled, the student moved from official channels to social media and the press to call for justice. "It pisses me off talking about it because it's an awful experience," she said. "It affected my mental health for a really, really long time."

In the documentary footage, UNILAG professors speak openly about using a faculty club as a prime location for grooming students for sexual assault. One journalist is propositioned by a professor while simply standing in a hallway. A lecturer demands that a student pray to accept Christ with him, while he moves to stimulate himself sexually. Professors close their office doors, attempting to harass, grope, and blackmail their targets.[26]

In one exchange, a UNILAG professor and wayward church pastor, Dr. Boniface Igbeneghu, tries to kiss a student in exchange for university admission, asking her about her sexual history and making the quid pro quo clear. "This is the benefit," he says. "It's not free for the girl now. Is she not paying for it with her body?"

When *Sex for Grades* was released, in October 2019, outrage was quick and powerful. The day the documentary aired, Nigeria's First Lady, Aisha Buhari, demanded that more action be taken to fight sexual harassment in universities and faith communities. "This simply has to change," Buhari said. "It is no longer enough to sweep allegations under the carpet or force victims to withdraw their allegations, victimize, or stigmatize them." Within two days of the broadcast, Nigeria's Senate reintroduced the 2016 Sexual Harassment in Tertiary Education Institution Prohibition Bill, sponsored by the deputy Senate president and fifty-seven other senators.[27]

But *Sex for Grades* wasn't the first time sexual harassment by university professors had prompted anger, an online campaign, and attempts to pass the bill. In 2018, a twenty-three-year-old Nigerian MBA student named Monica Osagie had used a mobile-phone app to capture a grim exchange in which a professor, Richard Akindele, had tried to negotiate how many times Monica would need to have sex with him for an A grade. "Is it not five we agreed? Our agreement is five," he said in the recording, which went viral on YouTube.[28] Monica suffered backlash in person and online, but women across Nigeria tweeted support with the hashtag #StandingWith-MonicaOsagie and called on government and university leaders to respond to her allegations.

In May 2018, the Nigerian Senate passed a motion calling for a full investigation and condemning sexual harassment in higher-learning institutions, naming Monica as their inspiration. Akindele was fired. In December 2018, he received a two-year sentence. Monica's complaint helped lay the groundwork for future court cases, and her story reinvigorated attention for the Senate's 2016 sexual harassment bill, which had stalled in Nigeria's House of Representatives. The House had rejected it for not also including workplace and religious institutions, and no lawmaker had attempted to revise the bill—until *Sex for Grades*.[29]

Facing a broken system, women's rights activists used digital content and online organizing to keep up pressure and put the bill back into play. If passed, it would make sexual harassment of students by teachers illegal, and put teachers who have sexual relationships with students in jail for anywhere from five to fourteen years. The bill proposes a fine of five million Nigerian naira (about US$13,000) if a court convicts the accused harasser, as well as fines and jail terms for university administrators who fail to conduct sexual harassment investigations. It also proposes serious consequences for students who make false allegations: suspension or expulsion.[30]

Sex for Grades helped achieve other victories. In response to the film, the Nigerian Human Rights Commission opened investigations into sexual and gender-based violence. And outrage stirred by the documentary helped lead to the creation of a sex offender registry. "One lecturer gets fired from one university and you get employed in the next one," Kiki said in our interview. "And we're just recycling these abusers." Dr. Igbeneghu, the UNILAG professor, was suspended and asked to step down as pastor from his church, despite his protests on Facebook that the documentary was a "setup" and a "hoax." Another professor captured on camera harassing students, Dr. Samuel Oladipo, was also suspended.[31]

Yet female students at UNILAG didn't want to see just two professors suspended—they wanted measurable changes to policies and enforcement. And they were ready to protest. But just as in the United States, authorities in Nigeria make frequent use of nondisclosure agreements to silence victims. "Somewhere in one of the documents they [students] signed when they gained admission is an indemnity form," Kiki told us. "They would go to jail if they protest. So it's like their wings are clipped."

· · · · · · · · · · · · · · · · · · ·

Throughout Nigeria, women's wings are clipped in schools, workplaces, and religious institutions because a bureaucratic and legislative system that should protect them simply isn't working.

It's been a long fight. Just as in Tunisia and Egypt, early women activists were central to Nigeria's campaign for freedom from colonization. In the 1929 "Women's War," tens of thousands of women in the southeastern part of the country joined across six ethnic groups to resist British corruption, taxation, and forced-labor demands, opposing fees that overwhelmingly targeted women workers.[32] Without a venue in the colonial government by which to gain a hearing, they protested in the streets. Their strategic campaign—called a "riot" by their oppressors—was one of Nigeria's many powerful examples of resistance to colonial control.

Much like today's Nigerian activists, the nationalist and women's rights leader Oyinkansola Abayomi, born in 1897 in Lagos, recognized the power of education to achieve women's liberation. After her first husband, a lawyer, was assassinated in a Nigerian courtroom, she became the founding teacher in 1927 of Queens College, Lagos, a girls'-only secondary school. She flouted societal norms by becoming the first woman in Lagos to drive a car. In 1944, with a dozen other women, she founded the first all-women political party, the Nigerian Women's Party, so that women would have a role in the nationalist fight—and a seat at the table after independence in 1960.[33]

Women in the north have also long been active in the fight for women's rights. One of the most prominent activists of her time, Kaduna State's Hajia Gambo Sawaba, born in 1933, was forced to end her formal education after primary school when her father died. After marrying at age thirteen, to a man who abandoned her following her first pregnancy, she became a lifelong activist for women's rights. She got involved in politics at age seventeen, campaigning against early marriage and forced labor, and advocating for Western-style education in Nigeria's north. She served as the deputy chairperson of the Great Nigeria People's Party and made her political mark when, during a lecture in the conservative north, she dared stand up and speak in a room full of men.[34] She died in October 2001, and although her life overlapped with Nigeria's independence, her work to fully secure women's equality remained uncompleted.

These days, when it comes to sexual harassment or assault, a complicated legal web—involving Nigeria's constitution, inconsistent state and federal legislation, unenforced penal laws in the south, and Sharia law in the north—obstructs justice for women. Take the hard-fought attempts at progress on the Sexual Harassment in Tertiary Education Bill. Despite the online uproar and advocacy by women's rights organizations—and although the National Association of Nigerian Students reported in February 2020 that it had received over two thousand complaints of university lecturers harassing female students, comparing the prevalence of sexual harassment in higher education to the COVID pandemic—critics objected that a new bill was unnecessary, arguing that laws like the Violence Against Persons Prohibition (VAPP) Act already adequately addressed sexual harassment and assault.[35]

The groundbreaking 2015 VAPP Act prohibits sexual violence and female genital mutilation, outlaws physical and economic abuse, and punishes rapists with life in prison.[36] But at the local level, it has gone largely unenforced. In Nigeria, federal legislation may pass the National Assembly, but it then must be adopted and enacted separately by each of the country's thirty-six states. As of this writing, fewer than half of Nigeria's states have passed the law, leaving millions of women without a consistent framework for fighting sexual and gender-based violence.[37]

The VAPP Act is not the only example of federal legislation falling short. In 2003, Nigeria passed a law guaranteeing all girls the right to basic education and outlawing marriage before the age of eighteen. But all of Nigeria's states needed to ratify it for it to take full effect. The governor of Kaduna, where the majority of Nigerian girls who are denied schooling live, signed the bill into law only in 2018—fifteen years after it was passed at the federal level, and after relentless campaigning by women activists on the streets and the airwaves.[38]

Even in the handful of states where the VAPP Act has passed, Nigeria's negligent legal system is notoriously unsupportive of survivors. A 2019 analysis found that Nigeria had fewer than eighty recorded rape convictions in its entire legal history.[39] Not much has changed recently. Lagos's first rape crisis center, Mirabel, has treated more than eleven hundred survivors of rape since 2014; only four perpetrators have been convicted.[40] Cases take so long to wind their way through the courts that victims often give up.

Nigeria's legal system fails women every day—almost by design, according to #ArewaMeToo's Fakhrriyyah. "How, then, do you expect a country to take women's issues seriously when these people, these men making all of these laws and policies, do not understand what women go through?" she said. "Or, which I think is more the reason, is because they benefit from the structures that are in place." The situation isn't likely to improve anytime soon. In the spring 2019 elections, the number of women in Nigeria's House of Representatives fell by almost half, dropping to just under 3.5 percent, one of the lowest rates in the world.[41]

. . . .

Leaders of the #ArewaMeToo movement realized that protests over individual cases of crimes against women, even if they went viral, would never be enough to end structural discrimination. A complicit government needed to be confronted more directly. In November 2019, as activists in southern Nigeria continued to fight for the bill prohibiting sexual harassment in education, #ArewaMeToo activists decided to challenge Nigeria's northern states to adopt the VAPP Act. "If you look at the prohibitions we have for rape in this part of the country, we look at penal courts—they are really insufficient," said Hassana Maina, the student activist in Borno. "They are really colonial laws that have been in existence for so long and have not been reformed."

Fakhrriyyah, Hassana, and other activists started an online campaign called #NorthNormal and held rallies in support of the VAPP Act on November 25, to mark the International Day of the Elimination of Violence Against Women.[42] This time they intentionally decentralized the advocacy, recruiting local leaders online. They looked for young people who were running community organizations, or anyone interested in fighting for structural reforms against sexual violence. Planning over WhatsApp, #ArewaMeToo leaders organized events in eight northern states: Abuja, Bauchi, Borno, Kaduna, Kano, Niger, Sokoto, and Yobe. Like Rania Said in Tunisia's #EnaZeda movement, Hassana soon found herself with a second full-time (and unpaid) job as an #ArewaMeToo organizer. "I was still a student and trying to coordinate everything," she said.

Then the trouble started. In Sokoto, the WhatsApp organizing group became overrun by rumors, posted by conservative critics, alleging that the group was promoting LGBTQ rights instead of responding to sexual violence. "Predators just do not want us to talk about this issue because they benefit from the silence," Hassana said. She responded by sending a copy of the VAPP Act to the group and urging people to read it. But the bad actors moved their allegations to Facebook. Soon, because of the potential backlash, it looked as if the Sokoto rally might not happen at all. "Sadiya, I really, I really admire her strength," said Hassana, referring to Sadiya Taheer, one of the Sokoto organizers. "She said, 'I have not been working for this for months for you to cancel this at the last minute because of some people. This is just not acceptable.'" The rally would go on.

Then Hassana's Borno event was threatened. Hassana was summoned by the police and told that although she'd submitted the correct paperwork to hold the rally, it had been canceled. She appealed to the police commissioner, but "nothing we could do would convince him," she said. Undeterred, she called an influential member of the statehouse she'd previously met; that official intervened, and #ArewaMeToo was given permission to hold its rally on the statehouse grounds.

But as the Borno event moved ahead, Hassana got a terrible call. When Sadiya and her team arrived at the State House of Assembly in Sokoto, only 7 of 150 women on the WhatsApp group had shown up. Most had stayed away out of fear. The police attacked the seven, accusing them of "lesbianism."[43] When Sadiya told the officers that the police commissioner had given permission to hold the rally, the police said the commissioner had expressly sent them to stop it. When Sadiya refused to give up her banner or her phone, the police assaulted her, hitting her repeatedly. Another activist, Idris Abbas, tried to film the attack and was arrested, his footage confiscated. A group of #ArewaMeToo volunteers went to the police station to advocate for Sadiya and found themselves detained as well.

Hassana leaped into action, calling the office of the state governor to push for the protesters' release. And yet again, the movement turned to social media to correct the narrative: "Twenty policemen all circled around me, and beat me up," Sadiya said in a video posted to her YouTube channel.[44] "I had to go see a doctor. I couldn't even stand up properly for a whole day." Despite continuous threats on Instagram, Twitter, and Facebook, she said she would not stop fighting.

· · · · · · · · · · · · · · · · · ·

When we last spoke, Hassana was still refusing to back down in the face of backlash and physical danger. "Since when I was little, my father would always tell me about the importance of believing in something and standing for it," she said. "I grew up reading books about role models like Nelson Mandela. It didn't feel like I should give up." Her next step: a move to Lagos to attend law school, in hopes the degree will empower her campaign for justice. She'd updated her Instagram bio to read, "About to start kicking asses in court."

In Lagos, meanwhile, Busola Dakolo's case against the "Gucci pastor" Biodun Fatoyinbo had taken a new, discouraging turn. In November, the same month #ArewaMeToo mounted its protests, an Abuja court ruled against Busola in her civil case, finding that it fell outside Nigeria's six-year statute of limitations for that kind of lawsuit. Further, the judge accused Busola's case of being "soaked in emotions" and maintained that to hold Fatoyinbo to account for misdeeds from over sixteen years earlier would be a "cruelty"—arguments commonly faced by survivors globally when they find the strength and resources to come forward, often many years after the initial trauma of the assault.[45]

Although her civil case was dismissed, Busola was determined to keep speaking, even if she might not see change for her generation of women. She prayed that Nigerian women would know that surviving sexual assault is "not a thing of shame, because we have to break the impunity." No matter how hard the struggle, she said, if her role as groundbreaker helps even one survivor come forward, "that gives me comfort, it gives me joy."

Also in Lagos, Kiki, the documentarian, was facing a new fight when last we spoke, this time with the Nigerian government, which was trying to pass a restrictive social media bill—a tactic used in other countries, including Egypt and Pakistan, to silence women activists.[46] "They say it's for hate speech, but we already have a law against hate speech," Kiki said. She recalled the many cases in which victims, denied access to government-funded TV stations or newspapers, were able to accuse powerful men of sexual harassment only when they went online. "It has been an empowering tool for us. And unfortunately, they are still trying to hamper our voices in real life, and they're now looking to hamper our voices on social media."

Kiki believed that Nigerian women inspired by #MeToo and let down by a broken legal system would continue to turn to the internet, where they were more likely to find strength in numbers and might turn outrage into justice. "Maybe you didn't see any mass protests as you'd see in other countries so far," she said, but "what we have for us that is safe is social media." She was grateful for the impact *Sex for Grades* was making but emphasized how crucial it was to keep up the pressure. "If you close your eyes for one second, it will die out," she warned. "I just want everyone to keep the energy. I want to see people actually change this system that has been allowing them to harass girls for years, years."

. . . .

The best bet for assuring that systemic change does happen in Nigeria? Young women leaders.

Timely international support could help Nigerian women turn #MeToo into a sustained, unified movement—one that reforms laws, ensures police enforcement, supports courtroom victories for survivors, and takes aim at the sexual harassment that keeps women out of higher education and professional life. But international donors often don't fund locally led organizations in countries like Nigeria, because their work doesn't fit neatly into Western funding categories, like microcredit or human rights. Many aid critics argue that the preponderance of development assistance still goes to Global North organizations because of racism and continued postcolonial discrimination. Funding can often be denied or delayed due to bureaucratic requirements or draconian monitoring and evaluation reporting, standards defined by functionaries in NGO headquarters that do not reflect the community's self-defined needs. Somehow, young Nigerian women willing to stand up to Boko Haram to change laws and empower women can't get US$10,000 without completing a small mountain of grant paperwork. For real change, local women leaders, not just US-based nonprofits, need to be funded. Put another way: aid needs to be decolonized.[47]

It should be obvious that Nigerian women know best what they need and what local barriers they face. They have extensive relationships with community and religious leaders, which are essential to achieving lasting impact. And when international NGO staff leave the country, it is local women leaders who remain to continue the hard work of challenging cultural norms.

Shifting more development aid to local organizations is a bipartisan idea. President George W. Bush's AIDS relief plan designated funding for community groups in developing countries that didn't normally receive US support. And it worked, helping those groups do the kind of hard work that can be achieved only through deep local relationships and community trust. Under President Barack Obama, USAID planned to increase funding to local NGOs and smaller organizations globally.[48] But today, not enough has shifted in terms of realigning aid to support local leaders.

The path to change will not be easy, as activists continue to face consequences from speaking hard truths out loud. Despite these challenges, their example shows that even in countries with limited internet access, and where reports of abuse are met with overwhelming cultural stigma, locally led #MeToo campaigns can succeed. Investing in Nigeria's next generation of women leaders, many of whom have helped drive the country's #MeToo movement—by working to pass legislation, enforce laws, change culture through education on sexual harassment and assault, and take back public space—would make a powerful difference.

Twenty-three-year-old Ololade Ganikale, a UNILAG graduate and survivor of childhood sexual assault, is one of those leaders.[49] In August 2018, Ololade founded the Hands Off Initiative, which works to break the cycle of sexual abuse and harassment by teaching children and young people about consent. "We want to make consent the curriculum for secondary schools in Nigeria, even if we can't start with primary schools yet," Ololade said when we first spoke in December 2019, as she worked in Abuja. After seeing a Kenyan "No Means No" video on YouTube, Ololade came to see social media as both inspiration and a real-time organizing tool. "I learned about the word 'feminism' on Twitter, and I started to read more about it," she later told us in Paris, in February 2020, where she'd just begun pursuing a degree in business while running Hands Off remotely. "It's really given me a voice to speak out. I unlearned being scared of reporting people." But her work is guided by a desire to see systematic change in real life. "As important as it is that we speak about this work online, it's also important for us to push our work offline," she said. "I'm sick and tired of hearing, 'We got justice for this victim.' I don't want it to happen at all. I know that it's going to take years and years of hard work to break the cycle of abuse in our society, but we have to start somewhere."

Damilola Marcus, a designer and the founder of the #MarketMarch campaign—a movement against street harassment—is another creative and inspiring leader. #MarketMarch grew out of Damilola's frustration with the jeering and groping she was constantly subjected to in Nigeria's marketplaces. She wasn't alone: a 2019 poll found that over 76 percent of Nigerian women had experienced sexual harassment and assault in street markets. Damilola believed that if women couldn't be safe in public spaces, they would never feel free in private spaces either. "We can't have any form of significant improvement for women's positions in society," Damilola said in an interview in Lagos, in August 2020, "if we do not have honest and brutal conversations around sexual harassment, sexual abuse, and the power dynamics that arise between men and women."[50]

In December 2018, she turned to Twitter to start that conversation and to organize women for a protest march in Lagos's sprawling Yaba market. Wearing yellow shirts reading "stop touching us," they called for an end to harassment and demanded that women have a right to safe public space for economic activity. Vendors taunted them and pelted them with water bottles and stones, but the event trended on social media and forced a national conversation on street harassment.[51]

Next, #MarketMarch took aim at the system failing to uphold the law. Upset at the lack of enforcement of the Lagos legal code that categorizes sexual harassment as a felony, Damilola started an online petition on the website Change.org. The petition calls on the police to ensure that current laws are upheld and to create an anti–sexual harassment squad that can punish perpetrators on-site, without a lengthy court process. Today, the petition has over seventy-three thousand signatures. As a result of #MarketMarch, women report far less harassment in Lagos markets where the organization has staged protests.[52]

Damilola has done this work with no funding other than proceeds from T-shirt sales, using free tools like WhatsApp and digital organizing to reach out to volunteers.[53] "I think social media removes that first barrier of what it means to do something about it," she told us. "#MarketMarch may not have happened if I had to go out and solicit for people to participate. I could just sit down and put the word out from my phone, and people would respond, people who were just like me, who felt what I was feeling."

Damilola said she saw a connection between her work and the campaigns in the north—a sense of solidarity that never could have happened without social media. "#ArewaMeToo was an eye opener, and it was a very positive moment for us to see that the feminists and those who are for women's liberation are not alone in the south," she said. "There's a significant group of voices in the north who are on the same page and looking to create a better Nigeria for women from all over Nigeria."

Fakhrriyyah told us that she was heartened by #ArewaMeToo's impact on the south, something she never expected when she started this work. "How #MeToo came to the conservative part of Nigeria before it trickled to other parts of Nigeria," she said, "you realize just how strong this movement was, because it publicly sparked the conversation around sexual violence on a national scale." Although #ArewaMeToo also operates on a shoestring budget, its leaders have serious ambitions.

When we last spoke, in June 2020, Fakhrriyyah was celebrating that another state assembly had passed the first and second reading of the VAPP Act for potential adoption.[54] "Our role was pretty much instrumental to creating that space," she said, but "where other organizations come in with their own funding, we're doing it without any resources being allocated to us." #ArewaMeToo plans to open a women's shelter to support rape survivors. It also aims to push state governments to respond to gender-based violence more seriously: to make budgetary provisions, improve the ministries that handle rape cases, and force "the police to take responsibility for their inability to investigate and to prosecute cases," according to Fakhrriyyah.

Fakhrriyyah's vision goes far beyond clicks and retweets: she wants to bring together #ArewaMeToo digital campaigning and traditional NGO efforts to continue achieving measurable, systemic change for Nigerian women. "We can't continue waiting for the government to establish these structures. We have to fill in the gap," she said. #ArewaMeToo's goal is to see "more people outspoken and forcing the hands of the government."

Increasing US funding to Nigerian-led women's rights groups would make a big difference for founders and activists like Ololade, Damilola, and Fakhrriyyah at a critical moment. For each of them, the fire is already burning—they could just use a little more fuel.

The leading philanthropist Jeff Skoll often quotes John W. Gardner, who served as the secretary of Health, Education, and Welfare under US president Lyndon Johnson and helped design America's "Great Society" initiative of the 1960s. Gardner's advice: "Bet on good people doing good things."[55] The US would do well to follow suit in Nigeria—to recognize that a Western organization's "theory of change" is nowhere near as powerful as the work of local journeywomen coming together.

Today, Busola, Kiki, Fakhrriyyah, and other Nigerian #MeToo activists persist in the fight, even when progress seems elusive. In June 2020, Busola continued to press her case online, posting to Instagram a letter from the Nigerian police saying they'd concluded their criminal investigation and given their report to the Ministry of Justice in Abuja for "onward prosecution."[56] Busola told us that she'd heard allegations that "foul play" had contributed to the investigation's delay, and said she was determined to use social media to keep attention on both her case and the larger cause of fighting sexual harassment and assault. "We might not see the right results in our generation," she said, "but we will definitely see results in generations to come."

The student harassment bill reignited by Kiki's work on *Sex for Grades* finally passed Nigeria's Senate on July 7, 2020, and was hailed as "landmark legislation" by Senate president Ahmad Lawan.[57] But as of September 2020, the bill still languished in the lower chamber. And for the bill to become law, the Nigerian president must sign it.

In 2020, Kiki was nominated for an International Emmy Award for her groundbreaking documentary.[58] She believes that voice by voice, #MeToo will help lead to justice for Nigerian women. "Africa Eye will release *Sex for Grades*, #ArewaMeToo will keep pushing in their own space, and then the Busola Dakolo case—I met her, she's really amazing—people keep pushing in their own space," she said in our interview. "The first push may not necessarily jolt everyone to go out and do something, but one of these stories will definitely touch one more person. And one day, it will be enough."

Pakistani artist Shehzil Malik created this poster for the 2019 Aurat March ("women's march" in Urdu) in Lahore, with her work triggering both discussion and backlash. At the now annual Aurat Marches across Pakistan, scores of women and allies have advocated for women's rights, bodily autonomy, and economic justice with vibrant signs and bold messages. Credit: Shehzil Malik

Chapter Five

PAKISTAN: DIGITAL JUSTICE
#میں_بھی

Mera Jism Meri Marzi ("My Body, My Choice").
—Anonymous Aurat March protester

On April 19, 2018, as #MeToo dominated headlines around the world, the Pakistani singer and actress Meesha Shafi decided it was her time to speak, too.

Much like American actresses in Hollywood had come forward as part of the #MeToo and TIME'S UP movements, Meesha turned to Twitter, posting a message to her followers: "Sharing this because I believe that by speaking out about my own experience of sexual harassment, I will break the culture of silence that permeates through our society. It is not easy to speak out [. . .] but it is harder to stay silent. My conscience will not allow it anymore #MeToo." She attached an image to the tweet with a longer statement, in which she named her alleged harasser: "I have been subjected, on more than one occasion, to sexual harassment of a physical nature at the hands of a colleague from my industry: Ali Zafar."[1]

Meesha was the first famous Pakistani woman to make public allegations against another leading celebrity. Zafar, married with two children, was also a Pakistani singer and actor, on television and in Bollywood. Meesha alleged that she'd been groped and sexually harassed by Zafar on two occasions, at her father-in-law's home and after a recording session.[2]

Zafar has always insisted on his innocence, releasing his own statement on Twitter three hours after Meesha's. "I am deeply aware and in support of the global #Metoo movement and what it stands for," Zafar wrote. "I am the father of a young girl and a young boy, a husband to a wife and son to a mother." He rebutted Meesha's allegations, insisting, "I categorically deny any and all claims of harassment lodged against me by Ms Shafi. I intend to take this through the courts of law." Those proceedings are ongoing. However, the Zafar case is instructive in understanding the challenges faced by women making allegations of abuse in Pakistan.[3]

Meesha's tweets forced a reckoning. Pakistani women had seen the #MeToo movement's global power online but had worried over the backlash they might face for speaking out about sexual harassment—a taboo in the country. For two household names to be involved was momentous, and emboldening.

After Meesha's disclosure, other women quickly came forward to accuse Zafar of misconduct. "Seeing Meesha's courage it's impossible for me to not speak now, not only in support of her but also to say she's not alone," Leena Ghani, a Pakistani makeup artist, said in her own Twitter statement only a few hours after Meesha's tweet. "In the many years I have known Ali, he has on several occasions crossed boundaries of what is appropriate behaviour between friends. . . . Inappropriate contact, groping, sexual comments should not fall in the grey area between humour and indecency." She added the hashtags #MeToo, #TimesUp, and #WeBelieveYou.[4]

Maham Javaid, a digital and print journalist in Pakistan for over a decade and a Human Rights Watch fellow, also posted about Zafar that day: "So @itsmeeshashafi's brave sharing of her experience reminded me of a story about @AliZafarsays from many many years ago, when Ali Zafar tried to kiss my cousin and pull my cousin into a restroom with him. Luckily my cousin's friends were there to push Ali Zafar off." She tweeted that no one had reported the incident because of the taboo against speaking about sexual harassment, and because they felt that allegations against a famous man were unlikely to be believed. "Thanks @itsmeeshashafi for reminding us that our stories matter."[5]

A blogger based in Islamabad, Humna Raza, also posted on Twitter alleging that when she had been at an event with her husband, eighteen months earlier, Zafar had groped her after she requested a selfie. She told a few friends, wondering if she had misinterpreted the interaction. After Meesha posted on Twitter, Humna's friends messaged her on WhatsApp to say they remembered her saying that Zafar had sexually harassed her, too. "I was making excuses from him in my head," Humna posted. "I took ages to decide whether I should write this, because my family, brother, everyone will find out. And will people even believe me? And am I messing with someone who might have too much power?"[6]

Meanwhile, other Pakistani celebrities, including the well-known actors Osman Khalid Butt and Urwa Hocane, expressed support for Meesha to their large followings on Twitter. Other influencers shared their own #MeToo experiences of sexual harassment in the industry, including the musician and social activist Momina Mustehsan, who wrote, "#MeToo needs a response," and, "very often, as we can see, women are violated by the very men they know, trust and often work with." The actress Ayesha Omar told Geo News that she was the victim of another abuser in the entertainment field, but was too afraid to reveal any details. "I hope I'm as brave as Meesha Shafi one day," she said. "The thing is that it's when people like Meesha come forward, that other people draw the strength to tell their stories."[7]

But making her allegations came at a cost. On April 25, Zafar's lawyers sent a letter to Meesha. They demanded she post an apology to Twitter within two weeks and delete her initial tweet accusing him, or he would file a defamation lawsuit seeking one billion Pakistani rupees in damages, a little over US$6.1 million. Meesha refused. Instead of apologizing, she announced on Twitter that Mohammed Ahmad Pansota and the longtime women's rights activist Nighat Dad would serve as her lawyers.[8]

Almost immediately, she began to receive death threats.[9]

· · · · · · · · · · · · · · · · · ·

On September 27, 2018, women across the United States huddled around screens to watch a Senate hearing in which President Trump's Supreme Court nominee, Brett Kavanaugh, was questioned over allegations that in high school he had attempted to rape Dr. Christine Blasey Ford. They had no idea women around the world were also watching.

Just days after the hearing, Fauzia Viqar, then the head of Punjab's Commission on the Status of Women, said she'd heard every word. "I was following the Brett Kavanaugh trial, and I was so upset," she said during an interview in Lahore, "not just because of the outcome, but also how Dr. Blasey Ford got berated by the Republican senators."[10] Fauzia had watched the hearings on YouTube while registering harassment reports from women across Punjab. She recognized the male senators' reactions instantly—responses she knew all too well from her own work.

Rukhshanda Naz, a longtime human rights defender and women's rights activist, did too. Dignified yet unguarded, Rukhshanda is fearless on Twitter, and in real life her presence makes you want to pull up a chair and learn. "I'm dealing with sexual harassment cases as well," she said, shaking her head, during an interview in Lahore.[11] "We find there is an acceptance, there is a tolerance for such cases in the name of tradition, in the name of family, or sometimes in the name of country."

Standing up for women's rights is a perilous business in Pakistan. In October 2018, months before she was named the Khyber Pakhtunkhwa region's first official tasked with stopping "harassment of women in public and private institutions," Rukhshanda spoke at a human rights conference dedicated to the legacy of the storied women's activist and lawyer Asma Jahangir, who had died earlier that year. With her sister Hina Jilani, Asma had founded Pakistan's first all-woman law firm, which fought to reform laws that trap abused women in marriages and norms that punish rape victims instead of their attackers. The sisters had also founded a women's shelter, after one of Hina's clients had been shot dead in front of her when the woman was trying to leave her abusive husband. Claiming a desire for family reconciliation, the client's mother had brought the gunman to the meeting herself.[12]

Threats had not stopped Pakistani women—and Indian women who had obtained visas to cross a hardened border—from coming together to honor Asma's life. Under the protection of heavy security, they led cheers from the stage: *We will win! Within our families we will win! Parliament main jeetangai! In court systems we will win! Are you ready?*[13]

Rukhshanda went straight from the human rights conference to a press conference—to protest against the Pakistani Supreme Court. Women's rights groups were up in arms over Chief Justice Saqib Nisar's recent remarks at an event in Karachi: "I was always told that a speech should be like a woman's skirt," he had said. "It should not be too long to not reveal anything, and neither too short that it doesn't cover the subject."[14] Tired of discrimination in Pakistani courts and sexist statements from its highest judge, women lawyers like Rukhshanda had decided to organize publicly.

Pakistan has never had a woman Supreme Court justice, the sole holdout among South Asian countries. As of 2016, only 5 percent of all Pakistani high-court judges were women. And the Pakistan Bar Council, the regulatory body that oversees the legal profession, has never had a woman member since its formation in 1973.[15] At the protest, women's rights activists from across Pakistan gathered in front of microphones on a simple stage as an all-male press corps arrived. The press conference had hardly begun when one of the women started tersely responding to a male journalist. After questions about a controversial dam project and other unrelated issues, the female speaker finally became so exasperated that she pushed herself away from the table and called an abrupt end to the event. Rukhshanda was incensed. "These men won't listen to us," she said, collecting her papers and purse to leave. "We are here talking about the rights of women and they won't even ask us questions about it."

. . . .

In Pakistan, the greatest obstacle to safety and justice for women is a broken legal system in which attackers go unpunished. Whether conducting police interviews or medical examinations, officials often don't have relevant training and refuse to prioritize collecting evidence that could lead to prosecution.[16] But building on the legacy of Asma Jahangir, Pakistani #MeToo activists are battling for equality and protections in courtrooms and online, combining strategic litigation with social media campaigning and raw determination.

At the 2018 conference dedicated to Asma's life, Nighat Dad, Meesha Shafi's lawyer, spoke about sexual harassment and online abuse. As executive director of the Digital Rights Foundation, an NGO in Pakistan dedicated to human rights and digital governance, Nighat saw in Meesha's case an opportunity to set a high-profile and public precedent, one that might inspire other women who'd been harassed in their workplaces to come forward. "Meesha decided enough is enough; I'm going to talk about this in public on Twitter," Nighat said when we met in Lahore, in October 2018. "We were like, yes, we can do this. Where the broken justice system had failed women for so many years, we can use these online spaces and get support."[17]

A purple-haired single mother who often self-funds her work, Nighat said technology and the internet had "given women space we don't find in the physical world."[18] Yet she added that "it's important not to leave it online, and use the laws that we have." She and her team decided not only to defend

Meesha in her defamation case but also to file a defamation countersuit and workplace harassment case against Ali Zafar. "During the process, we'll identify the gaps in the laws and policies."

The legal gaps are where Pakistani women get stuck if they dare seek justice, as laws to ensure their safety are almost never enforced. Unlike roughly a third of countries globally, Pakistan actually has legal provisions against sexual harassment—laws that rectified Pakistan's widely condemned 1979 Hudood Ordinances, passed by the dictator Zia-ul-Haq in the name of alleged "Sharisation" or "Islamisation." The ordinances conflated extramarital sex and rape, considered the testimony of one male witness to be equivalent to the testimony of two female witnesses, and punished thousands of survivors with incarceration for being unable to produce the required four witnesses to prove that their sexual assault was rape. The draconian law was reformed only in 2006—after an outcry by Pakistani women and international human rights activists—via the Women's Protection Bill, passed in response to the brutal 2002 gang rape of Mukhtar Mai, which had been ordered by a tribal council as punishment for a brother's alleged affair. Under the 2006 law, rape was punishable by a prison sentence of ten to twenty-five years, or by death.[19]

In 2010, Pakistan's parliament passed a law introducing workplace provisions, the Protection Against Harassment of Women at the Workplace Act. The legislation seemed to be groundbreaking, requiring that complaints be investigated within thirty days, and establishing civil provisions for punishment, with the maximum penalty being that the harasser would lose his job. But the law also outlines three limiting technical requirements for any case to be considered by a court: the victim has to be an "employee," the accused has to be an "employee" or an "employer," and the harassment has to have happened at a "workplace." If the case meets all three provisions, a woman can file a complaint with her workplace's committee—comprising three persons, one of which must be a woman—or with an ombudsperson appointed by the state.[20] If the three requirements are not met, the case is dismissed on that technicality, and a victim loses any opportunity to be heard. The result: the law excludes a variety of potential harassment situations, such as if a woman is harassed by another employee outside the official workplace, or if a female employee is harassed by a consultant.

In addition, Pakistan's Penal Code Section 509 defines sexual harassment as a criminal offense, and it applies both inside and outside the workplace.[21]

The law is expansive in its definition of sexual harassment and details punishments of up to three years in prison and fines payable to the state—not the victim—of up to five hundred thousand rupees, or roughly US$3,050. But this law requires a woman to wait out a backlogged court system and pay handsomely for a lawyer.

Essentially, Pakistani women have two paths to justice, both fraught with risk or obstruction. If a complaint fails to meet the requirements of the Workplace Act, it can be taken up by the criminal court system. But that promises great expense and great delay—*if* a case can get a fair hearing, a dubious prospect in a country where women face harassment even at the courthouse.

"Our lower courts are not a conducive environment for women to bring claims of sexual harassment," the Pakistani lawyer Hassan Niazi wrote in a November 2019 *Express Tribune* op-ed. "The court system involves women being harassed within court premises. Male court staff, male lawyers, and predominantly male judges give some prurient gazes that would make Harvey Weinstein blush."[22]

Survivors and their families also face social stigma. Rumors of a victim's past relationships can result in a perpetrator's going unpunished. As a result, many Pakistani women don't report sexual harassment or assault. Those who do often withdraw complaints after pressure from their families or communities, or are simply unable to win their cases in a system rigged against them.

And so Pakistani women are left largely without recourse, in a country where gender-based violence and harassment are prevalent inside and outside the home. In schools and workplaces, women and girls face everything from groping to demands for sexual favors in exchange for promotions. Even female legislators are not immune. In parliament, women can be jeered at and criticized for their appearance.[23]

Leaders like Fauzia and Rukhshanda are trying to work within government structures at the provincial level, in Punjab and Khyber Pakhtunkhwa. "Our own helpline takes complaints of harassment, addresses them to the best of our ability, and then passes [them] on to the ombudsperson's office," Fauzia said. "But I have to say the cultural wall against [punishing] harassment is so strong. . . . When it comes to powerful men, it's almost impossible." The Punjab Commission on the Status of Women has invested time and resources into recruiting more women into the workforce, educated employers about harassment, and offered awareness sessions to women and men. "A lot of times I personally see allies among men," Fauzia said. "Not all men are harassers."

In Khyber Pakhtunkhwa, Rukhshanda wants to see "institutions with teeth and resources." This is a woman who at age fifteen went on a hunger strike to persuade her father to allow her to continue her education—so it's not hard to believe she'd make a little go a long way. "If you are setting up a human rights or women's rights commission without giving autonomous status, resources, and without empowering them to take action against human rights violations?" She shook her head, knowing the deck would be stacked. "A survivor of any kind of violence in this country, they are helpless sometimes. . . . The criminal justice system is completely corrupt."

For Pakistani women, equity and safety at work usually remain elusive. And without the enforcement of basic protections for women in traditionally male workplaces or universities, Pakistani advocates say, women can't fully participate in society and achieve economic agency—at a loss not only for the women, but for the country.

In 2018, the World Bank reported that women make up only 22 percent of Pakistan's total labor force. According to the International Monetary Fund, harassment and violence against women cost Pakistan dearly: closing the gender gap in labor force participation could boost Pakistan's gross domestic product by 30 percent. Yet an Asian Development Bank study in 2016 reported that four out of ten Pakistani women who are not working say they cannot work because a male family member will not allow them to. "When women do speak up about harassment, our courts and law enforcement do not support them," Nighat Dad said. "And then men say: 'See, I told you, these spaces are not safe for you. You sit at home within the four walls of our house and then you are secure.' If women speak up, they lose the freedom and liberation of work."[24]

It's a message that women journalists are countering by breaking stories and driving attention when the legal system lags or fails—whether you're a celebrity or a girl fighting for her education.

. . . .

Hamna Zubair and Shiza Malik are part of a new generation of Pakistani women journalists prioritizing reporting on allegations of sexual harassment and assault. Millennial and digitally savvy, they're ready to use both traditional and social media to ensure that women's stories are finally told—and are kept in the spotlight as survivors fight for their accusations to be taken seriously and investigated.

When we first met Hamna at her Karachi office, she was an editor at *Dawn*, one of Pakistan's leading media outlets, whose progressive positions had resulted in multiple attacks on its offices. After passing through several heavily secured checkpoints in place to protect staff, we spoke in the busy newsroom about Hamna's reporting on Meesha Shafi's allegations against Ali Zafar. "It's the first high-profile accusation to have happened in Pakistan under the #MeToo movement," Hamna said.[25] "It also highlights the loopholes in Pakistan's sexual harassment laws." Like Nighat, in her own way as a journalist Hamna saw the case as an opportunity to explore a larger problem: that Pakistan doesn't "have a strong legal system that supports or empowers women. We have barely any legal-aid organizations, and all of these things are a real roadblock to women actually getting justice."

Concerned about both journalistic integrity and the ever-present threat of defamation litigation, Hamna carefully stressed that the case was ongoing. In navigating the complexities of this kind of coverage, she had built on the work of other reporters globally. "I definitely look to stories that have come out in the United States, landmark #MeToo stories like the story on Harvey Weinstein," she explained. "What are the best practices they've used? How did they manage anonymous sources?"

Despite the risks, Hamna said that *Dawn*'s leadership had supported her team's efforts to cover sexual harassment and #MeToo's impact in Pakistan. "I think everybody understands in the journalism world that you can't look away from this movement. It's not just a one-off case of sexual harassment," she said. "It's a landmark social and cultural movement of women reclaiming their space, having their voices heard, and saying this is a culture of misogyny and abuse that we will not tolerate anymore."

When it came to the transnational impact of #MeToo, Hamna rightly highlighted the work of generations of Pakistani women, which led to today's reckonings over sexual assault and violence. "The #MeToo movement in Pakistan and in India is not something that happened overnight. Just like it did in the US, it was a long time coming." She believed that social media was crucial to helping women speak out in unprecedented ways. "I feel like technology has really empowered women to talk to each other," she said, "whereas previously there were no real spaces in Pakistan for women to meet and share their ideas."

But in her reporting on a variety of sexual harassment and assault cases, Hamna had seen how women also experienced backlash online, no matter how famous they might be. "When Meesha Shafi did come forward with allegations, she was criticized," Hamna said. "She was trolled on social media. She was bullied. She had to deactivate her social media accounts, whereas there weren't a lot of consequences for Ali Zafar."

Shiza Malik, an Islamabad-based freelance journalist who has written for Vice, the *Daily Times*, and *Dawn*, has also used her reporting to help girls and women feel safer in coming forward, to show them that their allegations can get the public hearing they deserve, even if institutions—including schools—will not listen. Writing for Vice India, she helped bring attention to the #MeToo activism at the elite all-girls Lahore Grammar School (LGS), one of Pakistan's top educational institutions. On June 27, 2020, an LGS alumna wrote on Instagram that a teacher had sent her sexually explicit messages. Another alumna, Tehreem, twenty-one, saw the post and recognized the teacher's name. "I searched my phone and found screenshots of messages he had sent me four years ago and decided to post them," she told Shiza in a report published in July 2020. "My friends warned me against it, but I decided I had stayed silent for too long."[26]

Tehreem wasn't the only one ready to speak. Other students and alumni started posting allegations of sexual harassment to Instagram. One alumna wrote that when she was seventeen, an English teacher told her to subscribe to a dating website so they could talk about classroom assignments there. Current students posted stories about harassment by the same teacher. A debate teacher had also been reported for four years by students from almost every part of the school—without any action taken—for sending illicit messages. Another teacher had demanded that a student take a photo with him, promising he'd look at it in his bed every night. A different student claimed she had complained about the same teacher, only to be threatened with bad grades; the teacher had said he would "fix anyone who tried to defame him," the student wrote.[27] Much as the students featured in the Nigerian documentary *Sex for Grades*, these students in Pakistan were powerless to defend themselves from teachers who held all the authority.

"Cover-up is the usual reaction," an anonymous source at the school told *Dawn*. "But this is also because parents don't want to take action. A mother, who said her daughter complained about the school security guard ogling at her, said she solved the problem by making her daughter wear an abaya to school rather than complain."[28]

But now, the students were being heard. On June 30, Meesha Shafi posted her support on Twitter: "Proud to see all the women/girls break their silence, even though the world is SO ugly to those who speak up. Today, I feel like the pain and trauma I have suffered is worth so much! Your bravery is my reward. I am with you all!" That same day, the District Education Authority launched a sexual harassment investigation of the school. Yet again, the drama played out over Twitter, with the Punjab education minister tweeting, "I will deal with the case in Lahore Grammar School 1A1 myself. Have talked to the Principal this morning. Getting all the details. These Children are my Children. I will protect them. This case will be brought to a proper conclusion according to law. Make NO mistake about it."[29]

Yet on July 4, the same minister claimed that education officials could not investigate based on social media posts alone. Parents would have to file written complaints, even though female students had complained for years, to no avail.[30]

The students persisted. Posts went from Instagram to Twitter to Facebook and traveled well beyond the school community. Celebrities, activists, and other survivors started resharing the posts and commenting. "We saw that some big Twitter accounts with a lot of following and who are known to speak out on women's rights issues, those were the first women who actually put these stories out there," said Shiza in a September 2020 interview from Islamabad, noting how ably the students had used digital organizing.[31] "These girls, they contacted these social media influencers who had a voice, and found support. They found an audience through them."

Students began an online petition and escalated criticism against the teachers, the administration, and custodial staff. It was soon revealed that in violation of government rules, the school had no explicit sexual harassment policy, other than discouraging "inappropriate conduct." It also came to light in coverage by *Dawn* that in addition to teachers, boys from other top schools were sexually harassing LGS students. This included an ad-hoc group that called itself "Born to Kill," members of which were accused of gang-raping a female student. A teacher reported that the student had tried to kill herself after the attack.[32]

Nighat Dad told *Dawn* she wasn't surprised to hear of the boys' involvement. "We have seen incidents of blackmail and sexual harassment coming from male students—and we have seen this across the board," she said. "Even though this has happened before, during the [COVID-19] lockdown, things took a turn for the worse. There was a massive wave of pages on Facebook and Instagram where pictures of girls would be uploaded to blackmail them."[33]

Finally, in response to the outcry online, the school was forced to take action. On July 11, 2020, it fired four male teachers and suspended three female staffers, including the principal, who had disregarded previous reports of harassment.[34] Once again, social media had proved itself to be a vital tool in girls' and women's fight for justice. Had they not found a way to speak out online, traditional media would not have picked up the story, and it's likely that no action would have been taken.

An anonymous alumna of LGS told the newspaper *The National* that the global #MeToo movement had clearly played a role in emboldening students to raise their voices. "While there was always the implicit knowledge of harassment taking place on campus," she said, "the sensitisation happened after the movement became powerful post-2018. Schools need to start taking #MeToo seriously."[35]

· · · · · · · · · · · · · · · · · ·

When we spoke in September 2020, Shiza and Hamna were reeling from two horrific gang-rape cases that had shaken women across the country, leading to street protests. On September 4, a five-year-old girl in Karachi was on her way to buy cookies at a shop when she was kidnapped and sexually assaulted. Her small, lifeless body was found two days later, burned. Just five days later, when a Lahore mother of three ran out of gas on a motorway, she was robbed and gang-raped in front of her children. The police later confirmed that one of her attackers was a serial rapist. But the Lahore police chief, Muhammad Umar Sheikh, blamed the woman for her own assault, faulting her for not making sure her car had enough fuel and asking why she was out so late at night without a male companion. One of Pakistan's most well-known religious clerics, Maulana Tariq Jameel, posted a "condemnation" video online, blaming not the attackers but coeducation of men and women for causing such moral degradation.[36]

For Pakistani women, it was too much. Social media exploded with outraged posts using the hashtag #motorwayincident and calling for the police chief's removal. Shireen Mazari, Pakistan's federal minister for human rights, posted her own indictment on Twitter: "For an officer to effectively blame a woman for being gang raped by saying she should have taken the GT [Grand Truck] Road or question as to why she went out in the night with her children is unacceptable and have taken up this issue. Nothing can ever rationalise the crime of rape. That's it."[37]

When victims are blamed for their own brutal assaults, it's not a surprise that women hesitate to report. Discussing the Lahore case, Shiza said, "We know from the survivor that her first concern was she didn't even want to file a police report. She kept repeatedly requesting the police to keep her identity hidden." She added that social media had given women who were afraid of victim shaming more safety. "It's been a big game changer, because Pakistan is a very conservative society and the backlash and the fallout for the survivor is huge. So the very fact that social media offers them anonymity is the first step."

Hamna, who now works as a freelance writer and has been organizing online panels to talk about how to stop rape culture in Pakistan, said she hoped outrage on social media would result in concrete change. "I don't even think that we're talking about massive changes in legislation, because rape is a crime in Pakistan. Sexual harassment is a crime in Pakistan. Sexual assault is a crime in Pakistan. Domestic abuse is a crime in Pakistan," she said pointedly. "What I think needs to change is addressing corruption and bias and misogyny, from the regular police officer in the street to the inspector general of police."

In response to the September attacks and public outrage, Pakistan's prime minister, Imran Khan, called for harsher punishments for rapists, including public hanging and chemical or physical castration. Risking

COVID-19 exposure, at least one woman at a Karachi protest march seemed to agree, holding a sign that said "Chop Off Their Raping Tool." Written across her blue surgical face mask, in defiant black marker: *Mera Jism Meri Marzi*—"My Body, My Choice."[38]

. . . .

"My body, my choice" is known across the United States as a pro-choice slogan in the abortion debate. But the phrase has no such meaning in Pakistan. In 2018, when an anonymous woman wrote *Mera Jism Meri Marzi* across her poster for the first Aurat March—"Women's March," in Urdu—she meant it to say that she had autonomy over her own body, that she had the right to not be sexually harassed or assaulted.[39] She had no idea the slogan would unleash outrage across Pakistani media.

The poster triggered countless talk show debates, accusations of "Western debauchery," and religious sermons on modesty. Certainly, commentators said, no "modest" woman should have been at the Aurat March at all. (Today, afraid of violent retribution, the poster's designer deliberately remains unknown.)[40]

The historic 2017 Women's March in the United States, organized in response to the election of Donald Trump to the presidency, inspired similar events worldwide, including solidarity marches in Karachi, Lahore, and Islamabad. In a first for Pakistan, about five thousand women gathered in a Karachi park on International Women's Day in March 2018. Holding up homemade signs running the gamut from sarcastic to angry to funny, they called for an end to gender-based sexual harassment and violence.[41]

Media outlets credited the turnout to the growing #MeToo movement in Pakistan and to the recent passing of the women's rights champion Asma Jahangir, with women marching to honor her legacy. Women came in kurtas, niqabs, and T-shirts reading "girls just want to have fun-damental human rights."[42] Mothers brought daughters who carried placards demanding their right to an education, universities organized protest groups, and a few transgender women marched. So did some men, showing support as allies.

It was not the Aurat March's demands for gender equity that inspired backlash, however, but the *Mera Jism Meri Marzi* poster and another woman's sign: *khud khana garam kar lo!*—"Reheat the food yourself!"[43]

"'Heat up your own food'—that made men go nuts," said the artist and activist Shehzil Malik, laughing, when we spoke in October 2020.[44] "All my friends' husbands were so furious at that." Based in Lahore, Shehzil is a thirty-something activist and award-winning designer and illustrator. For the 2018 Aurat March, organizers asked her to design some posters, which quickly became iconic after being plastered on walls across cities. They depict women raising their hands, a woman's strong face, a flower in her blazing hair. During an interview from her Lahore home, Shehzil said she'd wanted to change how Pakistani women saw themselves and their rights. For the march, she took her love of science-fiction-inspired art and her skills in advertising and applied them to human rights, feminism, and South Asian identity. Much of her art depicts her own experiences: street harassment for riding a bike, the fear women feel in public spaces where they could be assaulted.

Shehzil takes great delight in art that inspires public conversations. Another infamous Aurat March poster asked men to stop sending unsolicited sexual photos, using the term of art "dick pics." "I never in my wildest dreams could have imagined an old Pakistani man saying the words 'dick pics' on, like, national television," Shehzil said. "Like these men have no idea. Maybe you should be getting mad that girls are receiving them as opposed to putting it on a poster saying stop sending them to me."

Shiza Malik, who helped organize the 2019 Aurat March in Islamabad, credited the #MeToo movement with helping give women—and men—a new vocabulary: "In the last two to three years, because of the Aurat March, because of all the debates that we've been seeing on mainstream media, on social media, it's opened up a space to talk about these things."

The marches were full of women who'd finally found the courage to speak—and loudly. Unfortunately, misogynists weren't going to go quietly. An online campaign targeted the women who'd dared to display the signs. Critics posted their faces and names on social media and threated to kill and rape them. They manipulated photographs from the marches and faked vulgar messages, in an attempt to sabotage the movement. Female protestors were "doxed" online, their personal information posted publicly for any harasser to find.[45]

Despite the backlash, the second Aurat March, in 2019, exploded—with women organizing in even more cities across Pakistan, including Faisalabad,

Hyderabad, Peshawar, Mardan, Quetta, Multan, and Lakarna.[46] Rural women, students, journalists, activists, and celebrities protested together.

Nighat Dad helped organize the Lahore event, where women sang, perplexed passersby took cell phone videos, and Meesha Shafi spoke. Longtime feminist activists like Hina Jilani marched with the next generation of feminists.[47] For many women, it was the first time they'd dared claim public space—a transformative moment for Pakistan's movement to end sexual harassment and rape culture.

"The credit for today does not go to just one woman alone," Nighat proclaimed as the event closed.[48] A collective of feminist organizations and individual activists had joined together for the planning. From a humble start, the Aurat March over the last three years has become a broader movement disrupting patriarchal norms in Pakistan, calling for enforcement of laws on sexual harassment and assault and for legal, economic, and political equality for women.

. . . .

Whether through protests, social media activism, journalism, the legal system, artwork, or participation in government, Pakistani women are determined to keep demanding a solution to the scourge of sexual harassment and violence, whatever the cost.

There have been setbacks. In May 2019, Fauzia Viqar was arbitrarily and unexpectedly dismissed from her role as chairperson of the Punjab Commission on the Status of Women. Rumor had it she was removed for political reasons, though authorities gave no clear justification and indicated that future chairpersons should not be paid a salary, but volunteer. Again, advocates turned to Twitter. Jamshed Kazi, who at the time was country director in Pakistan for UN Women, tweeted that he was "dismayed to hear the sudden removal of Ms Viqar," and other civil society organizations voiced concerns. Even the PCSW Twitter account started tagging other activists, government officials, and multilateral organizations.[49]

Nighat Dad defended Fauzia in the newspaper *Dawn*, citing Fauzia's contract and legislation requiring the government to pay the commission chairperson at a specific, clear scale. "I see this notification as invalid," Nighat said, "because Government was supposed to inform the citizens the reasons why it is taking this decision. It is their democratic right to know."[50] UN Women thankfully hired Fauzia, ensuring that she wouldn't be lost to the movement.

In October 2019, the Lahore High Court rejected Meesha Shafi's appeal to overturn the Punjab government's dismissal of her complaint against Ali Zafar. The court's finding: her lawsuit did not meet the three-part criteria to be considered a civil workplace harassment case, as Meesha wasn't an "employee" and the incidents didn't happen in a "workplace."[51] Her legal team argued that the nature of the entertainment industry made the law impossible to apply. They continue to pursue a criminal case and a defamation countersuit against Zafar, both of which are slowly winding their way through the courts.

In the meantime, Zafar invoked Pakistan's criminal defamation and "electronic crimes" laws. Both provisions carry serious weight, with a two-year jail sentence for defamation and, under the Prevention of Electronic Crimes Act (2016), up to three years' imprisonment for an individual who makes online statements likely to "harm the reputation" of a person.[52] Such laws have been deployed globally by perpetrators of harassment, who use them to intimidate victims into silence.

When we spoke again with Nighat Dad in October 2020, several of Meesha's civil sexual harassment case witnesses had been served notices of potential criminal charges for defamation, filed by Zafar. On October 9, Humna Raza withdrew her previous allegation publicly on Twitter, posting a handwritten and typed apology to Zafar that read, in part, "I would like to clarify that it was a confusion on my part."[53]

But some women are making hard-fought progress, even in the most challenging environments. Rukhshanda Naz remains in her role as Khyber Pakhtunkhwa ombudsperson for protection against sexual harassment of women at the workplace. In June 2020, working with UN Women, she released a toolkit to help train workplace investigators about sexual harassment complaints. "Our emphasis is on the execution and smooth implementation of the Workplace Harassment Law to make sure that the environment is safe for women to reach their full potential and contribute to the economy," Rukhshanda said during the online launch of the toolkit.[54] Her office continues to raise awareness of sexual harassment and to inform stakeholders and victims about their rights.

Where aid donors can support similar programs at both the regional and the federal government levels, they should. In the United States, the Trump Administration suspended $700 million in security assistance to Pakistan in 2018, in retaliation for the nation's poor record on controlling terror groups.[55] Alongside those cuts, American development aid to Pakistan also markedly decreased from 2017 to 2020, which was a missed opportunity to ensure critical support for women's rights.

Previously, US aid to Pakistan overlooked local organizations and leaders, primarily going through USAID contractors who had successfully navigated the agency's bureaucratic backwater. In the fetishization of issues, US assistance was often meager unless the funded project could be linked to fighting the "war on terror" or "countering violent extremism." But supporting women's rights and safety should not be shortchanged in return. Until the United States shifts its approach, philanthropy can and should fill the gaps.

Pakistan's current inclusion on the G7-initiated Financial Action Task Force "grey list," for failing to curb money laundering and terror financing, may also have the unintended consequence of negatively impacting women's organizations.[56] The country's placement on the list means it will only become harder to access international aid from multilateral institutions like the World Bank, the International Monetary Fund, and the European Union.

Such aid would be a shot in the arm for local leaders like Nighat Dad, who persists in working tirelessly while facing constant threats. Inspired by Meesha's case and the growing energy of the #MeToo movement, everyday women continue to seek out Nighat to ask how they can speak about sexual harassment in their workplaces. "They started looking to me as this woman that we'll go to, she'll defend us," sighed Nighat, who rarely sleeps and has a hard time saying no to any woman who needs help. "And I knew I can do it, but I cannot do it singlehandedly. We need a force and movement."[57]

In a model similar to that used by the US-based Time's Up Legal Defense Fund—which connects lawyers with low-wage workers—Nighat started talking to lawyers across Pakistan to build a pro bono team to represent sexual harassment cases and help women understand workplace law. Fifty lawyers joined the effort, including twenty men. Always digitally focused, Nighat built an online portal called Ab Aur Nahin!—"Time's Up, No

More!" in Urdu—to connect victims to lawyers in their city. Her group also created templates to make it easier for women to file cases with courts and ombudspeople.

Nighat's volunteer team has already had success translating #MeToo into progress for everyday women, using strategic litigation to further precedent-setting harassment and defamation cases in Pakistan. She hopes that Meesha's case will one day have an even bigger impact on the enforcement of sexual harassment laws across the country.

With dedicated funding, Nighat could do much more. Pakistan is at a tipping point, a moment of reckoning on women's workplace safety and equity. Nighat said she could accelerate her work and achieve measurable outcomes if she had the financial help needed to continue her pioneering legal and social media efforts—and keep her clients and herself safe. "This is a great moment for us because there is a lot of criticism on #MeToo: it's a hashtag, so what's next?" Nighat said. "What's next is using the law that we have and taking the cases to court."[58]

. . . .

Ideally, international leaders and donors will throw their support behind Pakistan's burgeoning #MeToo movement. In the meantime, Pakistani women are not waiting to be "saved."

In 2020, one of the Aurat March's main demands was economic justice for women. In 2017, the World Economic Forum ranked Pakistan second to last in terms of gender equality, due to its abysmal performance in women's economic participation, political empowerment, and enrollment in higher education. The only country that ranked lower was war-torn Yemen.[59] The journalist Shiza Malik said she saw a clear through line from harassment to loss of economic agency for women. "If a woman is facing harassment on the street, if she's facing harassment in the workplace," she said, "it directly contributes to her economic marginalization."

March organizers released a comprehensive manifesto online, covering everything from sexual harassment and assault to media representation and the political rights of the LGBTQ community. They also—to the chagrin of the conservative religious community—announced that the year's Aurat March slogan would be *Mera Jism Meri Marzi*.[60]

The march's aims and slogan incited so much backlash that some provincial parliaments voted to ban further demonstrations, and religious groups filed court petitions in Lahore, Karachi, and Islamabad to stop the march. Maulana Fazl ur Rehman, leader of the religious right-wing political party Jamiat Ulema-e-Islam, told Al Jazeera that he objected to the marches on the grounds of decency. "If they want to bring awareness to the issues that are faced today in society, if they are associated with rights for women granted to them in Islam and the constitution, we have absolutely no problem with that," he insisted. "What occurred last year was against the norms of culture and society. So much so that I cannot even bring myself to speak of them."[61]

The Aurat March organizers did not clutch their pearls in response. "It's not a vulgar slogan; it means it's my body and my choice," Nighat Dad said when we last spoke in October 2020. "And when we say this, that means don't violate the dignity of my body. Don't rape me, don't kill me in the name of honor. I'm not your honor. I'm a human being who has the same constitutional rights as other people."

Shiza Malik noted, "They didn't have a problem with women coming out and asking for their rights, but they wanted them to ask for their rights politely and dressed modestly." Hamna Zubair agreed. "The backlash against also says something, doesn't it? I mean, you have so many male critiques of Aurat March," she said. "Those criticisms, like it's being elite, or it's being foreign funded, which is not true—it just really comes from a place of trying to discredit it. And I think that's a testament to how powerful this is, because they know that this is a very potent symbol for women."

Symbols can be powerful statements—but in Pakistan, they can also lead to violence. A few days before the 2020 march, with all their court petitions rejected, a fundamentalist mob vandalized an Aurat March mural in Islamabad and threatened the artists. Clerics claimed the painting was "fahashi," or obscene. In a common practice in Pakistan, the religious gang painted over the women's faces so they would be "decent"—and dehumanized.[62]

"Anything you draw, they will hate that woman's depiction of art," said Shehzil Malik, whose designs for the 2020 march were also contested but still triumphantly went up on walls and posters across Pakistan. She saw the fundamentalists' response as similar to "what they do with the Black Lives Matter movement" in America. "Oh, you shouldn't say it this way. And it's very frustrating because you're like, oh, now you're going to tell me how we should talk about our own oppression?"

Aurat March organizers sent the event's slogans to the High Court for approval and held public forums that included conservative religious groups. It wasn't enough for Pakistan's entrenched patriarchy. Religious conservatives tried to stop the Islamabad march on the day itself, staging a Haya March (Modesty March) as a counter-rally. Militant groups from the Lal Masjid, a mosque long known for violence and armed skirmishes with authorities, assaulted Aurat March participants, throwing shoes, bricks, and stones at the women. The police intervened, but one woman was injured. Again, activists took to Twitter to call for action: "Mullahs are stoning the participants of #AuratAzadiMarch a march that was and is peaceful. Where is the security that was promised? Where was the police that was promised?"[63]

Despite being shaken, the Aurat March protesters did what women across Pakistan do every day—they picked themselves up and kept fighting. The march continued. And by the end of International Women's Day 2020, the marches had only grown, with thousands of women gathering in Karachi, Lahore, Islamabad, Multan, Quetta, Sukkur, and Hyderabad.[64]

In Lahore, members of Asma Jahangir's legal aid organization marched, holding signs with the feminist trailblazer's photo and chanting slogans into a bullhorn. Fauzia Viqar defiantly called on leaders to transform paper promises and easy endorsements into action: "The March has gotten blessings by all political parties across the board, but I feel like this issue has to be made a focus for all governments." An older man attended, part of the generation that could be expected to reject gender equity, holding a sign that read, "Men of quality do not fear equality." The crowd shouted call-and-response cheers: *Jagi Jagi Aurat Jagi!*—"Wake up, wake up, women, wake up!"[65]

Setting precedents is hard, sometimes crushing work. But Nighat Dad was resolute: "I don't think that anyone can stop the march now."

Representatives from sixty-five industries from the Swedish #MeToo movement present reform proposals to Åsa Regnér, the minister for gender equality, during a meeting at the Historical Museum in Stockholm, Sweden, in March 2018. Credit: Magnus Hjalmarson Neideman/SvD

Chapter Six

SWEDEN: UPRISING

#tystnadtagning

**To dare is to lose your foothold for a moment;
to not dare is to lose yourself.**[1]

—Swedish proverb

IN OCTOBER 2017, CISSI WALLIN, A THIRTY-TWO-YEAR-OLD ACTRESS AND WRITER from Stockholm, was scrolling through the newsfeed on her computer in a Tribeca diner while vacationing with her husband and toddler in New York. After browsing the headlines, she became transfixed by a story in which several prominent Hollywood actresses had publicly accused the film producer Harvey Weinstein of sexual assault and harassment. As she sat with her family, digesting one brave account after another, she closed her eyes and wondered silently, *What if people would believe me now?*[1]

A decade before, when Cissi was twenty-one and at the dawn of her career, she had met Fredrik Virtanen, then a well-known, middle-aged journalist at *Aftonbladet*, one of Sweden's largest newspapers. Cissi, a country girl from western Sweden, had flourished in her theater studies as a high schooler and found sudden fame at a young age, having starred in a popular feature film just the year before. She also had designs on becoming a writer and was thrilled to happen upon Virtanen, one of the most celebrated writers in the industry, at a fashionable Stockholm nightclub.[2]

Cissi got into a taxi with Virtanen for what she thought would be an after-party at his apartment. When they arrived, no one else was there. She recalled sipping one glass of wine at his kitchen table. Then, she says, everything turned black. When she woke, she alleged, Virtanen was trying to pull off her clothes, and he raped her orally while she was unable to move or fight back.

Virtanen would later dispute this, saying that he might have been guilty of clumsy behavior but denying all allegations. Cissi didn't share her account of what had happened right away. It took her until 2011, five years later, to finally go to the police. "Only then," she recalled, "did I have the energy."[3] But her complaint was dismissed and charges were never brought, rendering Virtanen innocent under the law.

Cissi occasionally spoke publicly about having been drugged and sexually assaulted by "a man in the media." The events of that night haunted her, affecting everything from what she read in the newspaper to where she felt comfortable walking in the city. She would take detours whenever she saw Virtanen in her neighborhood, running away, hiding, crying.[4] But in a nation like Sweden, which has strict rules prohibiting the media from publicly identifying someone merely accused of a crime, she had never thought about naming him.

Until October of 2017.

As is now well known, in response to the *New York Times* story Cissi read while sitting with her family in the diner, an unprecedented movement had begun. On October 15, ten days after the story's publication, the American actress Alyssa Milano invited survivors to share their accounts of harassment and abuse on social media, channeling the "Me Too" campaign developed by the human rights activist Tarana Burke years before. "If you've been sexually harassed or assaulted," Milano tweeted, "write 'me too' as a reply to this tweet."[5]

The next day, as the #MeToo hashtag went viral and women across the United States began pouring out tales of sexual abuse, Cissi—after consulting with her lawyers and family—decided to come forward publicly and share her story. As hundreds of thousands of others have since done, she logged on to Instagram, took a deep breath, and posted her account for all to see, naming her alleged assailant. "The powerful media man that drugged and raped me in 2006 is Fredrik Virtanen," she wrote. "I reported to the police in 2011, but I have not had the energy or courage to out him. Until now."[6]

When she clicked "publish," Cissi couldn't have known what would follow: that her post would be viewed by half a million people in twenty-four hours, inspiring eleven other women to come forward, many with disturbingly similar accusations against Virtanen; that she and her family would face death threats for daring to voice her alleged perpetrator's name; that her words would prompt a series of uprisings from women in every major industry in Sweden—with reverberations that persist today.

· · · · · · · · · · · · · · · · · ·

Sweden, a country of ten million people nestled between the Baltic and North Seas, has long been considered a beacon of gender equality. Feminism is openly celebrated there. Paid parental leave and universal childcare have created a gender-balanced labor force. Unlike in other Western economies, where women vastly outnumber men at playgrounds and parent association meetings, the streets teem with fathers pushing strollers and tending to children. Women hold nearly half of parliamentary seats, resulting in what government officials call the "first feminist government in the world." In 2006, the World Economic Forum ranked Sweden first in the world on its gender equality index, and it has remained near the top of the list ever since.[7] By nearly every metric available, Sweden seems as close to a feminist utopia as exists today.

The Swedish self-image as a paragon of progressivism initially led activists there to doubt the resonance of the #MeToo hashtag. "When the #MeToo movement came," the Swedish actress and activist Sofia Helin said, "I was skeptical." *This will be over in a month*, she recalled thinking, *and then it will all be back to normal.*[8]

Yet the #MeToo movement crashed onto Sweden's shores with a vengeance, proving that even the most "feminist" country in the world was not yet equal for women. Despite the perceptions of Sweden as a gender-balanced paradise, tensions bubbled beneath the surface. The older generation of women's advocates in Sweden had long questioned how well policies like shared parental leave and childcare could protect women given the persistence of traditional gender norms and unchecked harassment. Jenny Nordberg, a Swedish journalist, noted that although women "work alongside men and move freely in society, ultimately, it's still always viewed as a woman's responsibility to protect herself from men. In that sense, women are not yet fully protected by the justice system."[9]

Ida Östensson, a thirty-five-year-old feminist leader and founder of the Swedish advocacy organization Make Equal, explained how these norms shaped her own upbringing in a small northern town, ultimately propelling her to a lifetime of feminist activism. At a very young age, she said, girls and boys were taught strict gender roles detailing "how you can act, how you can talk, what space you can take, what you can do in your spare time."[10]

Ida's dream growing up was to be a skateboarder like her brothers, but she found herself ostracized by that predominantly male community. And like so many others, she faced relentless sexual harassment, starting when she was a young student. "We had this long glass corridor where you had to pass to go to different lessons," she recalled, and about "70 percent of the times I walked through, I got either called something or touched in a way I didn't want to." At the age of fourteen, she said, she was sexually abused by her sports coach, one of the people she trusted most. "All of us have our own experiences of sexual abuse and violence," she noted quietly.

Years before the #MeToo hashtag went viral, Ida and other activists had sought to address harmful gender norms in their country, laboring to put the issue of sexual harassment and assault on the national agenda and starting a nationwide online campaign called "Everything We Don't Talk About." Ida also lobbied the legislature to adopt a "Yes Means Yes" law, criminalizing all sex without consent as rape, even when violence, coercion, and threats were not involved.[11]

Ida and her colleagues were fighting an uphill battle for reform—a battle largely ignored in a country that ranked far above others on benchmarks of gender equality. But this complacency was shattered in October 2017, from the moment Cissi clicked "publish" on her #MeToo story.

. . . .

The film and television actress Sofia Helin, who is well known across Europe for her marquee role on a successful crime-drama series, was one of the first to read Cissi's Instagram post. Sofia had struggled with her experiences of sexual abuse in the industry. Like countless others, she had been silenced with a monetary settlement years before. Sofia weighed whether she, like Cissi, should come forward, recognizing the power she commanded as a public figure. "I felt that it was my duty to do something," she recalled. But unlike Cissi, she didn't want to name her alleged attacker. "I didn't want to be part of a movement where you just point a finger at one person and say: it's him and no one else," she told us. "If you do that, everybody else just relaxes and then goes on." To her, the whole structure was stacked against women and cried out for reform.

To expose that structural failure, Sofia initially decided to share her story with ten fellow actresses. Within forty-eight hours, "it just exploded," she said. "I got so many messages. They spoke about what they had experienced. It was shocking, and overwhelming." Emboldened, Sofia decided to write an article about misogyny and abuse in the Swedish film industry, but she didn't want to sign her name to it—or to stand alone. So she started a closed Facebook thread, which caught fire among the acting community, with one actress after another joining a petition for change and sharing personal testimonies of harassment, abuse, and assault.

Word of this private Facebook group had traveled to Malena Rydell, editor of the *Svenska Dagbladet*, one of the largest newspapers in Sweden. Malena had been tracking these issues for many years, having cut her teeth as the editor of a Swedish feminist magazine back in 2005. She decided the actresses' stories could be worth publishing, but she proceeded with caution, given the sensitive nature of the allegations. "We had a deal with them," Malena recalled over lunch in a Stockholm cafeteria.[12] The paper wouldn't identify any specific man, hewing closely to journalistic ethics rules that prohibited naming the accused. And the names of the actresses would be attached publicly to a petition for change, but not to any specific #MeToo story, further protecting their anonymity. "It was important to us to do this thoroughly, press-ethics-wise," Malena said firmly. "No one knew who gave which testimony." Within days, more than seven hundred actresses had signed the petition.

Malena published a gripping account of these stories in her paper, which has a circulation of seven hundred fifty thousand.[13] She had no inkling of the impact the story would have. "There was a much bigger reaction than I expected," she marveled. "We've seen a lot of petitions. People usually don't care." But the sheer number of the women's stories was overwhelming, as was the revelation that some of the most powerful women in Swedish society had experienced sexual harassment and abuse. Soon more and more actresses came forward, tweeting under the hashtag #tystnadtagning, or "silence action."

Although the accusations lodged by Cissi Wallin just a few weeks before had received media coverage, the collective nature of the actresses' action—with hundreds of women willing to speak out—provoked an un-precedented response from the highest levels. The same day the story was published, the Swedish minister of culture reached out to entertainment leaders to discuss the problems it highlighted, declaring her disgust and out-rage. The article even reached the prime minister, Stefan Löfven, who spoke publicly about his shock and vowed to take action. "When so many people express this," he said, "it becomes even clearer that we have to do something really radical."[14] Malena was astounded. "I knew a lot about feminist issues and had reported on them," she recalled, "but I couldn't see this coming."

The story sparked outrage not only in the halls of the capitol but also among women across the country. Caroline Snellman, a top lawyer in Stockholm who had come up in the ranks at several white-shoe law firms, was stunned by the actresses' stories and the conversation that ensued. Most people in Sweden didn't talk about their experiences of sexual ha-rassment and assault, which were perceived as individual problems and swept under the rug. But the astonishing number of stories from the film industry showed that "it's a structural problem, not an individual one," Caroline stressed.[15]

She knew that this misbehavior was also rampant in the legal profes-sion, so she decided to mimic the actresses' group, starting her own lawyers' thread on Facebook. Within hours, her group had grown exponentially: she created it on a Friday, and by Saturday morning five thousand lawyers had joined.

Like Sofia, who had organized the testimony of her fellow actresses, Car-oline insisted that members of the legal community post their stories anony-mously, to emphasize not the individual accounts but the systemic nature of the offenses. The volume of stories showed that the problem of sexual abuse in the workplace was widespread not only in the film industry, but also in more buttoned-up professions. Accounts came in from lawyers who'd worked at "all the nice, big firms," Caroline recalled, from corporate coun-sels to nongovernmental organizations. "It was everyone."

Forty-eight hours after Malena published the account of sexual abuse in the film industry in *Svenska Dagbladet*, the lawyers asked that she report on their uprising as well. Their testimony totaled more than one hundred pages, so Malena and her colleague Erika Hallhagen worked through the weekend to comb through the stories and publish a follow-up piece. Once it went live, the lawyers began tweeting under their own hashtag: #medvilkenrätt, or "with what right."[16]

The second article propelled news coverage to a new level, moving the story from a phenomenon of the movie business into the heart of society. Ida Östensson, who had for years labored with other activists to get media coverage for campaigns against sexual abuse and discriminatory gender norms, was struggling to keep up. "I think all of us worked eighteen hours every day," she remembered. Longtime women's leaders felt an urgency to act because "everyone was finally listening." Perhaps most surprising was the reaction of men: thousands of them contacted Ida Östensson's organization, Make Equal, expressing horror at the number of stories and asking what they could do to help. "It was overwhelming," she recalled. Seeking a brief respite, she packed up and headed to Spain to visit her parents.

Respite was not on the horizon. Women from a wide range of industries quickly began organizing en masse, creating their own social media groups and sharing their stories online. While on her way to Spain, Ida was contacted by representatives from women in half a dozen fields; they, too, had stories to tell. These women wanted to do more than testify to their experiences; they also aimed to collaborate within and between sectors to marshal collective willpower toward concrete demands for policy change. With only a spotty internet connection and a cell phone, Ida worked furiously to create a new Facebook group to link organizers from a vast array of sectors, from tech workers and teachers to archaeologists and architects.

Using a virtual platform, these women spent hours on top of their day jobs coordinating a strategy to keep momentum going. Over the next months, a new sector uprising would go public every few days, ensuring that women in each industry would get well-deserved media coverage—and cementing the notion that sexual abuse was rife in every workplace in the nation. Women from all walks of life came together to work cooperatively, launching one media campaign after another. In addition to #MeToo, they used humorous, industry-specific hashtags that quickly went viral. Restaurant workers used #vikokarover ("we are boiling with rage"). Health care employees posted under #nustickerdettill ("now it will hurt"). The game industry used #vispelarintemed ("we do not play along"), the banking industry #inteminskuld ("not my debt"), the sports sector #timeout, unions #inteforhandlingsbart ("not negotiable").[17] Even women in sex work spoke out against nonconsensual abuse, posting under the hashtag #intedinhora ("not your whore"). In just eight weeks, women in sixty-five industries across Sweden had joined the Facebook group, all of them launching their own uprising with the coaching of others who had gone before them.

The relentlessness of their campaign ensured that it dominated the front pages. What was once swept under the rug was now openly discussed at watercoolers and dinner tables across the country. The focus on the collective experience of women—rather than the individual wrongdoing of particular men—made the structural barriers that women faced in the workplace impossible to ignore. "You could see a pattern emerge," Malena said. "Everybody could embrace it."

The sheer number of women posting online and sharing their stories also made the universality of women's experiences of harassment and abuse undeniable. People could "no longer talk about 'certain men' who do this," remarked one organizer, nor could they question the motives of individual women. These abuses and crimes were being committed in every corner of society.[18]

As in other countries, technology was crucial to the dramatic rise and expansion of the #MeToo movement in Sweden. Facebook provided a virtual platform available to millions, facilitating the velocity with which the movement spread across the nation. The speed and availability of information was remarkable: what would otherwise have taken months or weeks to organize across sectors could be communicated and shared within minutes. The transnational dimension of the movement also made it powerful. "We had a history of hashtags before #MeToo," said Caroline Snellman, who led the lawyers' uprising. But "having the global movement—being connected to the world—made it more than a personal story or a Swedish story." This global movement was what "broke the dam."

In addition, social media platforms gave women the privacy they needed to organize on a sensitive topic that previously was largely shut out of the public square. The ability to connect in a closed digital forum meant women could share what had happened to them without fear of professional repercussions or personal reprisals, affording protection to those who otherwise would have been endangered simply for speaking out. Though women were succeeding in raising awareness and setting the terms of the debate, online resistance to their efforts was fierce. In certain industries, such as forestry, women decided they couldn't be identified in the media because of the risks they faced. "The sectors didn't have official spokespersons. They had to be anonymous because of threats," recalled Elin Andersson, a communications professional who put her day job on hold to help organize the Facebook group. Elin said wryly of the trolls, "You never knew what these people could do."[19]

Cooperation across sectors also allowed women with a broad range of backgrounds to help one another as the campaign evolved over the next several months. The PR professionals carefully curated the timing of each uprising to ensure maximum media attention. When a member of the Facebook group came under threat for speaking out, a team of lawyers was ready to offer legal advice. "It was amazing to see the support we could give each other," Elin said, "and the level of expertise in this group."

The democratizing effect of technology meant that anyone with an internet connection could get involved and make her voice heard. This not only significantly increased the number of women involved but also changed the very composition of the Swedish women's movement. "I would say that 90 percent of the people involved were not [part of] the feminist movement before," said Ida, who had spent her entire career on the front lines. "It changed the feminist landscape. You have new names, new feminists, very prominent people" now involved. These new recruits drew even more participants into the women's movement. "The Instagram feminists appeal to a broader spectrum of women than the usual intellectual feminists," one organizer observed. "And they had a huge following."[20]

The viral movement also added new credibility by lifting up the voices of the grassroots. Women's advocates in Sweden had long campaigned for the rights of workers in restaurants, health care, and other industries, but they didn't always have personal experience or background in those fields. Now they had leaders in every sector for which they advocated.

As in the United States, many women in positions of power in Sweden felt compelled to support women from all different walks of life—including those without resources or cultural cachet. Activists in the movie business and legal profession quickly recognized that although their stories were the ones capturing media attention, it was even harder for women to fight sexual abuse in transient workplaces or where employees were living paycheck to paycheck. "We realized that the early uprisings [represented] privileged groups, like actors and lawyers," Caroline Snellman said. So women in media, law, and the financial fields helped those without the ability to take days off to organize, or for whom media attention would be harder to capture.

Privileged white women also recognized the intersectional layers of discrimination faced by women who were members of minority groups, particularly women of color. Some specifically sought to lift these voices. "I look at this like Nintendo, or Mario Kart," Caroline explained. "There are different levels. If you're a Christian, heterosexual, white male, you're playing at the easiest level in our society. Maybe I'm at level two, as a Christian, heterosexual, white woman." But imagine a Muslim, lesbian woman in Sweden who had immigrated from North Africa: "That's level-ten difficulty," she observed. "And I can only see how much easier it is to be at level one. I can't know what it's like to be at level ten." Women with privilege argued to the media that these women's voices also deserved to be heard, in both naming the problem and identifying the solutions.

As the movement grew over the next several months, activists shifted from sharing their experiences to demanding policy reform and cultural change. Representatives from the sixty-five sectors came together to call for reforms, including more support for survivors, consent education in schools, mandatory training for police and social service providers, and more government investigations of workplace harassment complaints.[21] Organizers in Sweden were contacted by activists from other nations, including Finland, Germany, the Netherlands, and South Korea, seeking advice on how to replicate their success.

Staggering numbers of women had come together—not to castigate individual men, but to demand that societal institutions address the web of harassment and discrimination constraining the lives and opportunities of women. And thanks to technology, the size and spread of the movement was greater than ever before. #MeToo was "the biggest women's movement in Sweden since women got the right to vote in 1919," the reporter Maria Schottenius said.[22]

And no institution—no matter how sacred—would be immune.

· · · · · · · · · · · · · · · · ·

Scandinavia is known around the world for its history of social democracy, aurora borealis sightings, economical IKEA furnishings, and ubiquitous ABBA tunes. But the region is most renowned for the annual awards it bestows through its storied Nobel Foundation, which has recognized international excellence in top disciplines—including chemistry, economics, medicine, literature, physics, and the pursuit of peace—since the Stockholm-born Alfred Nobel first endowed it in 1901. Every year, the Nobel Foundation's esteemed members have sifted through countless nominations for some of the greatest accomplishments in human history, from Albert Einstein's identification of the photoelectric effect and Marie Curie's discovery of radioactivity, to Mother Teresa's ministrations to the impoverished and Martin Luther King Jr.'s eloquent campaign against racism. Perhaps no other institution inspires as much pride in Swedes as the Nobel Prize.

Before the #MeToo movement in Sweden was triggered by Cissi Wallin's Instagram post, the Swedish Nobel Academy, which awards the Nobel Prize in Literature, was arguably the most revered cultural institution in the nation. Across Sweden, its prestige was unmatched. "People treated the academy almost in a religious way," said Matilda Gustavsson, a reporter at the Swedish daily *Dagens Nyheter*.[23] Being affiliated with the academy was to be revered as royalty. Its proceedings were shrouded in secrecy, and members were appointed for life.

Matilda, a top cultural reporter, had long heard rumors about a man named Jean-Claude Arnault, the powerful artistic director of an academy-supported cultural forum and the husband of academy member Katarina Frostenson. Arnault, a French-born photographer in his seventies, relished his perch in an institution on which the cultural establishment relied for support, validation, and resources. But there was a darker side to the power he wielded: Arnault was also known within cultural circles to be a harasser of women, who often warned one another of his behavior. As with the rumors about Harvey Weinstein that circulated through Hollywood, although the allegations were widely known, they were not covered seriously before the #MeToo movement. The stories were instead "treated as something lightweight and gossipy," Matilda remembered. She couldn't imagine any newspaper covering them.

Reading coverage of the Weinstein story in the *New York Times* altered Matilda's perception of what could be considered newsworthy. "The Weinstein story made me realize it was possible to uncover a story like this," she recalled. She still worried, however, about writing something that would out a well-known figure in Sweden, given the country's strict ethical guidelines prohibiting media from naming alleged perpetrators before conviction. Even with the example of the *New York Times* outing Weinstein in the United States, "it was hard for me to imagine a story in Sweden where Arnault was named."

Cissi's post about Fredrik Virtanen shattered that barrier. "To name [Virtanen] was to break a social rule," Matilda explained. As others inspired by Cissi's courage began to come forward, a handful outed a few powerful men. And as in other countries, naming names had an outsize effect. "Whether you think that was a good thing or a bad thing," Matilda said, "it's an explanation for why the MeToo hashtag exploded in Sweden." And it's what made Matilda's investigation of Jean-Claude Arnault possible.

"People were so afraid of that man," she said. "The hardest part was to convince them to come forward and speak his name. Some of the women I talked with said, 'You will never be able to publish this.'" But the outcry in Sweden and around the world awakened these women to the power of their collective action. "They had seen that, maybe for the first time in history, it was possible that there could be consequences," Matilda recalled. One by one, she persuaded many of Arnault's victims to talk on the record.

Matilda labored for six weeks on her story, painstakingly validating every account with eyewitness testimony and corroborating evidence. She convinced her editor to publish the article without naming Arnault but including enough information that it was possible to figure out who the alleged perpetrator was. All told, eighteen women came forward, their stories carried prominently in *Dagens Nyheter* on November 21, 2017.[24]

The reaction was swift. The academy, whose proceedings had been secret for two centuries, convened an emergency meeting, after which Sara

Danius—a literary scholar and critic who was the first female head of the academy in its history—held a public press conference to provide transparency about what had been discussed. Danius shared personal testimony she had heard from academy members, as well as their wives and daughters, about their own experiences with Arnault's behavior, validating the credibility of the allegations and insisting they were worth taking seriously. Danius was matter of fact in her presentation but later described herself as "extremely shaken," having been through similar experiences herself. "She basically came out to the press and said, '#MeToo—this happened to us as well,'" Matilda told us. Importantly, Danius also launched a formal investigation, hiring a law firm to discover what academy members knew—and should have known.[25]

Danius's response to Matilda's story "meant so much to the women I spoke to for my article," Matilda recalled. One of those women—who remains anonymous to this day, but whom we will call "Lydia"—agreed to be interviewed for this book. Although Lydia had been unwilling to go on the record for Matilda's article, her account mirrored the complaints of those who had been willing to go public, many of whom were young women exploited by a powerful man through harassment, abuse, and disturbing encounters that turned violent and nonconsensual.

Years before, Lydia had endured her own harrowing experience with Arnault. Then a single mother and doctoral student, she met Arnault at a bar, where he impressed her with his close relationships with her supervisor and other professors at her institution. Taken with him, she agreed to accompany him to his Stockholm apartment. But their encounter turned violent when he grabbed her neck and forced her to perform oral sex, causing her to vomit. When he released her neck, as she was gasping for air, he raped her vaginally.

At the time, it didn't occur to Lydia to inform the police. After all, she had willingly gone to Arnault's apartment; she did not realize that what had happened could still be rape. She also worried that Arnault would make things difficult for her professionally; her friend had told her about instances in which he had "ruined" women who had complained of his behavior. She was so fearful that when he contacted her again, she responded, despite her revulsion. The abuse continued until she worked up the courage to refuse his calls, notwithstanding the danger she felt her rejection would put her in. Until that point, she had told only close friends and her therapist. When Matilda first contacted her, she was far too afraid to allow her story to be published—even with the knowledge that several other women were coming forward.

The reaction to Matilda's story, however—as well as to Cissi's Instagram post—gave Lydia the courage to finally file a report with the police. "It was because of #MeToo that I could report him," Lydia told us. "I couldn't have imagined the supportive reaction [to the article] before it was published." The solidarity she felt with the other women who were victimized compelled her to act. "I was shocked when I saw the magnitude of his offenses," she remembered. She decided to file a formal report not only because she "sought justice" for herself but also "as a way of putting an end to what he had been doing to other women." Because of Lydia's decision to file a police report, the trial of Jean-Claude Arnault shifted from the court of public opinion to the judicial system.

The response to Danius's decisive press conference, however, was decidedly more mixed. It quickly became clear that a feud had broken out behind the academy's walls—between those who supported Danius's investigation and serious treatment of the allegations, and those who disbelieved the women's testimony and vowed to stand by Arnault. What happened next was almost as stunning as the initial allegations: after two months of silence, as the Arnault investigation proceeded, three academy members stepped down from their lifetime appointments—something that had never happened in the academy's history. "The rules were that you just exit in a coffin," recalled Klas Östergren, a former board member and the first to resign.[26] But he had decided he could not lend his name to an institution with members who could contemplate protecting a sexual predator: "It was important to me to look my daughter in the eyes and say, 'I did what I could do.'"

Six days later, Sara Danius was ousted.[27]

On the very same staircase where she had stood a few months before, expressing support for the seriousness of the eighteen women's allegations, Danius revealed that she had lost the confidence of the remaining academy members—many of whom supported Arnault—and would leave.

Women around the country were outraged. The #MeToo movement had finally reached the pinnacle of Swedish society, puncturing an institution so storied that even a known sexual abuser could escape consequences for two decades because of the prestige of his affiliation. The idea that the woman seeking accountability for his abuse of power would have to resign—while those supporting Arnault stayed on—was intolerable. Following Danius's resignation, the respected image of academy members was shattered. "Public trust for the Academy is perhaps below rock bottom," Björn Wiman, the culture editor of *Dagens Nyheter*, observed at the time.[28]

For women in every sector of Swedish society, who had been organizing online for months, the time had come to make clear that the rules had changed. On April 19, 2018, thousands of women took to the streets, outraged that a prominent female leader was paying the price for the sexual crimes of a powerful man. Many wore a *knytblus*, or "pussy bow" blouse, an homage to Danius, who was known to be fond of that sartorial style, and a physical manifestation of the viral hashtag campaign #knytblusförsara, which had swept social media.[29]

Mere days after the protest, the Swedish Academy all but collapsed under the weight of the opposition it faced. The legacy of reverence for the institution disintegrated, with media from around the world covering the scandal and disarray. A press release soon announced that the Nobel Prize in Literature would not be awarded for the first time in nearly sixty years—a cancellation that previously had happened only in wartime.[30]

But a war of sorts was, in fact, underway: between those who supported the #MeToo movement and those who found it to be an overreaction and clung to a set of cultural norms that blamed women for assault and trivialized their experiences—or, worse, disbelieved them. Despite the positive reaction to #MeToo in many quarters, and evidence that public opinion was shifting, a backlash that had been brewing online began to find purchase among prominent members of society. Some who expressed concern over #MeToo were sympathetic to the travails women had shared but also worried that the movement had gone too far—especially as esteemed people and institutions began to face consequences.

This skepticism was particularly acute in the case of public allegations made by Cissi Wallin and others who were willing to name the men who had harassed or attacked them, subjecting the accused to trial by public opinion rather than to a court of law. Unlike the online uprisings—which focused on the collective experiences of women, rather than the crimes of individual men—naming perpetrators before conviction struck some as dangerous. This apprehension was especially pronounced after the suicide of a theater director, Benny Fredriksson, who had been accused of harassment and abuse in posts on social media and was ostracized as a result.[31]

Without Cissi's initial willingness to name names, however, it is unclear whether the #MeToo movement would have commanded the attention it did. "What Cissi did when she wrote about [Virtanen]—whether you like it or not—was spark Sweden's #MeToo movement," Matilda Gustavsson asserted. The naming of famous men was crucial. "That's what helped make it so big," said Elin Andersson, one of the Facebook group organizers. Lydia, who decided to file a police report against Arnault, concurred: "Cissi's testimony was of enormous importance to me," she said. "It's very unusual for women in Sweden to step forward publicly and come forward with names. I am not at all certain I would have had the courage to report," she emphasized, if Cissi hadn't. While seeking justice through public recrimination undoubtedly lacks the strictures of due process, at the time that Cissi came forward, the judicial system had eluded most of those brave enough to report abuse. Recall, after all, that Cissi's initial police complaint back in 2011 was dismissed entirely. If such complaints were true, where, exactly, were survivors supposed to turn when the justice system failed them? And how else could they help protect other women against future harm?

Although the #MeToo movement had put those questions on the agenda, it didn't always provide answers. The controversy over Arnault's trial, which began in September 2018, was a case in point. "In Sweden, people weren't even really aware of what rape is," Lydia said. "The general belief is when you are walking somewhere in the dark, a perpetrator approaches you that you don't know, and you are violently beaten and then raped." But the rape perpetrated against her was a different—and much more common—experience. "It took place in an apartment, and it began as consensual" before it turned violent, Lydia explained. But a lot of people didn't know that someone could be convicted of rape for engaging in nonconsensual sex—in part because before, so many weren't.

As the trial proceeded, Lydia was in the eye of a storm, even as her identity as the complainant was concealed. "There was a huge debate in Sweden about the trial," she recalled during our phone interview two years later. Several famous authors came forward to defend Arnault, as did Horace Engdahl, a prominent member of the Swedish Academy who had reportedly pressed for Sara Danius's ouster.[32] Lydia couldn't escape the public debate about whether her perpetrator had done anything wrong. "Since I am anonymous, people can start talking about the Arnault trial anywhere, and they don't know that I stand beside them," she said. "Standing in the grocery store, in the gym, hearing people talking about me . . . even some relatives who didn't know I was in the trial started to attack the victim during dinner." Lydia paused to take a breath. "It was horrible," she said quietly.

In the end, Arnault was convicted and given the minimum sentence of two years in prison; after he appealed, his sentence was increased by six months. To Lydia, this result was a breakthrough. "That the community recognized and acknowledged that something unjust had been done" made the pain of the public trial worthwhile, she said. "I hope it gave hope to other women when it comes to reporting sexual offenses."

Matilda, the journalist who broke the story about Arnault, also reflected on the outcome with amazement. She had no way of predicting the reverberations her initial article would incite. "I've been shocked almost every day since then," she said. But she is convinced that, despite the controversy it sparked, the eventual conviction of Arnault represented a step forward. While disagreement over the case persists to this day, "I think the movement has done something to change people's perceptions of this subject," Matilda said. "It made a lot of people realize that this is a very significant problem, and it's something that you need to take seriously."

. . . .

Perhaps the biggest shift in Sweden following the #MeToo uprisings has been cultural. A country that once saw itself as a leader on gender equality finally had to reckon with the discrimination that women still faced in all walks of life—not only harassment and abuse, but also challenges including pay inequality, underrepresentation in leadership positions, and inequality in asset ownership. "No one can say this is not a problem in Sweden" any longer, said Ida Östensson, the Make Equal activist, who had labored on these issues for years. "Everyone saw their mother, daughter, cousin, or friend write '#MeToo' or testify to discrimination. People now can't close their eyes anymore."

Lydia, whose willingness to come forward ultimately put Arnault behind bars, said that women's stories revealing how entrenched inequality and abuse were at the highest levels of Swedish society made the issue impossible to ignore. "In Sweden, we had this conception of ourselves as a feminist country," she said. "We have these victories when it comes to maternal and paternal leave, and so on. But somehow when it comes to sexuality, there was this gray area that we had not been talking about."

Two years after the #MeToo uprisings, Swedish women and men described a new understanding of consent and personal accountability. Whereas before perpetrators could get away with crimes or misbehavior, "now there is a cost," said Caroline Snellman, who led the lawyers' uprising. Women had awakened to their power, and in the age of social media, their silence could no longer be guaranteed. Perhaps the biggest achievement of the movement was that the guilt and shame attached to sexual assault and harassment had begun to shift. "The fantastic thing about the #MeToo movement was that we listened to each other and believed in their stories—not questioning or putting the blame on women," said Elin Andersson, who helped create the initial Facebook group. "Women won't tolerate it anymore." And their activism continues, with groups still working toward a full slate of gender equality reforms, within and across industries.

Employers have also begun to recognize their responsibility to address harassment and abuse and to level the economic playing field for women, in ways that could be emulated in other countries, including the United States. Caroline, the lawyer, drew an analogy between this shift and the campaign several decades ago to recognize corporate responsibility for corruption. "Today, as a CEO, I can do jail time because someone in my company who's working in Asia or Africa bribes someone. It's still my responsibility," she said. Sexual harassment is also a misuse of power—and one for which leaders should be held accountable. "Why wouldn't you treat these problems the same?" she said. "Corruption is a threat to democracy and fair play. So is sexism."

The private-sector demand for expertise in gender equality reforms is growing. According to Ida Östensson of Make Equal, before #MeToo, companies might have asked for a one-hour training on gender equality; now some of the biggest companies in Sweden are "asking us to build e-learning platforms for all of their employees, from directors all the way down, and to work with them for one or two years."

Activists, though, said that these cultural changes weren't enough, and that government reform was needed. The government "puts in some money—say, $50 million—and it sounds like a lot," Elin Andersson said. "But in reality, it's not, when it comes to the size of this problem." Ida agreed. "It's not about saying this is important," she stressed. "They have to show it with money. It costs money to change" these outcomes. Even the consent law, while a victory, was just a starting point. "It's not enough to put it into the books," Ida said. "We also have to have trainings, from the judiciary system to the police force."

Notably, important policy reforms have already taken place, and the pace of change in Sweden has been comparatively rapid. In many countries, even when the #MeToo movement has opened the door to a difficult and public debate on sexual abuse and gender inequality, the road from public awareness to policy change promises to be long. Yet in just two years, women's activists in Sweden have marshaled a comprehensive policy framework to combat workplace harassment, discrimination, and inequality. "I totally changed my agenda," Minister of Culture Alice Bah Kuhnke told the Swedish news site *The Local*, referring to a ten-point plan she put in place to tackle discrimination, including new guidelines for Swedish cultural institutions.[33] The Swedish parliament has enacted a law clarifying that sex without consent is illegal, even when threats or force are not involved—making Sweden only the tenth country in Western Europe to recognize nonconsensual sex as rape. The government is also increasing resources for its national agency on gender equality, which aims to rectify power imbalances between women and men across society.[34] Such victories suggest that conditions in Sweden are ripe for reform—and progress is in sight.

But the road ahead will not be easy, even in a country with a reservoir of policies supporting women's rights. Unresolved questions of inequality, power, and the process by which perpetrators should be held accountable persist. Perhaps no story exemplifies these remaining challenges more than Cissi Wallin's.[35] In response to her initial Instagram post, Fredrik Virtanen went on a public rehabilitation tour and was granted a sympathetic television interview in which he discussed the harm caused to his reputation and well-being because of the allegations. In that same interview, Cissi was asked not about how the incessant media coverage since her claims had affected her, but instead whether she had considered the pain that Virtanen's family would face when she came forward. The perspectives of the eleven other women who had gone public with accusations against Virtanen were largely ignored. Their claims were never pursued, nor were any charges brought.[36]

Even as the #MeToo uprisings shifted norms and laws related to gender inequality, the controversy over Cissi's willingness to raise her voice and name her alleged abuser continued unabated—even more so when Virtanen pursued defamation charges against her for her Instagram post. As with the trial of Jean-Claude Arnault, the entire nation watched captivated as legal proceedings against Cissi unfolded; unlike in Arnault's case, however, this time it was a woman's behavior on trial.

In December 2019, eight years after the police dismissed Cissi's rape complaint, and two years after she finally summoned the courage to name Virtanen—sparking a movement that connected activists across geographic and socioeconomic lines, and propelling a wave of reforms that are just beginning to take shape—Cissi was found guilty of defaming the man she said had raped her and was ordered to pay him thousands of dollars in damages.[37] The court acknowledged that victims naming their offenders had helped raise awareness of sexual abuse, but it did not find Cissi's doing so to be justifiable, noting that Virtanen's ability to defend himself against the allegations was "limited."

The progress that women in Sweden have made is substantial. The rapid changes there suggest that even more reform is on the horizon. But the personal costs for those who put their physical safety, professional reputations, families, and mental health at risk are substantial as well. Their opportunity to defend themselves—and the women who are too often abused in their wake—is also limited.

Virtanen, who had been forced out of his position as a columnist at *Aftonbladet* shortly after the media reported on the avalanche of accusations against him, had left the country by the time of the court's ruling and went on to write a book about his experiences called *Utan Nåd* (Without Mercy), in which he denied the claims of all twelve women but confessed to life-long struggles with alcohol, drug abuse, and self-hate. He also appealed the court's sentence on the basis that the damages he'd won weren't high enough.[38]

Even before the verdict, Cissi had lost her twelve-year position as a columnist for *Metro*, a popular newspaper. But she is forging ahead. Like Virtanen, she is pursuing an appeal of the court's judgment, seeking a legal right for women to raise their voices. "Our perpetrators are the ones who make up and create the structure," Cissi observed. "#MeToo shows very strongly that there is a great deal of dissatisfaction with and huge distrust of the legal system." She believes it is absurd to live under a rule of law where women are prosecuted, convicted, and sentenced by the state for having made allegations of sexual offenses. Cissi is also training as a social worker so she can work with vulnerable women, and she wrote a book to tell her own story. The power of her public testimony propels her forward. "Coming out the other side and feeling that I have value anyway—in that, there is an indescribable force," she said. "It is precisely the awakening that many are experiencing now."[39]

Despite the consequences that Cissi faced, she paved the way for women across Sweden to raise their voices. "To testify against powerful men is something that has always in history come with a price for women," observed Matilda Gustavsson, who broke the Arnault story. "And they've been ignored or their testimonies have been turned against them or they've been shamed or exposed in different ways." But she remained optimistic about the promise of the collective power women had assumed over the previous few years. "It's a big thing that women are speaking up, and doing this can change the world."

Caroline Snellman, the lawyer, whose activism in the women's movement continues to grow, has come to terms with the hate mail and threats she faces. "When you're pushing for things you really believe in, there are going to be sacrifices," she told us. "People don't give up power, privilege, without a struggle." But she, like so many others, has awakened to her power and refuses to back down. "I can either sit in the back seat, or I can put myself forward and be part of the change."

Her choice—and the choice of millions of others—is clear.

Members of Las Tesis, a Chilean feminist collective, perform their protest anthem *Un Violador En Tu Camino* ("A Rapist in Your Path") with US Women's March organizers at the January 2020 Washington, DC, march. Credit: Reuters/Mary F. Calvert

Chapter Seven

GLOBAL AGENDA: PROTEST INTO PROGRESS

THREE YEARS AFTER THE #MeToo HASHTAG FIRST WENT VIRAL, WHAT STARTED as a wildfire has evolved into a slow burn—one that shows no signs of being extinguished. While #MeToo revelations no longer dominate above-the-fold headlines, hastening some to declare the movement over, this facile take overlooks the global reverberations wrought by the most diverse and transnational wave of the women's movement to date. "Measuring success or failure based on continued discrimination or individual setbacks, I think, misses the historic shift in courts, legislatures, and social norms," said Michelle Bachelet, the first woman president of Chile and the current UN high commissioner for human rights, in an interview about the effects of the global #MeToo movement.[1]

Examples of this shift abound. As we saw in China, Egypt, Nigeria, and Sweden, women's activism has produced legal verdicts in which perpetrators who had previously escaped accountability are facing consequences for the first time. In India, where sexual abusers have long evaded repercussions for their crimes, Kuldeep Singh Sengar—a prominent member of the legislative assembly in the Uttar Pradesh province, who assaulted a young woman— initially faced no consequences, while the survivor and her family were attacked for coming forward. But after this impunity inspired protests across the country, the legislator was finally held accountable and convicted of kidnapping and rape. In the United Kingdom, allegations of sexual assault against the British lawmaker Charlie Elphicke were initially overlooked by his colleagues, with the Tory Party restoring him to his leadership position as whip after an initial suspension.[2] Pressure from activists, however, forced the authorities to take action, resulting in his conviction for three counts of sexual abuse and elimination from office. These judicial victories for survivors augur a new era of accountability.

As we saw in Nigeria and Tunisia, many nations have also enacted legislative reforms to bolster prohibitions against sexual harassment and assault. In 2018, activism ignited by the French #MeToo movement—which organized using the hashtag #BalanceTonPorc, or "Rat on Your Pig"—spurred parliament to pass two new laws punishing sexual harassment, one imposing obligations on employers to strengthen workplace regulations, and the second creating the first-ever national law criminalizing street harassment. That same year, in Morocco, activists who posted stories under the hashtag #Masaktach, or "I will not keep silent," won a new law imposing harsher penalties for violence against women, including rape, sexual harassment, and domestic abuse. In Ethiopia, rising social media activism led the country's parliamentarians to approve a law regulating workplace sexual harassment and sexual violence, and providing new remedies for survivors.[3]

As we saw in Brazil, in some countries the explosion of online organizing has translated into substantial increases in women's political participation and a new class of women leaders fighting for change. In 2018, a record-breaking number of women ran for office in that country. In Lebanon, 113 women became parliamentary candidates, an eightfold increase over the 12 women who ran in 2009. In Mexico, during the same time period, almost 3,000 women ran for office, producing full gender parity in parliament for the first time. In the United States, the 2018 midterm election yielded the largest and most diverse class of women elected in American history, with more than 475 women registered to run for seats in the House of Representatives and a historic 22 women winning their party's nomination for the Senate—numbers that continued to rise in 2020. And in Sri Lanka, an astonishing 17,000 women competed for political seats, confirming that large numbers of women are daring to translate online organizing into greater political participation.[4]

The persistent activism prompting these changes has also produced shifts in global norms. In 2019, after two years of negotiations informed by testimony from the #MeToo movement, the International Labour Organization—comprising governments, employer representatives, and workers' rights organizations from around the world—adopted the first-ever international convention prohibiting violence and harassment in the workplace. In this historic agreement, governments across the globe accepted a broad definition of sexual harassment in the workplace applicable to workers in the formal and informal sectors, and agreed to ambitious commitments to address this scourge. In 2020, Uruguay became the first nation to ratify the convention, with many others sure to follow.[5]

Online activism continues to play an important role in these victories. Though the number of #MeToo tweets and social media posts has decreased from the high watermark of 2017, the aggregate obscures the impact of highly localized campaigns, in which women continue to come forward in their communities to name names and demand change. They are doing so not only in countries where such speech is readily permitted, but also in the unlikeliest of places, where those who speak out face grave danger. Consider the courageous women in Iran, whose rights have been severely restricted since the 1979 Islamic Revolution and who bravely refuted claims that laws requiring women to wear a hijab were the best defense against harassment by sharing their experiences of abuse at the hands of their leaders. Or women in Russia, who have flooded social media with stories of sexual harassment and violence in the face of harsh crackdowns on protesters and the weakening of laws prohibiting gender-based violence. Even in Saudi Arabia, women have shared their accounts of sexual abuse and demands for change on Twitter, despite a long-standing government effort to arrest, imprison, and even torture female human rights defenders campaigning for reform.[6]

While the force of this new wave of the global women's movement is undeniable, so too is the intensity of a rising backlash that threatens to limit its gains. As women's rights activists have used the internet and social media to organize for change across borders, so have those seeking to maintain the status quo. Online harassment of women is pernicious and alarmingly widespread: one global survey found that over half of women and girls between the ages of fifteen and twenty-five had experienced online abuse, with four in ten enduring online harassment since their teenage years. Too often, this abuse succeeds in silencing women; over three-quarters of those who experienced online harassment said it affected their online participation, leading them, for instance, to reduce or self-censor their social media posts.[7]

This online backlash is personified by the rise of a class of misogynist leaders—from Jair Bolsonaro in Brazil, to Vladimir Putin in Russia, to

Recep Tayyip Erdogan in Turkey, to Donald Trump in the United States—
whose paths to power were predicated on promises to restore a bygone era
of male domination. It is no accident that many of these leaders have themselves faced accusations of sexual assault, and no surprise that they have
offered dismissive responses that foment a culture of impunity. President
Bolsonaro, for example, responded to allegations of violence by suggesting
that his accusers were not desirable enough to assault, saying one was "not
worth raping, she is very ugly." President Trump, accused of sexual misconduct by twenty-six women, responded similarly, saying in response to one
accuser, "She's not my type," and stating that another was too unattractive
to rape—thereby implying that men are entitled to assault women and nor-
malizing criminal behavior. This misogyny is reproduced in policy changes
rolling back progress on women's rights, including moves by Russian president Putin to weaken national laws criminalizing domestic violence; by the
Turkish and Polish governments to withdraw from the Istanbul Convention, a groundbreaking international agreement aimed at curtailing violence
against women; and by the Trump administration to eviscerate regulations
under Title IX of the Education Amendments of 1972 preventing and addressing sexual violence on campus.[8]

The fury and scale of the backlash, however, betrays the extent to which
cultural standards have already changed. After all, without these profound
shifts, there would be nothing for those clinging to outdated norms to react
against. "To me, that's not backlash," the *New York Times* journalist Jodi
Kantor, who with Megan Twohey broke the Harvey Weinstein story that
helped catalyze the explosion of the #MeToo movement, said in an interview
from Manhattan.[9] "That's the sound of social change." That said, continued
progress is not guaranteed, particularly given the embedded societal traditions undergirding the pernicious abuse exposed by this digital wave of the
women's movement. Translating these stories into a concrete agenda will
require commitments by government officials, multilateral organizations,
private-sector leaders, and philanthropists, as well as continued activism by
individuals to hold powerful actors to account.

What should this agenda look like? Activists who have long fought
against sexual violence emphasize that any #MeToo agenda must be rooted
in justice for survivors who for so long have been overlooked, disbelieved,

disparaged, and even penalized, and whose diverse voices and staggering numbers now render them impossible to ignore. The opportunity for change afforded by this awakening to women's experiences with violence is not lost on longtime activists. "The growth of #MeToo across the world among survivors did not surprise me," Tarana Burke, founder of the #MeToo movement, said in an interview in New York.[10] "I know how many of us are out here. But I could not see a time where nonsurvivors or nonallies would be interested in any way."

The undeniable power of women's voices has at last inspired widespread recognition of the pervasiveness of sexual harassment and abuse. Leaders dedicated to ending sexual violence are determined to honor these survivors' experiences by ensuring that their needs are at the heart of any prescription for action, as reflected by the groundbreaking "Survivors' Agenda" that Burke's organization released in partnership with others in 2020, which was informed by survivor surveys and calls for comprehensive services, policy reform, norm change, and accountability efforts.[11]

In addition to seeking justice for survivors, #MeToo leaders around the world have expanded their campaign into a broader agenda to challenge the power imbalances that perpetuate sexual harassment and assault in the first place. This theme came up often in our research for this book, not only in conversations with local advocates in Brazil, China, Egypt, Nigeria, Pakistan, Sweden, and Tunisia, but also in interviews with women who have shattered barriers as leaders and long served at the forefront of the women's rights movement. "Real change cannot happen unless the underlying causes of inequality and the marginalization of women are addressed and ultimately altered," Ellen Johnson Sirleaf, a Nobel Peace Prize laureate and former president of Liberia who was the first female head of state elected on the African continent, said in an interview from her home in Bomi County. "More needs to be done to expand the movement so that it becomes a catalyst and an integral part of a larger agenda for improvement in the status and role of disenfranchised women, legally, politically, and economically." Tina Tchen, a longtime women's rights lawyer who helped found the TIME'S UP movement and now serves as its president and chief executive, told us, "You can't address sexual harassment in a silo. That's another one of the failings of the past. We have to look holistically at these issues."[12]

Some believe that this broadening of the #MeToo movement has already taken place, given the overlapping nature of the fight against sexual abuse and broader campaigns for gender equality, which seek to show how harassment and assault undermine women's agency across economic, political, and social life. "#MeToo has given a bit more energy to these efforts," said Julia Gillard, who broke barriers as the first woman elected prime minister of Australia and who, while in office, delivered a speech on the floor of parliament about misogyny that went viral.[13] "It's put a spring in the step of a lot of women's activists, because there's a sense of solidarity with others around the world—a sense of a wave that really reinforces that you're not engaged in your activism alone."

To define an agenda for meaningful and lasting change for women, we take our lead from those on the front lines of this movement globally. Importantly, these women are challenging not only the epidemic of sexual harassment and assault but also the centuries-old systems of inequality—on the basis of gender, race, caste, ethnicity, religion, colonialism, and a host of other factors—that have allowed the abuse of women to flourish. "We are dealing with lots of biases, we are dealing with patriarchy, we are dealing with institutional and systemic bias," said United Nations deputy-secretary general Amina Mohammed, who served previously as Nigeria's minister of environment and led the UN's 2030 Agenda for Sustainable Development process and the creation of the Sustainable Development Goals.[14] "Unless we really get ahold of it at its root, and shake it up, it's going to be very difficult." Author and journalist Rebecca Traister, who chronicled the #MeToo movement in the United States and has marveled at its global spread, agreed when we spoke with her. "We're in the midst of a long-term global struggle about who gets to have power—who gets to participate, who is forced to stay on the margins, who's considered a human being, who has rights."[15]

This contest over power—who has it and who doesn't—unites activists at the forefront of the modern women's movement and differentiates this moment from prior eras. The global women's movement of the nineteenth century was largely focused on citizenship through enfranchisement—often limited initially to those in certain racial and social groups, to the exclusion of indigenous women and women of color. That movement marked the beginning of a global campaign for gender equality. In the twentieth century, the movement concentrated on the recognition of women's rights under human rights doctrine, culminating in the 1995 UN Fourth World Conference on Women in Beijing, where Hillary Clinton, then the First Lady of the United States, memorably declared that "women's rights are human rights," and where 189 countries agreed to a historic Platform for Action calling for the equal participation of women. But despite this groundbreaking international consensus, women's rights on paper were in too many places ignored in practice—disempowering women in law, in policy, and under social and cultural norms that undermined their implementation.

Today, many women leading the digital wave of the global women's movement are calling for more than equal rights: they are demanding an equal share of the power it will take to fully realize them. "Women's rights are still human rights," Hillary Clinton observed in an article in *The Atlantic* reflecting on the current movement. "But rights are nothing without the power to claim them."[16] The modern #MeToo agenda aims to rectify the power imbalances that have fueled the normalization of harassment and violence against women for centuries, and that put the most marginalized women at the greatest risk of abuse. "Sexual harassment isn't about sex—it's about gender and power," Jodi Kantor said. "It is the symptom of a skewed power dynamic."

Notably, a feature of this struggle for power is the commitment to ensuring it for every woman. "The #MeToo message emphasizes that women—regardless of nationality, ethnicity, race, position, and wealth—are affected by sexual harassment and violence and deserve accountability," said Phumzile Mlambo-Ngcuka, the former deputy president of South Africa and the current UN undersecretary general and director of UN Women, highlighting how the modern women's movement is more intersectional and inclusive than ever before. Examples of this intersectionality abound. Consider the TIME'S UP campaign in the United States, organized by influential celebrities in early 2018 following the Harvey Weinstein revelations, complete with a red-carpeted launch at the Golden Globe awards. Activists saw TIME'S UP not as a campaign only for those at the top, but as a reflection of a common struggle. Days after its launch, Mónica Ramírez of the Alianza Nacional de Campesinas (National Alliance of Farmworker Women) published a full-page letter supporting the movement in *Time* magazine, on behalf of seven hundred thousand female farmworkers.[17] "It was women who were not privileged—those usually unseen—who were speaking out in sister-hood," Tina Tchen of TIME'S UP said in our interview with her, in which she explained her organization's focus on achieving safe, fair, and dignified workplaces for all women. "I think that really fueled the commitment to a broad-based movement that was as equally for low-wage women as it was for women with more prominence."

. . . .

The global call for justice and accountability for all women requires a new agenda—one in which we move from women's rights on paper to women's power to implement them in practice. We've come to refer to the building blocks of this women's power agenda as the "Five Rs": A women's power agenda must afford meaningful *redress* for those harmed by sexual harass-ment, abuse, and discrimination. It must also include legal *reform*, a call for women's equal *representation* in all spheres, and a fair allocation of *resources*—three elements championed by Margot Wallström, the former Swedish foreign minister and UN special representative on sexual violence in conflict, and the first leader to articulate a "feminist" foreign policy deeming women's advancement as critical to global prosperity and stability.[18] Finally, any successful effort must foster a fundamental *recalibration* of the social norms and conventions that have allowed sexual abuse to go unchecked and inhibited women's power in the public and private spheres. Achieving this agenda will require leadership at the global, multilateral, local, and individual levels—and sustained collective action by activists to ensure progress and accountability.

Redress

Redress—justice for survivors of sexual harassment and assault—is a pre-condition of a survivor-focused agenda. It is also a metric by which we can measure progress toward a shift from securing rights on paper to ensuring the power to enforce them. For centuries, notwithstanding the existence of criminal or civil penalties for sexual abuse, those accused—particularly those with the most power—have had the legal system tipped in their favor, or the power to place a finger on the scale.[19] They have also enjoyed widespread pub-lic sympathy, while the reputations, sexual histories, and integrity of survivors have been put on trial. This injustice is a function of a fundamental imbalance of power in which women's words and experiences have counted less than men's. It also explains why, before the internet-based #MeToo movement afforded both anonymity and strength in numbers, so few women were willing to come forward to name what was plainly happening all around us.

Delivering justice for survivors requires a functioning and balanced legal system—one that protects the rights of survivors and the accused and is free from discrimination and stereotypes about women's veracity and sexuality. As a first step, governments should ensure that adequate legal protections against harassment and assault are in place in every country. In 2020, three years into the #MeToo movement, an astounding fifty countries still had no prohibitions on sexual harassment in the workplace. Fifty-eight percent of the world's nations lack explicit provisions criminalizing marital rape.[20] It's long overdue that we rectify these legal inequalities.

Even where laws criminalizing sexual harassment and abuse are on the books, as we saw in Egypt, Nigeria, and Pakistan, too often they are crafted in a way that precludes justice. Legislators should eliminate rules that rig the system against survivors and shield abusers from accountability, including provisions that permit judicial discretion to reduce charges and inhibit prosecution of sexual abuse. Nations should repeal needlessly burdensome evidentiary requirements that preclude prosecution, such as stipulations in Lebanon, Malawi, Panama, Peru, and Yemen mandating a specialized medical examiner's report—which can be difficult to obtain—to prove a sexual assault case. In January 2021, women's activists in Pakistan won an overdue victory, defeating the invasive and scientifically debunked "two finger" test, where rape victims were examined to determine whether their hymen, and therefore virginity and "honor," were still intact.[21] "Yes means yes" laws requiring explicit consent for sexual activity should replace outdated codes that authorize sexually intimate behavior without a person's first obtaining permission. And lawmakers should ban workplace tactics in developing and developed countries that prevent survivors from coming forward and seeking redress for harm, such as mandatory nondisclosure agreements as a condition of employment and forced arbitration that precludes recourse in a court of law.

Governments should also review rates of reporting, prosecution, and conviction for sexual abuse to assess the degree to which laws are being implemented and justice is being served. Current numbers reveal that survivors are too often denied accountability. In India, there were 127,800 open rape cases in 2017, leaving offenders free to repeat their crimes; only 18,300 cases made their way through the system to closure that year. That same year, in Finland, where an estimated 50,000 women are raped annually, there were only 209 rape convictions. In the United States, where the Rape, Abuse, and Incest National Network (RAINN) estimates that only a third of rape cases are reported—often because victims doubt that the judicial system will treat them fairly—just 5.7 percent of rape reports led to an arrest, and only 0.7 percent resulted in a felony conviction. In Nigeria, a 2019 analysis found that the country had fewer than eighty recorded rape convictions in its entire legal history.[22] These shockingly low prosecution and conviction rates should, at a minimum, invite regular assessment of the extent to which the justice system meets the needs of survivors and reform where it doesn't.

Survivors of sexual harassment and abuse—especially those who have far fewer privileges and resources than the accused—also deserve legal representation to help them level the playing field within the judicial system. In the United States, TIME'S UP created a legal defense fund to support low-wage women who lack the means to fight abusers who resort to expensive defamation suits as a tactic to avoid accountability, a ploy used around the world.[23] "The issue of legal representation came up because of women getting threatened by the lawyers of the powerful men they were accusing, which was part of, as we call it, the predators' playbook," Tina Tchen said. "We really needed an institution to do this on an ongoing basis for the defense of women accused of defamation and affirmative representation for those in need—including the huge numbers of working women who are at the lower end of the pay scale, for whom employment lawyers cannot afford to take their cases." Women's rights activists in Egypt, Nigeria, Pakistan, and Tunisia have created their own similar, often informal networks to connect victims with otherwise unattainable legal expertise—and usually on shoestring budgets. More resources are needed to help others around the world obtain representation and a fair shot at justice.

In addition, where appropriate to local contexts, lawmakers should explore alternatives to the penal system, including restorative justice approaches, which in some instances are preferred by survivors who wish to remain outside the criminal legal system. These methods can provide accountability for abusers—allowing them to recognize harm caused, take responsibility, and make efforts toward repair—while respecting victims' needs, like a desire for privacy. For example, in New Zealand, survivors frustrated with the limitations of the criminal justice system created a model program called Project Restore, focused on redressing harm and reducing re-offenses.[24] The program, which involves experts from the survivor advocacy community, is run by trained facilitators and a clinical counseling team and accepts referrals from the court system, survivors, and offenders alike.

To be clear, these approaches are not meant to replace appropriate criminal and civil punishments in countries and communities where survivors are still fighting to realize any kind of systemic justice. But the programs have been successful in certain regions and can help mitigate legitimate concerns about discriminatory incarceration. These methods can also help answer the question of how to ensure pathways to reintegration for abusers who have committed harm and want to reform their behavior and rejoin the workplace or community.

Programs seeking justice for survivors should include support for victim-compensation systems—including access to reproductive and mental health care, housing, and employment opportunities—which can provide services critical to healing from trauma. One program premised on this idea is the Global Survivors Fund for victims of sexual violence in conflict zones, created by the Nobel Peace Prize laureates Dr. Denis Mukwege, who spent his life repairing obstetric fistulas in women who survived wartime rape, and Nadia Murad, an Iraqi human rights activist who survived sexual slavery at the hands of ISIS. This survivor-centered fund is dedicated to providing assistance to those who suffered abuse in an effort to help them rebuild their lives. While this approach is nascent, movement leaders argue that more must be done to ensure justice for those harmed. "We have not given enough money to reparations for women who have experienced rape and sexual violence," said Margot Wallström, the former Swedish foreign minister and UN special representative on sexual violence in conflict.[25]

Compensation also should be considered for those for whom sexual harassment in the workplace has altered, truncated, or harmed their careers.

At its root, sexual harassment is a manifestation of discrimination against women, who are precluded from succeeding in or often driven from the workplace by their abusers. As a consequence, women's careers may be derailed, or they may be forced to change industries, factors that weaken lifetime earnings and contribute to persistent pay gaps between genders. "While some of the stories being told about harassment and assault included sexual or physical harm, or emotional harm, so much of what is actually being talked about is workplace equality and participation, and the systemic inequality within an economic and professional sphere," said the journalist Rebecca Traister. The public and private sectors have a role to play in devising compensatory systems to help women regain the career potential and earnings eviscerated by sexual harassment and abuse, elements of justice for survivors that are often overlooked by systems focused more on outcomes for wrongdoers than for those they've harmed.

To be sure, justice for survivors should not come at the expense of the bedrock principle of due process for the accused, the cornerstone of any fair judicial system. Some predators have inappropriately cloaked their wrongdoing in a shield of due process concerns. Yet the proliferation of women in the #MeToo movement who have chosen to name their alleged assailants publicly on social media instead of through the criminal or civil justice systems—in effect, trying the accused in the court of public opinion rather than in courts of justice—raises important questions about fairness that should be answered. Any attempt to address these concerns must be balanced against the fundamental unfairness of a legal system stacked so heavily against survivors that only a tiny fraction of those harmed prevail against their abusers—a reality that drives women to seek justice in alternative fora in the first place. Redressing the failures of the legal system to provide justice to survivors is a clear way to decrease the number of claims addressed through extrajudicial means.

In addition to improving law enforcement approaches, to encourage an honest reckoning with generations of harm, governments might consider creating entities modeled after South Africa's Truth and Reconciliation Commission, a restorative-justice body created after the defeat of apartheid, which could grant amnesty from civil and criminal prosecution in exchange for public testimony and afford a path forward for survivors and wrongdoers.[26] While this approach may not succeed everywhere—particularly in nations lacking basic legal rights for women—it could prove fruitful where that fundamental baseline is in place.

Reform

Any agenda to advance women's power must tackle persistent legal and structural barriers to women's equality that perpetuate a broader power imbalance between genders and foster conditions for sexual harassment and abuse. Without efforts to reform these obstacles across economic, political, social, and cultural life—and to ensure the robust implementation of those reforms—women will not have the power to ensure their own safety.

The number of legal provisions enshrining this broad power imbalance into law is astounding. Today, over one hundred countries have laws on the books that impede women's participation in the workplace, from reserving certain professions to men and limiting women's wages or hours to requiring spousal consent for work.[27] Restrictions on women's right to travel freely and unaccompanied by men, to own and inherit property, or to serve as a head of household consign women to dependency on male relatives and employers who are more powerful under the law, thereby rendering women vulnerable to exploitation and abuse. "When there are insufficient legal means to address the pervasive abuses to women and systemic inequality, little will change meaningfully to move the needle towards equality and justice," said Ellen Johnson Sirleaf, the former Liberian president. The elimination of legal inequalities between the genders is a precondition to creating a level playing field in the workplace and across public life—so that women have the power and agency to defend against sexual abuse to begin with.

In addition to legal reform, addressing structural barriers that undermine women's agency should be part of any effort to rectify the power imbalances that lead to abuse. This means ensuring that women and girls have access to the building blocks for self-determination—including health care and education—free from sexual harassment and assault. As we saw in China, Nigeria, Pakistan, and Tunisia, many educational systems today are rife with abuse against women and girls, who are preyed on by superiors demanding sexual favors as a precondition to educational success. This inequality puts girls at a severe disadvantage in obtaining the training they need to compete effectively in the workplace and across public life. "Schools should be safe from attacks—whether they come from terrorists or teachers," Malala Yousafzai, the Nobel Peace Prize laureate and Pakistani education activist, said in an interview shortly after obtaining her degree from Oxford University.[28] "Girls are dropping out because it's not safe."

Failure to reform educational systems in which sexual harassment and assault are endemic perpetuates gender inequality, which in turn creates the conditions under which abuse flourishes. "Girls are still being profoundly left behind in education," said Julia Gillard, the former Australian prime minister, who became the chair of the Global Partnership of Education after leaving government. "If we don't get that foundation stone right, then the rest can't follow. These are pivotal issues not only in a moral sense but also in a very practical sense—because that kind of disgraceful environment will mean that girls don't get anywhere near an equal or fair chance at education."

Countries must also reform harmful traditions that disempower women and girls, such as child marriage, a practice that affects one in five girls globally, or about twelve million every year. In the least developed countries, as many as 40 percent of girls marry before the age of eighteen. Child marriage is an enormous obstacle to equality because it inhibits girls from attending school, thereby reducing their ability to participate in the labor force and consigning them to dependency on men. Such practices perpetuate a power imbalance between the sexes across generations. "We need to dismantle those underlying root causes if we really want lasting change," said Michelle Bachelet, the former Chilean president and current UN high commissioner for human rights.

Some argue that legal and structural barriers to women's power, which reflect deeply rooted social norms, are insurmountable or reflective of cultural differences that warrant deference. Evidence suggests, however, that although creating a level legal and structural playing field for women and girls is undoubtedly a long-term endeavor, progress is possible, and cultural understandings of human rights are mutable. Consider domestic violence, an issue that was once understood as cultural and viewed as a private family matter. Twenty-five years ago, legal and structural codes reflected this view; only a handful of countries classified domestic abuse as a crime, and there was a stark lack of shelters and services for survivors around the world. Today, more than 150 countries have laws criminalizing domestic violence, driven in part by the recognition of women's rights as human rights during the last wave of the global women's movement in the late twentieth century.[29] And a growing number of countries are creating shelter systems for survivors. While more work is needed to implement these reforms, they have spurred progress—and a similar shift is afoot today. "Countries across the world have already enacted legal reforms," Phumzile Mlambo-Ngcuka, the head of UN Women, said in an interview reflecting on progress made since the onset of the #MeToo movement. "Three years in, the movement continues to bring important change." The legal and structural reforms that have already rippled out from the current wave of the movement suggest that further improvement is not only possible but likely.

Representation

The representation of women in leadership positions must be a cornerstone of any agenda to build women's power. Activists at the forefront of the movement seeking justice for survivors are calling for more than reparations and services; they are demanding a fundamental restructuring of who is in charge and has a seat at the table. "A lot of times, the people who are making the policies are not survivors," said #MeToo's Tarana Burke, a fierce champion of the Survivors' Agenda. "They're not doing it from a place that respects survivors as leaders. It's from a place of pity, rather than about empowerment, rebuilding, and reshaping." The recognition of this representation gap is remaking the agenda for change. "We're not just going to our leadership and saying, 'These are the policies we want to see,'" Burke said. "We're also saying, 'These are the kinds of people we want to be in leadership.'"

Gender parity in representation is also a precondition to ameliorating the power imbalance across economic, political, and social life that has allowed the centuries-long proliferation of sexual harassment and abuse and cultivated an aura of impunity. "#MeToo led to all sorts of conversations about gender and representation and equality," Jodi Kantor said. Sexual harassment and abuse has invisibly sapped gender equality, driving women out of workplaces and public spaces for generations. One solution: an increase in women's political representation. "Sexual harassment only diminishes when there is more gender equality—when there are more women in charge," she said.

Activists around the world who have awakened to the power of their voices are increasingly determined to use them in the political system, as participants or candidates. In countries like Pakistan, Aurat March organizers have also founded a new political party, the Women's Democratic Front. "The #MeToo movement is inherently a political movement," said Phumzile Mlambo-Ngcuka, the former deputy president of South Africa and head of UN Women. "It is an expression of women's rights to participate in political and public life without having to fear discrimination, sexual harassment, or violence." The scale of the underrepresentation of women in political life is staggering: as of 2020, out of 193 countries, only 22 have a female head of state, and just 4 have reached gender parity in parliament.[30] Some have called for remedial measures to address these gaps, including quotas, which have been shown to be effective around the world and are often a product of robust organizing by local women's rights movements demanding tangible representative change.

"I am a big advocate for political parties having quotas and systems to prioritize the selection of women if they lack them," said Julia Gillard, the former Australian prime minister. In 2014, Tunisia's post-revolution constitution included a commitment to gender parity in government, with quotas enacted from the municipal to parliamentary levels, a requirement that was expanded to party electoral lists in 2016.[31] Such measures are especially important in light of persistent cultural barriers to women's leadership. As Margot Wallström, the former Swedish foreign minister, noted, "We see that there is heavy pushback for women candidates everywhere—smear campaigns and hate campaigns on social media against the women candidates. They need our support."

Other activists are calling for gender equality not only in government, but also in the private sector, where endemic sexual harassment and abuse have left a harmful legacy of women's disenfranchisement from the labor force. "We want to see governments calling for women's parity in all spheres, including corporate boards and throughout the economy," Phumzile Mlambo-Ngcuka said. Gender equality in leadership is critical to increasing women's power. As a matter of fundamental fairness, this demands action by private- and public-sector leaders alike, from requirements for diverse and inclusive recruiting pools to incentives for achieving gender balance in senior positions. "If we genuinely believe that merit and capacity are equally distributed between the sexes, and we look at any institution and we aren't seeing half male and half female leadership, then that must mean that women of merit didn't get to come forward," Julia Gillard said.

Research suggests that increasing women's leadership matters because doing so is not only fair but also strategic: women's participation increases profits, improves stability, and places policies to promote gender equality higher on the agenda.[32] "While it's not true of every female leader at every time, there is increasingly good evidence that the involvement of women in decision-making also changes the nature of it, and makes for a more pro-woman and profeminist agenda," said Gillard, who founded a Global Institute for Women's Leadership at King's College in London after retiring from government service. "I'm a big believer that you don't solve problems unless you're talking about them. That is really the incredible strength of the #MeToo movement: until you name them, shine a light on them, get active around them, they don't get solved. #MeToo has done that for sexual harassment—and we are doing far more of that than we used to around women in leadership."

Resources

Ensuring that women have equal access to resources is another critical component of increasing women's power.[33] A shift from women's rights on paper to women's power in practice requires changes in laws and policies, but also in budgets. It should no longer be acceptable for officials to assert their commitment to eradicating sexual abuse and discrimination while failing to commit sufficient funding to address a scourge that threatens half the population.

The failure to adequately finance initiatives to fight this problem is pervasive at the national and local levels. Countries from Canada to Russia to South Africa perpetually underfund law enforcement efforts and services for survivors, from forensic experts to rape crisis centers. In the United States, an estimated three to four hundred thousand unopened rape evidence kits languish in storage facilities, allowing assaulters to evade prosecution and cause further harm. The refusal to prioritize the backlog of untested rape kits in criminal justice budgets is symbolic of the silencing and dismissal of women's experiences of abuse, which in turn make women less likely to come forward. As the #MeToo movement disrupts this vicious cycle, advocates are demanding that leaders who have finally promised reforms dedicate the resources necessary to implement them.[34]

Gender equality initiatives are also significantly shortchanged in the funding of foreign assistance. According to the Organization for Economic Cooperation and Development's Development Assistance Committee, which represents thirty of the top government donors globally, only 4 percent of development aid is spent on gender equality as a primary objective, even among governments that proclaim support for women's rights. Between 1995 and 2011, before the onset of the #MeToo movement, global financing for efforts to prevent violence against women—an injustice that has been shown to depress GDP growth and economic development—actually declined. Leaders like Secretary of State Hillary Clinton, who spent her career fighting for resources to advance gender equality, believe these gaps shortchange both women and broader efforts to promote growth and stability. "We should be linking women's rights, and human rights writ large, to our foreign policy, and particularly our development agendas," Clinton emphasized in an interview.[35]

This effort begins with ensuring that those who put their safety and lives on the line to advance women's rights enjoy the same level of international support as those who promote freedom of speech, press, or assembly. "Dedicated support and engagement with women's human rights defenders are critical to ensuring that women's voices are part of the civil debate and also important to ensure women's voices in democratic decision-making," said Michelle Bachelet, the former Chilean president.

Paltry funding for gender equality is also endemic at the multilateral level, where government and international institutions frequently pool funds cooperatively to amplify their respective efforts. Too often, government and multilateral leaders make rhetorical commitments to improve the status of women without increasing resources to fulfill those promises or implementing mechanisms to ensure accountability. Compare the budget for UN Women—the only UN agency dedicated to gender equality—which stands at only $500 million, with the budget for UNICEF, focused on children's rights and needs, which stands at $1.5 billion.[36] And unlike almost every other major twenty-first-century global challenge—from climate change to food security to antiterrorism to global health efforts—there is no pooled fund or global pledging campaign to support efforts to eliminate inequalities faced by 50 percent of the world's people, an oversight that demands action.

Data-driven accountability measures in budgetary processes are also lacking. Systems for tracking national expenditures toward international targets, such as the UN Millennium and Sustainable Development Goals, often omit the issue of gender equality as a category of aid flow.[37] In many instances, national data agencies fail to track expenditures or programs on the basis of gender, race, and other factors, further obscuring disparities. By overlooking the substantial benefits produced by investment in women's power—and, in some cases, failing to count women in the first place—many multilateral efforts continue to ignore the economic and development potential of half the population.

At the top of the list of needs cited by local leaders on the front lines of the modern movement: adequate resources for women's rights organizations, which remain dramatically underfunded around the world. "Women-led organizations are pivotal to advancing gender equality in their countries; they are fearless at the forefront of change, often with very little support and chronic underfunding," said Phumzile Mlambo-Ngcuka, the leader of UN Women, one of the least-resourced agencies in the United Nations.

The underfunding of women's rights organizations is particularly short-sighted given how effective they are at producing change. Research by the Canadian scholar Laurel Weldon of Simon Fraser University shows that strong and autonomous women's movements have been a powerful force in changing attitudes about violence against women, promoting economic empowerment, expanding the presence of women in leadership, and advancing democracy. "We've now put pen to paper on what feminist activists have been witnessing on the ground in their local communities for the last fifty years," said PeiYao Chen, vice president of the Global Fund for Women.[38] "With the rise of online activism, these movements are getting more organized and louder than ever, and they warrant further investment from policymakers and stakeholders who are determined to close the gap on gender inequality worldwide."

Capitalizing on the promise of the work these organizations lead will require greater financing informed by the needs of activists on the ground—along the lines of the Canadian Equality Fund, which is dedicated solely to financing women's organizations and is guided by a diverse group of movement leaders. "The answer is supporting local leaders," said Malala Yousafzai, whose organization the Malala Fund supports more than sixty grassroots educators and advocates for girls' education globally. "We know they are best-placed to understand the challenges in their communities and develop solutions that work." UN deputy-secretary general Amina Mohammed agrees. "Who are the community leaders that really do take the decisions, whether they're in the homes or the markets?" she said in an interview from UN headquarters. "On resources and the impact they need to make, you need to think about the players that will get the most bang for the buck—it ends up being local women."

To promote progress, funding streams for initiatives to increase women's power should be substantial enough to help activists hold their governments and institutions accountable. Women need resources for advocacy to fundamentally shift the balance of power between genders, instead of micro investments that perpetuate the status quo. These resources should be sufficiently unconstrained so that grassroots leaders can respond to pressing needs and shifts in strategy without being overly burdened by reporting requirements that hamper flexibility. "Checks and balances are important and need to be in place, but we have to ensure that this is not done at the cost of the women's movement," Phumzile Mlambo-Ngcuka said. Women's organizations should also be supported by multiyear funding to further the long-term efforts required to shift deeply rooted norms. "You want to point to results," said Julia Gillard, the former Australian prime minister. "But short-term thinking is never going to get to the real, structural, underlying causes of inequality, including gender inequality."

Recalibration

Any successful effort to increase women's power must contend with the social and cultural norms that militate against it in the first place. The universality of social norms against women's power, which cross every culture and region of the world, is striking. Even where strong laws and policies are on the books and adequate resources are in place, deeply ingrained stereotypes about gender roles can inhibit their implementation and obstruct women's power. These gender norms cry out for recalibration, especially in light of evidence that women's leadership and inclusion strengthen decision-making processes across sectors. "Unconscious bias means we still look at women leaders and tend to conclude that they're not very likable, and we punish them very strongly if they step outside of perceived gender stereotypes of what a woman is like," Julia Gillard said. "We need to get rid of all stereotypes on being shrill, or flaky, or weak, or nasty."

Twenty-five years after the UN Fourth World Conference on Women in Beijing, even as women are healthier, better educated, and enjoy more legal rights than at any time in history, social norms against women's power persist. The data show that discomfort with women's power is widely shared not only by men but by people of all genders. The UN Development Programme's 2020 report, which relies in part on perception surveys, found that in many parts of the world, clear majorities of men and women show bias against gender equality and resistance to women's authority. About half of those surveyed said that men made better political leaders than women, and 40 percent believed that men were better business executives.[39] "Again and again, we've seen anger, hostility, and sexism directed at women who have the audacity to seek power," said Hillary Clinton, whose time in public life was characterized by virulent opposition to the authority she wielded. "Deep-seated biases are even harder to change than discriminatory laws."

Cultural attitudes also undergird our tolerance and understanding of sexual harassment and assault. Despite the significant rise in the number of laws criminalizing violence against women since 1995, almost 30 percent of those surveyed by UNDP still agreed it was justifiable for a man to beat his partner.[40] "We haven't really had a very serious conversation with men. You know, we have tackled them, we put them away behind bars. We have done what we can, where we can," said UN deputy-secretary general Amina Mohammed. "But we haven't had the conversation that gets into the way that they're wired. And I think that that's something that we need to do going forward."

Even after the awareness raised by the #MeToo movement, many women continue to be doubted or vilified when they highlight concerns about sexual abuse. Witness the treatment of Dr. Christine Blasey Ford by the United States Senate, which refused to allow testimony corroborating her accusations of sexual assault against Brett Kavanaugh and subsequently confirmed his lifetime appointment on the Supreme Court.[41] "What underpins all of this is that women aren't usually believed—and haven't been for centuries," said Tina Tchen, of TIME'S UP. "In the past, when women talked about these issues, it hadn't been taken seriously and it hadn't been seen as the tip of the iceberg of a much more broken system."

Though research suggests that #MeToo has begun to shift attitudes about the pervasiveness of sexual harassment and abuse, considerable work remains. "It's clear that we still need to do much more to shift the cultural norms, stereotypes, attitudes, and behaviors that condone sexual harassment, to create the conditions for effective, long-lasting change," Phumzile Mlambo-Ngcuka said. "We will do that best when we engage many partners in that transformation."

To effectuate that shift, advocates are increasingly enlisting new allies in a push for cultural reform, rather than focusing solely on redress or policy change. "The move from having a complaint structure to a proactive culture-building approach, which makes this kind of conduct far less likely—those approaches are still in their infancy," Julia Gillard said. "But they are promising." Some organizations have pressed business leaders to step up in ways that government leaders haven't, urging them to do what is right—not just what is legally required. As Tina Tchen told us, "You can set a standard and a set of values and a code of conduct that's beyond the legal limits of the law."

To address the broader power imbalance in which sexual abuse flourishes, some activists are partnering with cultural influencers to help promote a popular reassessment of women's leadership and power, including portrayals that celebrate women exercising leadership and men serving as caretakers. "Until we rebalance understandings of domestic and care responsibilities," Julia Gillard said, "women are always going to be working a double shift," which will continue to affect the distribution of power between the genders.

Other advocates are demanding instruction in sex education that teaches children from the earliest ages about the importance of consent, as seen in groundbreaking grassroots efforts by activists like Hassana Maina and Ololade Ganikale in Nigeria. The notion that sexual activity must be wanted and expressly agreed to by all parties is still not widely taught. Without consent education, harmful societal norms about gender dominance and conquest take root and create the conditions under which abuse thrives. "What I want to see is comprehensive sex education that starts in kindergarten and goes until twelfth grade," said Tarana Burke, founder of the #MeToo movement, "so that I'm looking at a generation of young people who have been learning about respect and boundaries and consent since they were five years old."

Cultural transformation is undoubtedly a long process. But history teaches that norms can change even when they seem intractable, after hard-fought campaigns for justice. Consider the difference from one generation to the next after the fall of apartheid in South Africa, or the transformation in the acceptability of gay marriage in the United States. The cultural shifts already wrought by the #MeToo campaign promise to be another transformative moment—one in which women demand the power not only to claim their rights, but also to reshape the structures of the society in which we live. "With this younger generation, we're seeing women who are coming along and saying, 'I'm going to be myself, in every sense, and the system's going to have to adapt to me,'" Julia Gillard said. "And that's cultural change."

. . . .

The full scope and power of the modern wave of the women's movement is a story still being written. But this first chapter suggests that a fundamental shift is underway. Women have awakened to the strength of their collective voices and are armed with digital tools that allow more people to participate in the movement for equality than ever before. "This wave that we're living in at the moment—a feminist wave, which #MeToo has been so much a part of—has given women generally a much greater sense that their voices should be heard, and should be valued when they're heard. And that matters," Julia Gillard told us. While the road ahead will surely be marked by setbacks, women's newfound awareness of their own power—and demands for reforms to augment it—are unlikely to be undone. "Once you shine a light on something, you can't unsee it," Tarana Burke said.

Since the #MeToo movement went viral in 2017, those leading the charge and covering its spread have felt a demonstrable shift, one deeper and longer lasting than anyone anticipated. Two and a half years after the *New York Times* journalists Jodi Kantor and Megan Twohey broke the Harvey Weinstein story, Jodi recalled being in downtown Manhattan on the courthouse steps during his rape trial when more than one hundred women came together to perform the defiant Chilean anthem "A Rapist in Your Path," created by the feminist art collective Las Tesis. The song—which had ricocheted from Latin America to the Middle East and North Africa, to South Asia, and ultimately to the United States—was a testament to a movement that had truly gone global and could not be ignored.[42] "You could hear the demonstrators from inside the courtroom," Kantor said. "It was symbolic of the fact that the Weinstein trial was connected to this bigger thing that was happening in the culture—and you couldn't pretend that it wasn't."

Perhaps the most important strength of the modern wave of the global women's movement is not only its geographic breadth, substantive depth, and incredible speed, but also its intersectionality. It is no accident that the #MeToo and Black Lives Matter movements proliferated at a similar time, or that its leaders have worked in common cause with one another—a fusion that promises to shift the balance of power out of the hands of privileged men for good. UN deputy-secretary general Amina Mohammed believes that #MeToo helped create global momentum for "movements for justice, whether it was climate justice, or racism. People realized that they could use the power of technology to come together, rising up against what is just not acceptable," she said in our interview. "It went across all colors and cultures and religions." Journalist Rebecca Traister sees the same international, intersectional impact: "There's never been such an effective linking of so many different forms of oppression."

While the social norms undergirding pervasive harassment, discriminatory laws, and structural barriers persist, the changes the #MeToo movement has already won demonstrate that progress is on the march. Today, the rising generation of young people growing up online in the wake of #MeToo have a different understanding of standards of consent and gender roles than their parents and grandparents did—progress that will continue to bear fruit in the decades to come, in every region of the world, notwithstanding the backlash or government attempts to quiet the revolution. The relentless optimism of women leaders in these battles speaks louder than any crackdown ever could. "Centuries of patriarchy and discrimination take time to be eroded," Michelle Bachelet, the former Chilean president, observed. "But I'm confident that this change—this awakening—is unstoppable."

Argentinian protestors wear face masks to prevent the spread of coronavirus (COVID-19) and wave green handkerchiefs symbolizing reproductive freedom on the fifth anniversary of the #NiUnaMenos ("Not One Less") campaign protesting violence against women, in Buenos Aires, Argentina, in June 2020. Credit: Reuters/Agustin Marcarian

AFTERWORD

Awakening WAS WRITTEN BOTH IN THE WAKE OF THE RISE OF THE GLOBAL WOMEN's movement and also in the midst of a global pandemic—one that, unbeknownst to us, had only just begun as we embarked on a research trip to China in January 2020, when the coronavirus outbreak had already started. As we write this, the COVID-19 epidemic continues to wreak havoc on the lives, livelihoods, education, and safety of millions around the world. The virus has revealed deeply rooted inequalities on the basis of gender, race, ethnicity, immigration status, class, and many other factors, and has had particularly pernicious effects on women, threatening to inhibit their activism and roll back decades of progress.

Already, in just nine months, the impact of the pandemic on women has been devastating. Female employees have borne a disproportionate burden of job losses globally, with women's jobs, for which they were already paid less, almost two times more vulnerable than men's. Women—especially women of color and low-wage women—also comprise the majority of workers deemed essential, serving on the front lines and putting their health and survival at risk. As schools and childcare centers shuttered across the globe, women already saddled with a disproportionate burden of caregiving saw their responsibilities increase exponentially, fueling an exodus of female workers from the formal labor force, thereby undermining economic security and growth. And as officials imposed stay-at-home orders in the name of public health, women facing intimate-partner violence—for whom home is anything but safe—paradoxically were left vulnerable by the very policies intended to promote public safety. Despite these grave realities, too often government emergency-response efforts ignored the gendered dimensions of this pandemic, with the United Nations finding that only 12 percent of countries in 2020 introduced comprehensive measures to address women's needs, a gap that imperils not only women and their families but also broader prosperity and stability, which are inextricably tied to the fortunes of half the world's population.[1]

Without measures to address the persistent gender inequalities exposed and fueled by this crisis, women's capacity to raise their voices—to march, organize, run for office, and demand change—undoubtedly will be compromised. But the COVID-19 pandemic, which has caused so much destruction, could also deliver an opportunity to reimagine the world as we rebuild it—to reassess and transform the gendered norms and stereotypes that shape our economic structures and political institutions, and perpetuate the inequalities that inspired the rising activism detailed in this book. This project—to build back our economies and societies in a way that is fairer and freer for all—is the province not only of women's activists but also of those fighting racial injustice, environmental degradation, economic inequality, and other social ills to achieve a more just and inclusive world. Just as the #MeToo campaign went viral, so too has the US Black Lives Matter movement, in a surge that similarly spread to other countries, with ordinary people using twenty-first-century tools to decry police brutality, systemic racism, and intersectional forms of discrimination, and to demand basic human rights for all.

The pandemic raging while we drafted *Awakening* affords more than a chance to uncover and root out the inequalities that corrode our institutional and economic structures. It also serves as a useful metaphor for the critical importance of both citizen participation and global action in addressing the great challenges of our time—not only global health and climate threats, but also societal injustices like racial and gender inequality. Though social inequalities are often considered to be deeply rooted in particular countries and cultures, this book reveals how the disease of gender inequality is not contained to any one nation. It shows that just as gender injustice can spread across borders, so too can its cure. As with COVID-19, we cannot suppress this scourge by addressing it solely within our own nations—not when it teems in other regions and travels easily across country lines. "Social justice issues aren't so different from biological pandemics," observed the

Iranian-American author and journalist Roya Hakakian, in an interview at the height of the pandemic. "We need to understand that the success of the movement in one country relates to the success in another."[2]

The magnitude of the modern wave of the global women's movement, which we detail in these pages, is a story still evolving. Although it remains to be seen how the coronavirus pandemic will affect the rise in women's activism globally, there are hopeful signs that women will not be quieted—that, despite the challenges and ravages around us, women will not back down. Indeed, at the height of the pandemic—in the face of economic upheaval, school closures, rising domestic violence, and global unrest—American women of color donned face masks and turned out in record numbers to help elect Kamala Harris as vice president of the United States, making her the highest-ranking female, Black, and South Asian leader in American history, and ending two and a half centuries of male occupancy of this role. During that same period, women in Argentina, who protested against gender-based violence under the #NiUnaMenos campaign—a precursor to #MeToo—leveraged their newfound political power to win the legalization of abortion in a socially conservative region, a historic victory for a movement that has now spread throughout Latin America. And women in Iran—one of the most oppressive regimes in the world, where women's rights have been brutally curtailed for decades, and where survivors of sexual abuse have long been shamed into silence—rose up to join their sisters around the world and also say, "Me Too." Despite the pandemic, dozens of Iranian women voiced allegations against a powerful, internationally acclaimed artist, described in the *New York Times* as the "Harvey Weinstein of Iran," resulting in the government's consideration of a landmark bill to criminalize sexual assault and harassment. "A #MeToo Awakening Stirs in Iran," the *Times* headline blared.[3] This awakening is a global one—and despite the challenges women now face, their clarion call goes on.

SUPPORTING WOMEN'S RIGHTS GLOBALLY

WE HOPE READERS WILL BE INSPIRED BY THE WOMEN LEADERS IN THIS BOOK. WE invite you to learn more about and support their work on behalf of survivors and the legal, economic, political, and social equality of women around the world.

Global

The 'me too.' movement, founded by Tarana Burke, serves as a convener, innovator, thought leader, and organizer across the mainstream and grassroots to address systems that allow for the proliferation of sexual violence, with a focus on communities of color. **www.metoomvmt.org**

FRIDA provides young feminist organizers with the resources they need to amplify their voices and bring attention to the social justice issues they care about. It enables the support, flexibility, and networks to sustain young feminist visions. **www.youngfeministfund.org**

Global Fund for Women funds bold, ambitious, and expansive gender justice movements to create meaningful change that will last beyond our lifetimes. **www.globalfundforwomen.org**

TIME'S UP aims to create a society free from gender-based discrimination in the workplace and beyond, so that people of every race, ethnicity, religion, sexuality, gender identity, and income level will be safe on the job and have equal opportunity for economic success and security. **www.times upnow.org**

UN Women supports UN Member States as they set global standards for achieving gender equality, and works with governments and civil society to design laws, policies, programs, and services needed to ensure that the standards are effectively implemented and truly benefit women and girls worldwide. **www.unwomen.org**

Vital Voices supports women leaders who are solving the world's greatest challenges. Through individualized partnerships, the organization invests in women with local solutions proven to drive change, offering these leaders the support, recognition, and resources they need. **www.vital voices.org**

Brazil

The Marielle Franco Institute was established to preserve Marielle's legacy. The Institute aims to create a school project to support young Black LGBTQ women in Brazil and launch the Marielle Franco Center for Heritage and Memory. **www.support.institutomariellefranco.org**

Mulheres Negras Decidem (Black Women Decide) is an NGO to elevate the leadership of Black women in strengthening democracy in Brazil. Founded in 2018, the organization advances political training, education, and research. **www.mulheresnegrasdecidem.org**

Rede Nami is an NGO formed by women to use art as a vehicle for positive cultural transformation through the promotion of women's rights. Founded by artist Panmela Castro in 2010, the organization aims to end violence against women and promote the role of women in the arts. **www.redenami.com**

Think Olga and **Think Eva** are two sister organizations that share the same mission: to sensitize society to gender issues and intersections, and to educate and equip people to identify as agents of change in women's lives. Founded in São Paulo in 2013, both organizations use social innovation tools, including communication, technology, and education strategies, to create a positive impact on the lives of women in Brazil and the world. **thinkolga.squarespace.com**

China

Beijing Qianqian Law Firm is a nonprofit legal aid firm, founded in 2009 by decorated Chinese women's rights activist Guo Jianmei. The firm is committed to the advancement of women's legal rights in China through litigation and advocacy, including in the areas of equal land rights, public welfare, and domestic violence prevention. **www.woman-legalaid .org.cn/**

Free Chinese Feminists is an online collective of women, founded by the Chinese women's rights activist Lu Pin, that aims to elevate the rights of women in China through social media tools. **www.facebook.com /feministchina/**

Maple Women's Counseling Center is a Beijing nonprofit organization dedicated to providing legal and psychological support to survivors of domestic violence in China, establishing the first crisis hotline in the country. **www.maple.org.cn**

Egypt

The Doria Feminist Fund, founded by Mozn Hassan, mobilizes financial, political, and technical resources for feminist groups and scholars in the Middle East and North Africa region. The Fund works to ensure they have necessary resources to sustain and develop their activism, identify and determine their priorities independently, produce homegrown knowledge by and for their movements, and advocate for the rights of all women and LGBTQ+ individuals and groups in their countries. **www .doriafeministfund.org**

Due to government restrictions, most women's rights organizations in Egypt have been forced to cease formal operations. Global human rights organizations like **Amnesty International**, **Human Rights Foundation**, and

Human Rights Watch continue to fight for the rights of women human rights defenders and their cases internationally.

www.amnesty.org
www.hrf.org
www.hrw.org

Nigeria

African Women's Development Fund mobilizes financial, human, and material resources to support initiatives for transformation led by African women, women's rights organizations, and African women's movements. **www.awdf.org**

#ArewaMeToo, co-founded by Fakhrriyyah Hashim, works to change the socio-political and cultural fabric of Northern Nigeria, helping young women confront expectations of obedience and silence in the face of injustice and inequality. To support of their #NorthNormal, VAPP Act, and women's equality campaigns, contact **NorthNormal@gmail.com**.

Hands Off Initiative, founded by Ololade Ganikale, works to break the cycle of abuse and address the systemic problem of rape, sexual abuse, harassment, and assault in our societies. They do this by going to schools, universities, and communities to teach children, teenagers, and young adults about consent. **www.handsoffinitiative.org**

Stand to End Rape Initiative is a youth-led social enterprise advocating against sexual violence, providing prevention mechanisms, and supporting survivors with psychosocial services. **www.standtoendrape.org**

Pakistan

AGHS Legal Aid Cell, Asma Jahangir's law firm, strives to provide access to justice through free legal representation for the marginalized and persecuted; build a stronger constituency of activists, mainly women; challenge discrimination, violence, and threats against the vulnerable through legal action; end impunity for perpetrators of human rights violations; and reform laws and policies through the use of court interventions, research,

and partnerships from the grassroots level to policymakers. AGHS also started **Dastak**, which supports women and children who are victims of violence or are denied human rights and fundamental freedoms by providing protections and social services, including shelter.
www.aghslaw.net
www.dastak.org.pk

Digital Rights Foundation, founded by Nighat Dad, envisions a place where all people, and especially women, are able to exercise their right of expression without being threatened. **digitalrightsfoundation.pk**

Sweden

Make Equal features solution-focused equality experts who employ innovative methods and tools to advance practical equality work. Founded in 2010, the Stockholm-based organization works across Sweden and has reached over one hundred million people worldwide through its campaigns. **www.makeequal.se**

TakeTwo empowers individuals and businesses within the media and communications industries to create more diverse, inclusive, and gender-equal workplaces, as well as more equal and representative productions in film, advertising, PR, the news media, and other means of communications. **www.taketwo.world**

Tunisia

Association of Tunisian Democratic Women (ATFD), co-founded by Bochra Belhaj Hmida, works for the elimination of all forms of discrimination against women, the defense of acquired rights, the evolution of Tunisian legislation on effective equality between the sexes, the transformation of patriarchal mentalities, the empowerment of women to fight discrimination, and the civic and political participation of women. **www .facebook.com/femmesdemocrates**

Aswat Nissa, founded by Ikram Ben Said, works to promote a culture of gender equality; to fight all forms of gender discrimination; to foster women's participation in Tunisia's political spheres by bolstering their personal competencies and leadership; and to advocate for the integration of the gender approach in all public policy areas. To support the #EnaZeda movement, you can donate to Aswat Nissa. **www.aswatnissa .org**

Chaml Collective is a feminist collective created in 2014 by a group of young Tunisian women who feel the need to express themselves, to discuss issues related to women, and who, by their diversity, are eager to deconstruct the myth of "the Tunisian woman." **www.facebook.com /collectif.chaml**

ACKNOWLEDGMENTS

MANY PEOPLE SHARED THEIR WISDOM AND GUIDANCE WITH US AS WE WROTE THIS book, and we are thankful for all of them.

We are most indebted to women at the front lines of the modern women's movement who shared their voices and insight in these pages. Their willingness to meet with us—often at great risk—and relive difficult and painful experiences was invaluable to our efforts to capture the significance of this movement. We thank each of them for their courage. And we are deeply grateful to Tarana Burke for her leadership and inspiration, and honored by her contribution to this book.

We are thankful to the inimitable Gail Ross, whose belief in us made this book possible. Her indispensable guidance and wit sustained us throughout our two-year journey together, and we were extremely lucky to be in her good hands. We are also grateful to Dara Kaye, whose sharp edits helped to crystallize our thesis in the early stages of this project.

The wisdom of our editor, Colleen Lawrie, is reflected throughout these pages. Her support for our vision and notes of encouragement were as irreplaceable as her edits. We are deeply thankful for her partnership. We also thank Clive Priddle, Jaime Leifer, Anupama Roy-Chaudhury, and the PublicAffairs team for their commitment to this project; Rose Tomaszewska, Lucie Sharpe, and Zoe Hood at Virago in the UK; and the team at Ariel in Spain.

We are indebted to Jen Balderama McDonald, whose expertise with language and narrative storytelling strengthened our work immeasurably, and whose seamless collaboration across borders and time zones made the editing process a pleasure. We are also thankful to Lauren Collins Peterson for her invaluable contributions, Katie Carruthers-Busser for her guidance, and Julie Hersh for her terrific editing on our initial proposal.

We are deeply grateful to Pivotal Ventures, whose support for our research and writing made our work possible. We are indebted to the Cahill family, the Cutler family, Terri Balaran, and the Brown Advisory for their aid and belief in this project. And we very much appreciate the continued and generous support of the esteemed members of CFR's Women and Foreign Policy Advisory Council.

Our colleagues at the Council on Foreign Relations provided sage advice throughout this process. Special thanks are in order for Richard Haass, Jim Lindsay, Shannon O'Neil, and Trish Dorff for their invaluable guidance, and Lisa Shields, Anya Schmemann, and Susan Nelson for their support.

This book could not have been written without the Council's talented Women and Foreign Policy Program team, whose members traveled with us every step of the way, logging countless hours researching, fact-checking, and sprinting through airports across the globe. We are especially grateful to three incredible colleagues, with whom we were privileged to work: Rebecca Turkington, you're one of the most capable minds we've known, and a stellar travel partner—Cambridge is lucky to have you. Haydn Welch, your constant hard work, thoughtful contributions, and grace have made a powerful difference to this book. Alexandra Bro, your intelligence, judgment, and indefatigable commitment are a blessing to everyone around you. We are also incredibly thankful for the invaluable work of Erik Fliegauf, Delphi Cleaveland, and Hareem Abdullah in checking every last detail. And we are fortunate to count on the insight, collaboration, and constant support of our wonderful Council colleagues Jamille Bigio, Carrie Bettinger-Lopez, Gayle Lemmon, and Catherine Powell.

We are also grateful to the team at Twitter, including Lisa Roman and Elaine Filadelfo, for sharing their data and insight with us.

Many people were kind enough to lend their time, trust, expertise, and hospitality as we logged miles around the world. In Brazil, our sincere thanks go to Panmela Castro, Luiza Erudina, Juliana de Faria, Jandira Feghali, Miguel Fontes, Anielle Franco, Malu Gatto, Marcia Leporace, Daniel Lima, Ana Carolina Lourenco, Manuela Miklos, Daniela Monteiro, Taina de Paula, Antonia Pellegrino, Jacqueline Pitanguy, Andreza da Silva, Valdirene Silva de Assis, Renata Souza, Jazmin Stuare, Debora Thome, Sandra

Vale and Kristin Wylie. Special thanks to Gary Barker and Daniela Ligiero for opening their rolodexes, Natalia Cote-Muñoz and David Gervater for their guidance, and Juliane B. Leão for her impeccable translation, insight, and generosity during our travels together.

In China, we are grateful to Zheng Churan, Leta Hong Fincher, Sophia Huang, Guo Jianmei, Xiaonan Liu, Li Maizi, Mimiyana, Lu Pin, Liwen Qin, Rachel Tong, Liang Xiaowen, Luo Xixi, Hao Yang, Dina Yang, Ruikan Yang, Li Ying, and Wang Zheng. A special thank you to Liz Economy, Stewart Patrick, and Wenchi Yu for opening doors, Ao Yin for her excellent research, and Yuxin Lei for her indispensable translation and guidance on the ground.

In Nigeria, we are thankful to Busola Dakolo, Ololade Ganikale, Fakhrriyyah Hashim, Hassana Maina, Damilola Marcus, and Kiki Mordi.

In Tunisia, we are grateful to Shams Radhouani Abdi, Salma Ben Amour, Ahlem Belhadj, Hend Bouziri, Nawrez Ellafi, Amna Guellali, Bochra Belhaj Hmida, Ghaya Ben Mbarek, Sonia Ben Miled, Farah Ben Mna, Mona Mzid, Amal Bint Nadia, Ikram Ben Said, and Rania Said. We also want to say a special thank you to journalist Lilia Blaise, who was so thoughtful in her recommendations and learnings from coverage, and to our translator Héla Gaida, photographer Nicolas Fauqué, and our fixer Youssef.

In Egypt, our appreciation goes to Mozn Hassan, Nada Nashat, May El Shamy, Azza Soliman, and Yehia Soliman.

In Pakistan, our thanks to Sadaffe Abid, Jehan Ara, Sahar Atif, Kamala Bhasin, Yassim Butt, Nighat Dad, Jahanzeb Hussain, Saroop Ijaz, Sadia Khan, Shehzil Malik, Shiza Malik, Zillay Mariam, Rukhshanda Naz, Sarah Qureshi, Shabana, Saba Shaikh, Salman Sufi, Fauzia Viqar, Roshaneh Zafar, and Hamna Zubair. A special thank you to our photographer, translator, and daily inspiration, Insiya Syed, and to our dear host, Sameer Chisty, and his family. We also want to recognize the influence of the powerful work and writing of Rafia Zakaria.

In Sweden, we are grateful to Elin Andersson, Hannah Kaiser Barnes, Klas Danielsson, Malin Ekman, Matilda Gustavsson, Sofia Helin, "Lydia," Klaus Östegren, Ida Östensson, Alexandra Pascalidou, Malena Rydell, Victoria Saxby, Caroline Snellman, and Carolin Solskar.

We are especially grateful to the many leaders who took time to share their wisdom and insight with us, including Michelle Bachelet, Hillary Rodham Clinton, Julia Gillard, Phumzile Mlambo-Ngcuka, Amina Mohammed, Ellen Johnson Sirleaf, Tina Tchen, Margot Wallström, Malala Yousafzai, and the terrific journalists Roya Hakakian, Jodi Kantor, and Rebecca Traister.

We each also want to thank the people in our lives who made our writing and reporting possible.

From Rachel: I'm indebted to a long line of women who've inspired me through their example and whose teachings animate my work, including Marcia Greenberger and Judy Lichtman for their leadership and life lessons; Lissa Muscatine for her unwavering encouragement and belief in this project from the start; Melanne Verveer for her mentorship and an invaluable education by her side; Cheryl Mills for her fierce loyalty and incomparable insight; Jen Klein for her boundless friendship and reservoir of wisdom that have sustained me and my family through both good and hard times; and above all, Hillary Rodham Clinton, who inspires and supports each and every one of us.

I'm thankful for the teachers whose instruction has made a lasting imprint on my work and my life: Howard Berkowitz and John Roemer, for nurturing my love of books and commitment to social justice; Rosalind Rosenberg, for uncovering the everyday heroines of the women's rights movement; Wendy Williams, for showing me how law can transform lives; and Rabbi Kerrith Solomon and Ann Smith, for a master class in resilience.

To the Mesa Refuge, which offered a safe haven to facilitate the writing of this book: thank you for believing in this project. While circumstances in 2020 kept me from your beautiful Marin County campus, I am honored to be among the esteemed authors you've generously supported.

To the many friends who cheered me at each step of this journey, over meandering walks and adventurous runs, mugs of tea, long carpool lines and even longer text chains, and who never once doubted that I could write a book while homeschooling two children under quarantine: I'm more grateful for your friendship than you can know.

To Marcia Lander, my companion in caretaking and cherished member of our family: all of us have grown and thrived because of your constant love and support. I'm grateful for every moment, both large and small, and now to share, among many other things, a love of beautiful Rio de Janeiro. Muito obrigada.

I'm thankful to the Vogelstein family for the adventures in Buggieland that kept the children smiling on weekends when I wrote, and to the Cardin family whose devoted messages buoyed me at every step. You've all touched my life in countless ways, for which I'll always be grateful.

To the Brauner and Sossen families, especially my parents, Joan and Abe Brauner: I'm deeply thankful for innumerable weekends at the library that encouraged my love for books, and for your support for me and the children through the creation of this one. I'm indebted to my siblings, Diana and Josh Blumenfeld and Jason and Stacey Brauner, for their perpetual care and always being on the other end of the phone. And to my children, Parker and Sage, and our beloved Bella: thank you for your light and laughter, which bring indescribable joy and meaning to every day. Wherever life leads, may you always find an open door.

From Meighan: When I worked for Malala, every speech would start with the *Bismillah*, an invocation used by many Muslims at start of any undertaking. Translated, it simply states: *"In the name of God, the most gracious, the most merciful."* It always struck me, as Malala would speak it aloud in so many places where God was frankly often not invited, that it is such a universal prayer, one that could be said in my own faith community without anyone even blinking an eye. We have important differences, but also so much in common.

So, in my own way, I must start by thanking God, who has graciously and mercifully seen me through for the humbling process of writing this book, and who I believe sees these women, their survivors' stories, and their campaigns as righteous and worthy.

My best teachers have been girls and women globally, activists and human rights defenders I've been humbled to work with and witness in action, women like Malala and the still-too-small number of women Nobel Peace Prize laureates, dissident leaders from Hong Kong to Saudi Arabia, and countless girls insisting on a future of their own, whether in a classroom or refugee camp. Let me never forget whom I work for.

Thank you to the Cahill family, for your constant love, care, and encouragement to all who share your fierce commitment to bettering the world.

Your home and hearts are safe harbor. I could not have written this book without all of you.

To my journalist and author friends who went before or alongside, and swore I could hit this deadline too, even as I managed virtual school during a pandemic, without childcare, as a single mother: my precious sisters in faith and spirit Sarah Hurwitz, Lisa Sharon Harper, Andrea Codrington Lippke, Marlena Graves, Elizabeth Dias, Alyse Nelson, Shannon Sedgwick Davis, Kirsten Powers, and Julie Rodgers, and to Morra Aarons-Mele, Jenna Arnold, and Jay Newton-Small, thank you.

All my appreciation for the prophetic, weekly truth of the Freedom Road Global Writer's Group. You shared your hearts, your stories that needed to be told, whispered, shouted out loud.

To all my Saturday morning friends and Wednesday night women, thank you for your experience, strength, and hope. We belong.

Thank you to every employer who took a chance on me when I didn't have the right experience or credentials—your risk helps me look other women in the eye today and tell them that even if they too don't feel qualified, they are worthy and needed.

My gratitude to the Harvard Kennedy School and Shorenstein Center for inviting me to be a fellow and start to develop some of the ideas in this book, especially to Nicco Mele, and also Larry and Judi Bohn for their warm welcome to Boston.

Thank you to every friend and colleague who was ready with pep talks during the writing of this book: Kate Damon, Trish and George Filopoulos, Joe Gebbia, Andrea Hailey, Vivianne Hipol, Grazia and Gian Carlo Ochoa, "Uncle Bob" Roth for giving me and Mo strength in stillness, Taylor Royle, Maryum Saifee, and the "Shero" women of the Oslo Freedom Forum. We carry each other. I am rich beyond measure because of you all.

I'm thankful to my family for their support, and especially to the two miraculous siblings who came into my life during the writing of this book: my older brother, Rick, and my younger sister, Gabrielle. You remind me that God finds the most creative ways to answer prayers.

To my mother, who the moment she had any money to speak of, insisted we must travel, since she grew up with such limited opportunity. We saw the world for the first time together.

To both my parents, for your example of welcoming a Vietnamese family to live with us as part of the 1980 Refugee Act. You taught me that policies change real lives.

To my son, Moses, your love has been the greatest gift to me. Thank you for repeatedly proclaiming you will read this book, even if I think Harry Potter might be a better read. Your drawings across my many drafts frankly improved the writing.

And to my immigrant and Choctaw foremothers who struggled, survived, and proudly went before, I pray living my life in service, agency, and freedom honors all of your sacrifices.

NOTES

Authors' Note

1. Rajiv Chandrasekaran, "In Afghanistan, U.S. Shifts Strategy on Women's Rights as It Eyes Wider Priorities," *Washington Post*, March 5, 2011.

Introduction

1. Tarana Burke, interviewed by Rachel Vogelstein and Meighan Stone, May 28, 2020.

2. We use the term "women" to include anyone who identifies as a woman, including cis women, trans women, and feminine-identifying nonbinary people.

3. Jodi Kantor and Megan Twohey, "Harvey Weinstein Paid Off Sexual Harassment Accusers for Decades," *New York Times*, October 5, 2017, www.nytimes.com/2017/10/05/us /harvey-weinstein-harassment-allegations.html. "More than 12M 'Me Too' Facebook Posts, Comments, Reactions in 24 Hours," CBS News, October 17, 2017, www.cbsnews.com/news /metoo-more-than-12-million-facebook-posts-comments-reactions-24-hours/.

4. Erik Ortiz and Corky Siemaszko, "NBC News Fires Matt Lauer After Sexual Misconduct Review," NBC News, November 29, 2017, www.nbcnews.com/storyline/sexual -misconduct/nbc-news-fires-today-anchor-matt-lauer-after-sexual-misconduct-n824831. Ronan Farrow, "Les Moonves and CBS Face Allegations of Sexual Misconduct," *New Yorker*, July 27, 2018, www.newyorker.com/magazine/2018/08/06/les-moonves-and-cbs-face -allegations-of-sexual-misconduct. Robin Pogrebin, "Five Women Accuse Richard Meier of Sexual Harassment," *New York Times*, March 13, 2018, www.nytimes.com/2018/03/13 /arts/design/richard-meier-sexual-harassment-allegations.html. Julie Bosman, Matt Stevens, and Jonah Engel Bromwich, "Humane Society C.E.O. Resigns amid Sexual Harassment Allegations," *New York Times*, February 2, 2018, www.nytimes.com/2018/02/02/us /humane-society-ceo-sexual-harassment-.html. Irene Plagianos and Kitty Greenwald, "Mario Batali Steps Away from Restaurant Empire Following Misconduct Allegations," *Eater New York*, December 11, 2017, https://ny.eater.com/2017/12/11/16759540/mario-batali -sexual-misconduct-allegations. Robin Pogrebin, "Peter Martins Retires from the New York City Ballet After Misconduct Allegations," *New York Times*, January 1, 2018, www .nytimes.com/2018/01/01/arts/dance/peter-martins-resigns-ballet.html. Associated Press, "Journalist Mark Halperin Suspended from MSNBC over Sexual Harassment Claims," *The Guardian*, October 26, 2017, www.theguardian.com/world/2017/oct/26/mark -halperin-sexual-harassment-suspended-msnbc. "90 State Lawmakers Accused of Sexual Misconduct Since 2017," Associated Press News, February 2, 2019, https://apnews.com /article/a3377d14856e4f4fb584509963a7a223. See also Legislator Misconduct Database, GovTrack.us, accessed October 27, 2020, www.govtrack.us/misconduct. Elaine Godfrey, Lena Felton, and Taylor Hosking, "The 25 Candidates for 2018 Sunk by #MeToo

Allegations," *The Atlantic*, July 26, 2018, www.theatlantic.com/politics/archive/2018/07/the-25-candidates-for-2018-sunk-by-metoo-allegations/565457/.

5. Linus Unah, "The #MeToo Movement Has Reached Muslim-Majority Northern Nigeria," Al Jazeera, March 31, 2019, www.aljazeera.com/features/2019/03/31/the-metoo-movement-has-reached-muslim-majority-northern-nigeria/. Fakhrriyyah Hashim, "How Nigeria's Conservative Northern Region Came to Terms with Its MeToo Movement," Quartz Africa, July 22, 2019, https://qz.com/africa/1671204/nigeria-metoo-movement-shook-up-north-with-are wametoo/. Abbianca Makoni, "Northern Nigeria's MeToo Movement Is Blowing Up, and It All Started from One Tragic Tweet," *The Independent*, April 7, 2019, www.independent.co.uk/voices/metoo-arewa-nigeria-sokoto-gender-sexual-assault-social-media-a8858706.html. Fakhrriyyah Hashim, interview with Meighan Stone, June 15, 2020.

6. Rebecca Kay LeFebvre and Crystal Armstrong, "Grievance-Based Social Movement Mobilization in the #Ferguson Twitter Storm," *Journal for New Media and Society* 20, no. 1 (May 5, 2016): 8–28, https://doi.org/10.1177/1461444816644697.

7. Zeynep Tufekci, *Twitter and Tear Gas* (New Haven, CT: Yale University Press, 2017). See also LeFebvre and Armstrong, "Grievance-Based Social Movement Mobilization."

8. Seth F. Kreimer, "Technologies of Protest: Insurgent Social Movements and the First Amendment in the Era of the Internet," Faculty Scholarship at Penn Law, 1175, 2001, https://scholarship.law.upenn.edu/faculty_scholarship/1175. Catherine Clinton and Christine A. Lunardini, *The Columbia Guide to American Women in the Nineteenth Century* (New York: Columbia University Press, 2000). Carol Elizabeth Lockwood, *The International Human Rights of Women: Instruments of Change* (Washington, DC: American Bar Association, Section of International Law and Practice, 1998). Hillary Clinton, speech at the UN Fourth World Conference on Women, 1995, "Women's rights are human rights, and human rights are women's rights," accessed January 23, 2021, www.un.org/esa/gopher-data/conf/fwcw/conf/gov/950905175653.txt.

9. John P. Rafferty, "Women's March," *Encyclopedia Britannica*, 2017, accessed October 28, 2020, www.britannica.com/event/Womens-March-2017. Data from Crimson Hexagon, Facebook, Instagram, and Twitter, October 14–21, 2017, cited by CNN, Fox, Kara and Jan Diehm, "#MeToo's Global Moment: The Anatomy of a Viral Campaign," CNN, November 9, 2017, www.cnn.com/2017/11/09/world/metoo-hashtag-global-movement/index.html.

10. Gabriel Magno and Ingmar Weber, *International Gender Differences and Gaps in Online Social Networks*, Qatar Computing Research Institute, 2014, https://ingmarweber.de/wp-content/uploads/2014/06/OnlineGenderGaps.pdf. *Digital Globalization: The New Era of Global Flows*, McKinsey Global Institute, March 2016, www.mckinsey.com/business-functions/mckinsey-digital/our-insights/digital-globalization-the-new-era-of-global-flows#.

11. Jeremy Heimans and Henry Timms, *New Power* (New York: Doubleday, 2018).

12. Talkwalker (@Talkwalker), "#MeToo—with over a million uses in two days, here's how the hashtag spread across the world (Track the hashtag => bit.ly/2ggbr5i)," Twitter, October 17, 2017, https://twitter.com/Talkwalker/status/920223591089700864.

13. Adriana Carranca, "The Women-Led Opposition to Brazil's Far-Right Leader," *The Atlantic*, November 2, 2018, www.theatlantic.com/international/archive/2018/11/brazil-women-bolsonaro-haddad-election/574792/. Huizhong Wu, "In Nod to #MeToo, China Codifies Sexual Harassment by Law," Reuters, June 2, 2020, www.reuters.com/article/us-china-parliament-lawmaking-metoo/in-nod-to-metoo-china-codifies-sexual

-harassment-by-law-idUSKBN2390EY. Shayna Greene, "Egypt Cries 'Fake News' When Actress Tells Her Story of Sexual Harassment," MediaFile, October 3, 2018, www .mediafiledc.com/egypt-cries-fake-news-when-actress-tells-her-story-of-sexual-harassment/. Julie Turkewitz, "Nigerian Women Say 'MeToo.' Critics Say 'Prove It," *New York Times*, November 2, 2019, www.nytimes.com/2019/11/02/world/africa/nigerian-women-me-too -sexual-abuse-harassment.html. Sabrina Toppa, "They Accused a Pakistani Megastar of Sexual Harassment. Then They Were Sued for Defamation," *Time*, October 20, 2020, https:// time.com/5900710/pakistan-me-too-movement-lawsuits/. Hanna Hoikkala, Veronica Ek, and Niklas Magnusson, "Sweden Says #MeToo," *Bloomberg Businessweek*, December 20, 2017, www.bloomberg.com/news/articles/2017-12-20/sweden-says-metoo. Fairouz ben Salah, "#EnaZeda: Tunisian 'MeToo' Movement Met with Both Support and Smear Tactics," *Middle East Eye*, February 22, 2020, www.middleeasteye.net/news/enazeda-tunisian -me-too-movement-support-smear-campaigns.

14. Meighan Stone and Rachel Vogelstein, "Celebrating #MeToo's Global Impact," *Foreign Policy*, March 7, 2019, https://foreignpolicy.com/2019/03/07/metooglobalimpact internationalwomens-day/.

15. Jeremiah J. Castle, Shannon Jenkins, and Candice D. Ortbals, "The Effect of the #MeToo Movement on Political Engagement and Ambition in 2018," Sage Journals, June 5, 2020, https://doi.org/10.1177/1065912920924824. *Women in the Workplace 2020*, McKinsey Global Company, September 30, 2020, www.mckinsey.com/featured-insights /diversity-and-inclusion/women-in-the-workplace.

16. Erik A. Christiansen, "How Are the Laws Sparked by #MeToo Affecting Workplace Harassment?," American Bar Association, May 8, 2020, www.americanbar.org /groups/litigation/publications/litigation-news/featured-articles/2020/new-state-laws -expand-workplace-protections-sexual-harassment-victims/. Vindu Goel, Ayesha Venkataraman, and Kai Schultz, "After a Long Wait, India's #MeToo Movement Suddenly Takes Off," *New York Times*, October 9, 2018, www.nytimes.com/2018/10/09/world/asia /india-sexual-harassment-me-too-bollywood.html. Stone and Vogelstein, "Celebrating #MeToo's Global Impact."

17. Spanish Criminal Code, Articles 178 and 180, accessed January 7, 2021, www .legislationline.org/download/id/6443/file/Spain_CC_am2013_en.pdf. See also Graham Keeley, "Spain Toughens Law Against Sexual Violence," Al Jazeera, March 3, 2020, www .aljazeera.com/news/2020/3/3/spain-toughens-law-against-sexual-violence. Moroccan Violence Against Women Bill, Law no. 103-13, accessed January 23, 2021, www.morocco worldnews.com/2018/04/244641/unenglish-translation-of-moroccos-law-103-13-on -elimination-of-violence-against-women/. See also "Morocco: New Violence Against Women Law: Progress, but Some Gaps; Further Reform Needed," Human Rights Watch, February 26, 2018, www.hrw.org/news/2018/02/26/morocco-new-violence-against-women -law. *Sexual Harassment at the Workplace*, Japanese Ministry of Health, Labour and Welfare, accessed October 28, 2020, www.mhlw.go.jp/content/11900000/000378182.pdf. See also "Japan: End Workplace Harassment, Violence," Human Rights Watch, December 2, 2018, www.hrw.org/news/2018/12/02/japan-end-workplace-harassment-violence. See also Nisha Varia, "The #MeToo Movement's Powerful New Tool," Human Rights Watch, October 14, 2019, www.hrw.org/news/2019/10/14/metoo-movements-powerful-new-tool#.

18. Smooth Operator NK (@NKthiat), "Dans l'esprit des mouvements #balancetonporc et #metoo, @CodsOlivia et moi lançons #nopiwouma dans l'espoir de délier les langues et

de se soutenir mutuellement. Please follow—) @nopiwouma pour + d'infos. Nopiwouma@ gmail.com pour partager vos histoires," Twitter, November 13, 2017, https://mobile.twit ter.com/nkthiat/status/930062423310008320. See also Eliza Mackintosh, "The Me Too Movement Was Silent in Senegal. These Women Are Trying to Change That," CNN, 2018, accessed January 23, 2021, www.cnn.com/2018/12/19/africa/senegal-as-equals-intl /index.html. Alyssa Milano and Tarana Burke, "People Do Not Often Lie About Sexual Misconduct," *Meet the Press*, NBC News, October 7, 2018, www.nbcnews.com/meet-the-press /video/alyssa-milano-and-tarana-burke-people-do-not-often-lie-about-sexual-misconduct -1338716227914.

19. Lauren Wolfe, "Backlash Against Women's Equality Rolls Back Progress Worldwide," Women's Media Center, March 6, 2020, https://womensmediacenter.com/news -features/backlash-against-womens-equality-slows-progress-worldwide. "Why Strongmen Attack Women's Rights," Freedom House, June 18, 2019, https://freedomhouse.org/article /why-strongmen-attack-womens-rights.

20. Alka Kurian, "Long Before #MeToo, Women in Many Parts of the World Organized Successful Campaigns Against Sexual Violence," *The World*, March 7, 2019, www.pri .org/stories/2019-03-07/long-metoo-women-many-parts-world-organized-successful -campaigns-against-sexual.

21. Jodi Kantor, "Weinstein Is Convicted. Where Does #MeToo Go from Here?," *New York Times*, February 26, 2020, www.nytimes.com/2020/02/26/us/harvey-weinstein -metoo-movement-future.html. Michelle Garcia, "'The Rapist Is YOU': Feminists Revolt Outside Harvey Weinstein's Trial," Vice, January 10, 2020, www.vice.com/en/article /bvgzp3/the-rapist-is-you-feminists-revolt-outside-harvey-weinsteins-trial.

Chapter One. Brazil

1. Marco Aurélio Canônico, "Da Maré, vereadora fazia parte do 'bonde de intelectuais da favela,'" *Folha de S. Paulo*, March 15, 2018, www1.folha.uol.com.br/cotidiano/2018/03 /feminista-negra-e-cria-da-mare-quem-foi-a-vereadora-marielle-franco.shtml.

2. Lia De Mattos Rocha, "The Life and Battles of Marielle Franco," openDemocracy, March 20, 2019, www.opendemocracy.net/en/democraciaabierta/life-and-battles-marielle -franco/.

3. Atila Roque, "'I Am Because We Are': 100 Days Without Marielle Franco," Ford Foundation, June 22, 2018, www.fordfoundation.org/ideas/equals-change-blog/posts /i-am-because-we-are-100-days-without-marielle-franco/. Kevin Bales, *Disposable People: New Slavery in the Global Economy* (Berkeley: University of California Press, 2004), 121–149.

4. *Global Gender Gap Report 2020*, World Economic Forum, 2019, www3.weforum.org /docs/WEF_GGGR_2020.pdf. "Electoral Statistics," Tribunal Superior Eleitoral (TSE), updated October 2020, www.tse.jus.br/eleicoes/estatisticas/estatisticas-eleitorais.

5. Suyin Haynes, "The Assassination of Brazilian Politician Marielle Franco Turned Her into a Global Icon," *Time*, March 22, 2018, https://time.com/5210509/assassination -brazilian-politician-marielle-franco-global-icon/. Anielle Franco, interviewed by Rachel Vogelstein, January 30, 2020. Unless otherwise attributed, all quotations from Anielle Franco throughout this chapter come from this interview.

6. Donna Bowater and Priscilla Moraes, "Is a Women's Spring Blossoming in Brazil?," Al Jazeera, December 11, 2015, www.aljazeera.com/features/2015/12/11/is-a-womens-spring

-blossoming-in-brazil. See also Olga Khazan, "Sexism in Paradise," *The Atlantic*, December 21, 2015, www.theatlantic.com/international/archive/2015/12/brazil-women-abortion-sex ism/421185/.

7. Juliana de Faria, interviewed by Rachel Vogelstein, January 30, 2020. Unless otherwise attributed, all quotations from Juliana de Faria throughout this chapter come from this interview.

8. Pedro A. G. Dos Santos and Debora Thomé, "Women and Political Power in Brazil," Oxford Research Encyclopedias, January 2020, https://doi.org/10.1093/acrefore /9780190228637.013.1744. D. A. Maciel, "Ação coletiva, mobilização do direito e instituições políticas: O caso da campanha da Lei Maria da Penha" [Collective action, galvanizing the law and political institutions: The case of the campaign for the Maria da Penha Law], *Revista brasileira de Ciências Sociais* 26, no. 77 (2011): 97–111, https://doi.org/10.1590 /S0102-69092011000300010.

9. Marcela Xavier, "The Campaigners Challenging Misogyny and Sexism in Brazil," *The Guardian*, December 3, 2015, www.theguardian.com/global-development -professionals-network/2015/dec/03/sexism-misogyny-campaigners-brazil-social-media.

10. "Chenga de Fui Fui Survey," Think Olga, April 2015, https://thinkolga.com /projetos/chega-de-fiu-fiu/. See also Xavier, "The Campaigners Challenging Misogyny and Sexism in Brazil."

11. Fernanda Canofre, "Who's Afraid of Simone de Beauvoir? How a National Exam Had Millions of Brazilians Talking About Gender," *The World*, November 20, 2015, www .pri.org/stories/2015-11-20/whos-afraid-simone-de-beauvoir-how-national-exam-had -millions-brazilians-talking. Website of Hollaback!, accessed October 28, 2020, www .ihollaback.org/.

12. "Chenga de Fui Fui Survey."

13. Dom Phillips, "Men Tweeted Creepy Things About a Brazilian Girl on 'MasterChef Junior.' Here's How Brazilian Women Fought Back," *Washington Post*, November 6, 2015, www.washingtonpost.com/news/worldviews/wp/2015/11/06/men-tweeted-creepy-things -about-a-brazilian-girl-on-masterchef-junior-heres-how-brazilian-women-fought-back/. "#PrimeiroAssédio," Think Olga, 2015, accessed October 28, 2020, https://thinkolga.com /projetos/primeiroassedio/. See also Think Olga (@ThinkOlga), "Obrigada a tantas mulheres que encontraram força para dividir suas histórias. Vamos reunir num post na OLGA sobre o #PrimeiroAssedio," Twitter, October 21, 2020, https://twitter.com/ThinkOlga /status/656996210004381696.

14. Google Trends, "Research of the Year: My First Harassment," 2015, accessed October 25, 2020, https://trends.google.com.br/trends/story/2015_BR. Tom Phillips and Caio Barretto Briso, "Brazil: Outcry as Religious Extremists Harass Child Seeking Abortion," *The Guardian*, August 17, 2020, www.theguardian.com/world/2020/aug/17/brazil -protest-abortion-recife-hospital. Juan Paullier, "#MiPrimerAcoso, la creadora del hashtag que sacudió internet y la importancia de que las mujeres no callen," BBC Mundo, April 25, 2016, www.bbc.com/mundo/noticias/2016/04/160425_mexico_hashtag_mi_primer _acoso_violencia_mujeres_jp. Alvaro Jarrin and Kia Lily Cadwell, "Beyond #MeToo, Brazilian Women Rise Up Against Racism and Sexism," The Conversation, January 11, 2018, https://theconversation.com/beyond-metoo-brazilian-women-rise-up-against-racism -and-sexism-89117. Elisabeth Jay Friedman and Constanza Tabbush, "#NiUnaMenos: Not One Woman Less, Not One More Death!" North American Congress of Latin America,

November 1, 2016, https://nacla.org/news/2016/11/01/niunamenos-not-one-woman-less -not-one-more-death. Alanna Nunez, "Pregnant 14-Year-Old Girl Reportedly Murdered by Her Boyfriend," *Cosmopolitan*, May 14, 2016, www.cosmopolitan.com/politics/news /a40489/14-year-old-pregnant-girl-murdered-by-her-boyfriend/.

15. "#PrimeiroAssédio."

16. Antonia Pellegrino, interviewed by Rachel Vogelstein, January 27, 2020. Unless otherwise attributed, all quotations from Antonia Pellegrino throughout this chapter come from this interview.

17. Adriana Carranca, "The Women-Led Opposition to Brazil's Far-Right Leader," *The Atlantic*, November 2, 2018, www.theatlantic.com/international/archive/2018/11/bra zil-women-bolsonaro-haddad-election/574792/. Khazan, "Sexism in Paradise." Amy Erica Smith, *Religion and Brazilian Democracy: Mobilizing the People of God* (Cambridge, UK: Cambridge University Press, 2019), 61–79. "Segundo ato #MulheresContraCunha, contra o aumento de 54% do feminicídio de Negras," Portal Geledés, November 13, 2015, www .geledes.org.br/segundo-ato-mulherescontracunha-contra-o-aumento-de-54-do-feminici dio-de-negras/.

18. Manoela Miklos, interviewed by Rachel Vogelstein, January 30, 2020. Unless other-wise attributed, all quotations from Manoela Miklos throughout this chapter come from this interview.

19. *2016 Country Reports on Human Rights Practices—Brazil*, US Department of State, March 3, 2017, www.state.gov/reports/2016-contry-reports-on-human-rights-practices /brazil/. Max Bearak, "Dozens of Men Took Part in the Gang Rape of a Brazilian Teen. Then the Video Surfaced Online," *Washington Post*, May 28, 2016, www.washingtonpost .com/news/worldviews/wp/2016/05/27/dozens-of-men-took-part-in-the-gang-rape-of-a -brazilian-teen-the-the-video-made-it-online/. Donna Bowater, "Massive Protests in Bra-zil After a Girl Was Blamed for Being Gang-Raped in Rio," Vice, May 31, 2016, www .vice.com/en/article/3kwy9n/massive-protests-in-brazil-after-a-girl-was-gang-raped-in -rio. Suzana Camargo, "#MexeuComUmaMexeuComTodas reúne artistas e internau-tas contra assédio," *Conexão Pleneta*, May 2016, https://conexaoplaneta.com.br/blog /mexeucomumamexeucomtodas-reune-artistas-e-internautas-contra-assedio-sexual/.

20. Kristin Wylie, interviewed by Rachel Vogelstein, January 2020. Unless otherwise attributed, all quotations from Kristin Wylie throughout this chapter come from this interview.

21. Sonia E. Alvarez, "'Vem Marchar Com a Gente'/Come March with Us," *Meridi-ans* 14, no. 1 (2016): 70–75, www.jstor.org/stable/10.2979/meridians.14.1.05. Kaul Vieira, "Sementes de Marielle: Talíria Petrone leva a política de mulheres negras para Brasília," *Hypeness*, 2018, accessed January 23, 2021, www.hypeness.com.br/2018/11/sementes-de -marielle-taliria-petrone-leva-a-politica-de-mulheres-negras-para-brasilia/. "Many of these women led marches": according to Ana Carolina Lourenço, who was interviewed by Rachel Vogelstein, January 29, 2020. Unless otherwise attributed, all quotations from Ana Caro-lina Lourenço throughout this chapter come from this interview.

22. Simon Romero, "Dilma Rousseff Is Ousted as Brazil's President in Impeachment Vote," *New York Times*, August 31, 2016, www.nytimes.com/2016/09/01/world/ameri cas/brazil-dilma-rousseff-impeached-removed-president.html. Maria Betânia Ávila, "Um golpe patriarchal," TEORIAeDEBATE, June 15, 2016, teoriaedebate.org.br/2016/06/15 /um-golpe-patriarcal.

23. Daniela Monteiro, interview with Rachel Vogelstein, January 29, 2020. Unless otherwise attributed, all quotations from Daniela Monteiro throughout this chapter come from this interview. Haynes, "The Assassination of Brazilian Politician Marielle Franco Turned Her into a Global Icon."

24. Anne Jean Kaiser, "Brazil Sees Black Female Candidates Surge After Murder of Rising Star," *The Guardian*, September 30, 2018, www.theguardian.com/world/2018/sep/30/brazil-sees-black-female-candidates-surge-after-of-rising-star.

25. Dom Phillips, "Brazil: Two Ex-Police Officers Arrested over Murder of Marielle Franco," *The Guardian*, March 12, 2019, www.theguardian.com/world/2019/mar/12/police-officers-arrested-murder-brazilian-politician-marielle-franco.

26. Ernesto Lonsoño, "A Year After Her Killing, Marielle Franco Has Become a Rallying Cry in a Polarized Brazil," *New York Times*, March 14, 2019, www.nytimes.com/2019/03/14/world/americas/marielle-year-death.html.

27. "The Rio Protesters Fighting for Justice for Marielle Franco," BBC, March 23, 2018, www.bbc.com/news/av/world-latin-america-43510006.

28. Charis McGowan, "#NiUnaMenos Five Years On: Latin America as Deadly as Ever for Women, Say Activists," *The Guardian*, June 4, 2020, www.theguardian.com/global-development/2020/jun/04/niunamenos-five-years-on-latin-america-as-deadly-as-ever-for-women-say-activists. Haynes, "The Assassination of Brazilian Politician Marielle Franco Turned Her into a Global Icon." See also Black Lives Matter (@Blklivesmatter), "Our movement mourn's [*sic*] the death of radical, lesbian, Afro-Brazilian council member, Marielle Franco assassinated in Rio de Janeiro," Twitter, March 25, 2018, https://twitter.com/blklivesmatter/status/977956231938748416?lang=en. Black Lives Matter, "Black Lives Matter in Boston #SayHerName March on July 4," Press Release, June 27, 2020, https://blacklivesmatter.com/black-lives-matter-boston-sayhername-march-on-july-4/.

29. Renata da Silva Souza, interviewed by Rachel Vogelstein, January 28, 2020, and Tainá de Paula, interviewed by Rachel Vogelstein, January 27, 2020. Unless otherwise attributed, all quotations from Renata da Silva Souza and Tainá de Paula throughout this chapter come from these interviews.

30. Lara Bartilotti Picanço, "2018 Brazilian Election Results: Initial Takeaways on Political Renewal and the Role of Women," Wilson Center, December 10, 2018, www.wilsoncenter.org/blog-post/2018-brazilian-election-results-initial-takeaways-political-renewal-and-the-role-women. "About Renata Souza," website of Renata Souza, accessed January 23, 2021, www.renatasouzapsol.com.br/about-renata-souza. R. Queiro Ramos, "The Path to Black, Female, Favela Representation in the Rio de Janeiro State Legislative Assembly," *Rio on Watch*, January 31, 2019, www.rioonwatch.org/?p=50926. Dos Santos and Thomé, "Women and Political Power in Brazil."

31. Ernesto Londoño and Shasta Darlington, "Jair Bolsonaro Wins Brazil's Presidency, in a Shift to the Far Right," *New York Times*, October 28, 2018, www.nytimes.com/2018/10/28/world/americas/jair-bolsonaro-brazil-election.html. Picanço, "2018 Brazilian Election Results."

32. Jandira Feghali, interviewed by Rachel Vogelstein, January 29, 2020.

Chapter Two. China

1. Information about the events narrated in the opening paragraphs of this chapter come from the following sources: Jiayang Fan, "China's #MeToo Moment," *New Yorker*, February

1, 2018, www.newyorker.com/news/daily-comment/chinas-me-too-movement. Luo Xixi, interviewed by Rachel Vogelstein, October 31, 2020. Unless otherwise attributed, all quotations from Luo Xixi throughout this chapter come from this interview.

2. Simina Mistreau, "China's #MeToo Activists Have Transformed a Generation," *Foreign Policy*, January 10, 2019, https://foreignpolicy.com/2019/01/10/chinas-metoo -activists-have-transformed-a-generation/. Chen Ronggang, "China's #MeToo Movement Must End with Stronger Harassment Laws," *Sixth Tone*, January 28, 2018, www.sixthtone.com /news/1001618/china-%23metoo-movement-must-end-with-stronger-harassment-laws.

3. Karen Yuan, "#MeToo with Chinese Characteristics," *The Atlantic*, February 5, 2018, www.theatlantic.com/technology/archive/2018/02/metoo-in-china/552326/.

4. Fan, "China's #MeToo Moment."

5. Rong Tiesheng, "The Women's Movement in China Before and After the 1911 Revolution," *Chinese Studies in History* 16, no. 3–4 (1983): 159–200.

6. Gail Hershatter, "State of the Field: Women in China's Long Twentieth Century," *Journal of Asian Studies* 63, no. 4 (November 2004): 991–1065. Shen Lu, "Thwarted at Home, Can China's Feminists Rebuild a Movement Abroad?," *China File*, August 28, 2019, www.chinafile.com/reporting-opinion/postcard/thwarted-home-can-chinas -feminists-rebuild-movement-abroad.

7. Women's Research Group, All-China Women's Federation, Women's Status in China's Social Transition, 2006: 134–143. Research Group of the Third Survey on Women's Status in China, "Executive Report of the Third Survey on Women's Status in China," *Collection of Women's Studies*, 2011 (6): 12. See also Leta Hong Fincher, "China's Feminist Five," *Dissent* 63, no. 4 (2016): 84–90. Lu, "Thwarted at Home."

8. *Global Gender Gap Report 2020*, World Economic Forum, 2019, www3.weforum .org/docs/WEF_GGGR_2020.pdf. Rangita de Silva de Alwis, "Opportunities and Challenges for Gender-Based Legal Reform in China," Faculty Scholarship at Penn Law, 1708, 2010, https://scholarship.law.upenn.edu/faculty_scholarship/1708. Yojana Sharma, "In China, Universities Continue to Discriminate Against Female Applicants," *Chronicle of Higher Education*, August 27, 2013, www.chronicle.com/article/In-China-Universities/141275.

9. Beijing Declaration and Platform for Action, United Nations, 1995, https://bei jing20.unwomen.org/-/media/headquarters/attachments/sections/csw/pfa_e_final_web .pdf. Charlotte Bunch, "Beijing, Backlash, and the Future of Women's Human Rights," *Health and Human Rights* 1, no. 4 (1995): 449–453. Emily Rauhala, "Hillary Clinton's Long—and Complicated—Relationship with China," *Washington Post*, October 12, 2015, www.washingtonpost.com/news/worldviews/wp/2015/10/12/hillary -clintons-long-and-complicated-relationship-with-china/. Wang Zheng, "Feminist Struggles in a Changing China," in *Women's Movements in the Global Era: The Power of Local Feminisms*, ed. Amrita Basu (Boulder, CO: Westview Books, 2017), 151–178. "Human Rights Activism in Post-Tiananmen China: A Tale of Brutal Repression and Extraordinary Resilience," Human Rights Watch, May 30, 2019, www.hrw.org/news/2019/05/30 /human-rights-activism-post-tiananmen-china.

10. Leta Hong Fincher, *Betraying Big Brother: The Feminist Awakening in China* (New York: Verso Books, 2018). Liwen Qin, interview by Rachel Vogelstein, November 28, 2018. Unless otherwise attributed, all quotations from Liwen Qin throughout this chapter come from this interview.

11. Lu, "Thwarted at Home." Hong Kong Free Press, "Prominent Chinese Feminist Social Media Account Shuttered on International Women's Day," Global Voices Advox,

March 12, 2018, https://advox.globalvoices.org/2018/03/12/prominent-chinese-feminist -social-media-account-shuttered-on-international-womens-day/.

12. "Feminism and Social Change in China: An Interview with Lü Pin," China Change, August 26, 2019, https://chinachange.org/2019/09/16/feminism-and-social-change-in -china-an-interview-with-lu-pin-part-2-of-3/. Ting Guo, "Blood Brides: Feminist Activists Cracking China's Patriarchal Order," *Open Democracy*, July 9, 2015, www.opendemocracy .net/en/5050/blood-brides-feminist-activists-cracking-chinas-patriarchal-order/. Emily Rauhala, "China's Domestic Violence Law Is a Victory for Feminists. But They Say It Doesn't Go Far Enough," *Washington Post*, December 29, 2015. Lu, "Thwarted at Home."

13. Raul Jacob and Zhou Ping, "Chinese Toilet Campaign Falls Foul of Censors," *Financial Times*, February 28, 2020, www.ft.com/content/af0f2a5e-61e2-11e1-820b-00144fe abdc0. Li Maizi, interview by Rachel Vogelstein, September 26, 2019. Unless otherwise attributed, all quotations from Li Maizi throughout this chapter come from this interview.

14. Lü Pin, "Will China Have Its #MeToo Moment?," Amnesty International, November 24, 2020, www.amnesty.org/en/latest/campaigns/2017/11/will-china-have-metoo-moment/. Liang Xiaowen, interview by Rachel Vogelstein, July 26, 2018. Unless otherwise attributed, all quotations from Liang Xiaowen throughout this chapter come from this interview.

15. Katherine Fung, "The Chinese Feminist Fighting Patriarchy in China from Abroad," *The World*, May 16, 2019, www.pri.org/stories/2019-05-16/chinese-feminists-fighting -patriarchy-china-abroad. Wang Zheng, interview by Rachel Vogelstein, November 28, 2018. Unless otherwise attributed, all quotations from Wang Zheng throughout this chapter come from this interview.

16. Siodhbhra Parkin and Jiayun Feng, "The Movement Is Clearly Losing Momentum: Lu Pin on Chinese Feminism," SupChina, March 8, 2019, https://supchina .com/2019/03/08/the-movement-is-clearly-losing-momentum-lu-pin-on-chinese-feminism/.

17. Rauhala, "China's Domestic Violence Law Is a Victory for Feminists." "China to Increase Number of Female Toilets Across the Country," *ChinaDaily*, November 18, 2016, www.chinadaily.com.cn/china/2016-11/18/content_27418794.htm. Lu, "Thwarted at Home."

18. Mona Eltahawy, "#MonaTalksTo: Zheng Churan and Liang Xiaowen," #Mona-TalksTo, February 13, 2018, https://sister-hood.com/mona-eltahawy/monatalksto-zheng -churan-and-liang-xiaowen/.

19. "Meet the 5 Women's Rights Activists China Detained," *New York Times*, April 6, 2015, www.nytimes.com/interactive/2015/04/06/world/asia/06chinadetain-3.html.

20. "Meet the 5 Women's Rights Activists."

21. Traci Lee, "Hillary Clinton Calls China's President 'Shameless' over UN Meeting," NBC News, September 28, 2015, www.nbcnews.com/news/asian-america/hillary-clin ton-calls-chinas-president-shameless-over-un-meeting-n434761. Hong Fincher, *Betraying Big Brother*.

22. Lu Pin, interview by Rachel Vogelstein, July 26, 2018. Unless otherwise attributed, all quotations from Lu Pin throughout this chapter come from this interview.

23. Leta Hong Fincher, interview by Rachel Vogelstein, July 26, 2018. Unless otherwise attributed, all quotations from Leta Hong Fincher throughout this chapter come from this interview. Lu, "Thwarted at Home."

24. Sophia Huang Xueqin, email correspondence with authors, January 22, 2019. Unless otherwise attributed, all quotations from Sophia Huang Xueqin throughout this chapter come from this correspondence.

25. Mimi Lau, "New Alleged Victims Come Forward After Intern's Rape Claim Against Journalist at Chinese Provincial Government Newspaper," *South China Morning Post*, June 29, 2016, www.scmp.com/news/china/society/article/1982997/new-alleged-victims-come-forward-after-interns-rape-claim-against.

26. Simon McCarthy, "China's Sexual Harassment Problem," SupChina, December 4, 2017, https://supchina.com/2017/12/04/chinas-sexual-harassment-problem/.

27. Sophia Huang Xueqin, email correspondence with authors.

28. Michael Martina and Christian Shepherd, "China Revokes Academic Title of Professor Accused of Sexual Harassment," Reuters, https://jp.reuters.com/article/instant-article/idUSKBN1F30I4. Lu Pin, interview by Rachel Vogelstein. Wang Zheng, interview by Rachel Vogelstein, November 28, 2018. Philip Wen and Christian Shepherd, "Beijing Professor Dismissed as Sexual Harassment Allegations Spark Campus Activism," Reuters, January 12, 2018, www.reuters.com/article/us-china-harassment/beijing-professor-dismissed-as-sexual-harassment-allegations-spark-campus-activism-idUSKBN1F10J9.

29. Wang Zheng, interview by Rachel Vogelstein. Yuan, "#MeToo with Chinese Characteristics."

30. Margaret Anderson, "How Feminists in China Are Using Emoji to Avoid Censorship," *Wired*, March 30, 2018, www.wired.com/story/china-feminism-emoji-censorship/. Josh Horwitz, "#MeToo Activists in China Are Turning to the Blockchain to Dodge Censorship," *Quartz*, April 24, 2018, https://qz.com/1260191/metoo-activists-in-china-are-turning-to-the-blockchain-to-dodge-censorship/.

31. Lily Kuo, "#MeToo in China: Movement Gathers Pace Against Wave of Accusations," *The Guardian*, July 30, 2018, www.theguardian.com/world/2018/jul/31/metoo-in-china-movement-gathers-pace-amid-wave-of-accusations.

32. Ziyi Tang and Echo Huang, "A Platform for Female Factory Workers Has Disappeared from China's Twitter," *Quartz*, July 16, 2018, https://qz.com/1328627/a-chinese-platform-for-female-factory-workers-rights-has-been-blocked-on-weibo/. Sue-Lin Wong and Christian Shepherd, "Inspired by #MeToo Student Activists Target Inequality in China," Reuters, September 5, 2018, www.reuters.com/article/us-china-students-labour-insight/inspired-by-metoo-student-activists-target-inequality-in-china-idUSKCN1LL0FB.

33. Chinese Civil Code, Article 1010, adopted May 28, 2020, https://npcobserver.com/legislation/civil-code/. See also Bonnie Puckett, "China's New Civil Code Cracks Down on Sexual Harassment and Protects Individual Privacy Rights," *National Law Review*, August 28, 2020, www.natlawreview.com/article/china-s-new-civil-code-cracks-down-sexual-harassment-and-protects-individual-privacy. "Ten Guidelines for the Professional Behavior of Teachers in Colleges and Universities in the New Era," Ministry of Education of the People's Republic of China, November 14, 2018, www.moe.gov.cn/srcsite/A10/s7002/201811/t20181115_354921.html. Tang Ziyi, "China Publishes First Detailed Protocol for Handling Abuse by Educators amid Waves of Scandals," *Caixin Global*, www.caixinglobal.com/2018-11-16/china-publishes-first-detailed-protocol-for-handling-abuse-by-educators-amid-wave-of-scandals-101347870.html. Amy Qin, "Stop Asking Women About Pregnancy Status, China Tells Employers," *New York Times*, February 21, 2019, www.nytimes.com/2019/02/21/world/china-gender-discrimination-workplace.html. Jiayun Feng, "First Court Ruling in China Against Sexual Harassment on Public Transportation," SupChina, October 15, 2019, https://supchina.com/2019/10/15/first-court-ruling-in-china-against-sexual-harassment-on-public-transportation/.

34. Sui-Lee Wee and Li Yuan, "They Said #MeToo. Now They Are Being Sued," *New York Times*, December 26, 2019, www.nytimes.com/2019/12/26/business/china-sexual-harassment-metoo.html.

35. Guo Riri and Mimi Lau, "Fears for Young Marxist Activist Missing After Police Raid in China," *South China Morning Post*, October 11, 2018, www.scmp.com/news/china/politics/article/2167955/fears-young-marxist-activist-missing-after-police-raid-china. Mimi Lau, "Police Detain Chinese #MeToo Activist Sophia Huang Xueqin on Public Order Charge," *South China Morning Post*, October 24, 2019, www.scmp.com/news/china/politics/article/3034389/police-detain-chinese-metoo-activist-sophia-huang-xueqin-public.

36. "Feminist Voices in China: From #MeToo to Censorship," Roundtable, Council on Foreign Relations, July 26, 2018, www.cfr.org/event/feminist-voices-china-metoo-censorship. Leta Hong Fincher, interview by Rachel Vogelstein.

37. "Feminist Voices in China: From #MeToo to Censorship."

Chapter Three. Egypt and Tunisia

1. Narrative details of the events related in the opening paragraphs of this chapter come from the following sources: Lilia Blaise, "Tunisia's #MeToo Started Outside a High School. Will It End in Court?," *New York Times*, November 9, 2019, www.nytimes.com/2019/11/09/world/africa/tunisia-metoo.html. Maisie Odone and Hanen Zrig, "Thousands of Sexual Violence Victims Share Their Stories," *Meshkal*, November 5, 2019, https://meshkal.org/?p=533. "MP 'Masturbating' Near School Ignites Tunisia #MeToo Scandal," Agence France-Presse, October 14, 2019, https://news.yahoo.com/mp-masturbating-near-school-ignites-tunisia-metoo-scandal-181711100.html. Sonia Ben Miled, email correspondence with authors, November 20, 2020. Maya Oppenheim, "Tunisia Politician Appears to Masturbate Outside of School, Sparking #MeToo Movement," *The Independent*, December 2, 2019, www.independent.co.uk/news/world/africa/tunisia-metoo-zouheir-makhlouf-masturbate-car-video-a9229611.html. Layli Foroudi, "Setback for Tunisia's #MeToo Movement as New MP Gets Immunity," Reuters, November 13, 2019, www.reuters.com/article/us-tunisia-women-rights/setback-for-tunisias-metoo-movement-as-new-mp-gets-immunity-idUSKBN1XN2GX.

2. "Tunisia Passes Historic Law to End Violence Against Women and Girls," UN Women, August 10, 2017, www.unwomen.org/en/news/stories/2017/8/news-tunisia-law-on-ending-violence-against-women#. "Tunisia: Landmark Step to Shield Women from Violence," Human Rights Watch, July 27, 2017, www.hrw.org/news/2017/07/27/tunisia-landmark-step-shield-women-violence. Sarah Yerkes and Shannon McKeown, "What Tunisia Can Teach the United States About Women's Equality," Carnegie Endowment for International Peace, November 30, 2018, https://carnegieendowment.org/2018/11/30/what-tunisia-can-teach-united-states-about-women-s-equality-pub-77850. CREDIF, *Gender-Based Violence in Public Spaces in Tunisia*, 2016, 30, www.euromedwomen.foundation/pg/en/documents/view/6071/genderbased-violence-in-public-space-in-tunisia.

3. Ikram Ben Said, in interview with Meighan Stone, February 13, 2020. Amal Bint Nadia, in interview with Meighan Stone, February 22, 2020. Unless otherwise attributed, all quotations from Ikram Ben Said and Amal Bint Nadia throughout this chapter come from these interviews.

4. Rana Jawad, "'Masturbation Photos' Prompt Tunisia's #MeToo Anger," BBC, December 1, 2019, www.bbc.com/news/world-africa-50558967?ref=newsnetworks-dot-com.

5. Sonia Ben Miled, in interview with Meighan Stone, February 21, 2020. Unless otherwise attributed, all quotations from Sonia Ben Miled throughout this chapter come from this interview. She also supplied information about events at the December 2019 press conference held by Aswat Nissa.

6. Rania Said, in interview with Meighan Stone, January 9, 2020. Unless otherwise attributed, all quotations from Rania Said throughout this chapter come from this interview.

7. Information about the events at ENS, unless otherwise attributed, come from the following sources: Lou Bens and Haïfa Mzalouat, "#EnaZeda: Aymen Hacen à l'ENS, dix ans d'impunité," *Inkyfada*, January 7, 2020, https://inkyfada.com/fr/2020/01/07/harcelement-ens-aymen-hacen/. "Les 4 Verites S02 Episode 12 27-12-2019 Partie 02," December 27, 2019, video, www.youtube.com/watch?v=5Vf23nrbH8I&feature=share. Salma Ben Amour, interview with Meighan Stone, February 22, 2020. In addition, all quotes from Salma Ben Amour, unless otherwise attributed, come from this interview.

8. Elise Capogna, "Tweet Clash: From Lyon to Tunis," *Tribune de Lyon*, December 20, 2019, https://tribunedelyon.fr/2019/12/20/tweet-clash-de-lyon-a-tunis/. Bens and Mzalouat, "#EnaZeda."

9. Blaise, "Tunisia's #MeToo." Aswat Nissa (@AswatNissa), "Some pictures of the #EnaZeda protest," Twitter, November 13, 2019, https://twitter.com/AswatNissa/status/1194674146761793537. Foroudi, "Setback for Tunisia's #MeToo Movement."

10. Aswat Nissa (@AswatNissa), "Live from the press conference," Twitter, December 18, 2019, https://twitter.com/el_karama/status/1207314456696545280.

11. Ghaya Ben Mbarek (@Ghaya_BM), "A bailiff, sent by Zouheir Makhlouf," Twitter, December 18, 2019, https://twitter.com/Ghaya_BM/status/1207289120277569538. "Zouhair Makhlouf Envoie Un Huissier De Justice À L'association Aswat Nissa," *Tuniscope*, December 18, 2019, www.tuniscope.com/article/190906/actualites/societe/makhlouf-455014#.XfqGYKKf7kc.twitter. Aswat Nissa (@AswatNissa), "In the middle of the press conference," Twitter, December 18, 2019, https://twitter.com/AswatNissa/status/1207331968909746182.

12. Marc Fisher, "In Tunisia, Act of One Fruit Vendor Sparks Wave of Revolution Through Arab World," *Washington Post*, March 26, 2011, www.washingtonpost.com/world/in-tunisia-act-of-one-fruit-vendor-sparks-wave-of-revolution-through-arab-world/2011/03/16/AFjfsueB_story.html. Adeel Hassan, "A Fruit Vendor Whose Death Led to a Revolution," *New York Times*, December 17, 2014, www.nytimes.com/2014/12/16/us/arab-spring-a-fruit-vendor-who-started-a-revolution.html.

13. Angus McDowall and Tarek Amara, "Tunisia's Ousted President Ben Ali Dies in Saudi Exile," Reuters, September 19, 2019, www.reuters.com/article/us-tunisia-ben-ali/tunisias-ousted-president-ben-ali-dies-in-saudi-exile-idUSKBN1W4206.

14. Edmund Blair and Samia Nakhoul, "Egypt Protests Topple Mubarak After 18 Days," Reuters, February 10, 2011, www.reuters.com/article/us-egypt/egypt-protests-topple-mubarak-after-18-days-idUSTRE70O3UW20110211.

15. Nermin Allam, *Women and the Egyptian Revolution* (Cambridge, UK: Cambridge University Press, 2017), 32, 36, 37. Nabila Ramdani, "Women in the 1919 Egyptian Revolution: From Feminist Awakening to Nationalist Political Activism," *Journal of International Women's Studies* 14, no. 2 (2013): 41.

16. Dorra Mahfoudh and Amel Mahfoudh, "Mobilisations des Femmes et Mouvement Féministe en Tunisie," *Nouvelles Questions Féministes* 33, no. 2 (2014): 14–33. Sami Zlitni

and Zeineb Touat, "Social Networks and Women's Mobilization in Tunisia," *Journal of International Women's Studies: Arab Women Arab Spring* 13, no. 5 (2012): 47. Halima Ouanada, "Women's Rights, Democracy and Citizenship in Tunisia," in *Global Citizenship Education: Critical Perspectives*, ed. Abdeljalil Akkari and Kathrine Maleq (Cham, Switzerland: Springer Nature Switzerland, 2020), 131. Mounira Charrad, "Tunisia at the Forefront of the Arab World: Two Waves of Gender Legislation," *Washington and Lee Law Review* 64, no. 4 (2007): 1513–1528. "'It Was a Way to Destroy Our Lives': Tunisian Women Speak Out on Religious Discrimination," International Center for Transitional Justice, June 14, 2016, www.ictj .org/news/tunisia-women-speak-out-religious-discrimination-TDC. "Tunisie: Quand Bourguiba enlevait le voile des femmes," Le Point Videos, April 27, 2016, www.lepoint .fr/video/tunisie-quand-bourguiba-enlevait-le-voile-des-femmes-27-04-2016-2035192_738 .php. Ursula Lindsay, "Some Gains, Many Sacrifices: Women's Rights in Tunisia," Al-Fanar Media, July 10, 2017, www.al-fanarmedia.org/2017/07/scholars-debate-legacy-state -feminism-chances-overcoming-islamist-secularist-divide/#.

17. Khedija Arfaoui, "The Development of the Feminist Movement in Tunisia 1920s–2000s," *International Journal of the Humanities* 4, no. 8 (2007): 56. Rana Magdy, "Egyptian Feminist Movement: A Brief History," Open Democracy, March 7, 2017, www .opendemocracy.net/en/north-africa-west-asia/egyptian-feminist-movement-brief-history/. "Decentralization and Women's Representation in Tunisia: The First Female Mayor of Tunis," Tadamun, June 24, 2019, www.tadamun.co/decentralization-and-womens-representa tion-in-tunisia-the-first-female-mayor-of-tunis/?lang=en#.X71RIc1KgdV. Samar El-Masri, "Tunisian Women at a Crossroads: Cooptation or Autonomy?," Middle East Policy Council, June 14, 2015, https://mepc.org/tunisian-women-crossroads-cooptation-or-autonomy.

18. Mariz Tadros, "The Politics of Mobilising for Gender Justice in Egypt from Mubarak to Morsi and Beyond," *IDS Working Paper* 2014, no. 442 (2014): 10. Elizabeth Dickinson, "Anatomy of a Dictatorship: Hosni Mubarak," *Foreign Policy*, February 4, 2011, https:// foreignpolicy.com/2011/02/04/anatomy-of-a-dictatorship-hosni-mubarak/. "Hosni Mubarak: A Living Legacy of Mass Torture and Arbitrary Detention," Amnesty International, February 25, 2020, www.amnesty.org/en/latest/news/2020/02/hosni-mubarak -legacy-of-mass-torture/. *Time for Justice: Egypt's Corrosive System of Justice*, Amnesty International, 2011, www.amnesty.org/download/Documents/32000/mde120292011en.pdf. "Tunisia: Women Victims of Harassment, Torture and Imprisonment," Amnesty International, June 2, 1993, www.amnesty.org/en/documents/mde30/002/1993/en/. Tarek Amara, "Relatives, Torture Victims Give First Public Testimony to Tunisia Truth Commission," Reuters, November 17, 2016, www.reuters.com/article/us-tunisia-rights/relatives-torture -victims-give-first-public-testimony-to-tunisia-truth-commission-idUSKBN13C2IF. Carlotta Gall, "Women in Tunisia Tell of Decades of Police Cruelty, Violence and Rape," *New York Times*, May 18, 2015, www.nytimes.com/2015/05/29/world/africa/women-in-tunisia -tell-of-decades-of-police-cruelty-violence-and-rape.html.

19. Mariz Tadros, "Challenging Reified Masculinities: Men as Survivors of Politically Motivated Sexual Assault in Egypt," *Journal of Middle East Women's Studies* 12, no. 3 (2016): 323–342. *"Circles of Hell": Domestic, Public and State Violence Against Women in Egypt*, Amnesty International, 2015, www.amnestyusa.org/files/mde_120042015.pdf. Xan Rice, "Egyptians Protest over 'Virginity Tests' on Tahrir Square Women," *The Guardian*, May 31, 2011. Kainaz Amaria, "The 'Girl in the Blue Bra,'" NPR, December 21, 2011, www.npr.org/sections/pictureshow/2011/12/21/144098384/the-girl-in-the-blue-bra. Sharon

Otterman, "Women Fight to Maintain Their Role in the Building of a New Egypt," *New York Times*, March 5, 2011, www.nytimes.com/2011/03/06/world/middleeast/06cairo.html. Karim Faheem, "Harassers of Women in Cairo Now Face Wrath of Vigilantes," *New York Times*, November 6, 2011, www.nytimes.com/2012/11/06/world/middleeast/egyptian-vigilantes-crack-down-on-abuse-of-women.html. Leila Fadel, "Vigilantes Spray-Paint Sexual Harassers in Cairo," NPR, November 1, 2011, www.npr.org/2012/11/01/164099058/vigilantes-spray-paint-sexual-harassers-in-cairo.

20. Mozn Hassan, interview with Meighan Stone, March 20, 2020. Unless otherwise attributed, all quotations from Mozn Hassan throughout this chapter come from this interview.

21. For more discussion of women's activism against sexual harassment during this time, see Hoda Elsadda, "Travelling Critique: Anti-imperialism, Gender and Rights Discourses," *Feminist Dissent* no. 3 (2018): 88–113. Loubna Hanna Skalli, "Young Women and Social Media Against Sexual Harassment in North Africa," *Journal of North African Studies* 19, no. 2 (2014): 244–258.

22. For past feminist victories in Tunisia, see Lilia Blaise, "Tunisia Takes a Big Step to Protect Women from Abuse," *New York Times*, August 1, 2017, www.nytimes.com/2017/08/01/world/africa/tunisia-women-domestic-violence.html. Yerkes and McKeown, "What Tunisia Can Teach the United States About Women's Equality." "Tunisian Women Free to Marry Non-Muslims," BBC, September 15, 2017, www.bbc.com/news/world-africa-41278610.

23. "Egypt's New President Sisi Vows to End Sexual Assaults," BBC, June 10, 2014, www.bbc.com/news/world-middle-east-27786530.

24. "Egypt: Military Pledges to Stop Forced 'Virginity Tests,'" Amnesty International, June 27, 2011, www.amnesty.org/en/press-releases/2011/06/egypt-military-pledges-stop-forced-virginity-tests/. "Egyptian Authorities Using Sexual Violence on 'Massive Scale,'" BBC, May 19, 2015, www.bbc.com/news/world-middle-east-32790804. Hind Ahmad Zaki and Dalia Abd Alhamid, "Women as Fair Game in the Public Sphere: A Critical Introduction for Understanding Sexual Violence and Methods of Resistance," *Jadaliyya*, July 9, 2014, www.jadaliyya.com/Details/30930/Women-As-Fair-Game-in-the-Public-Sphere-A-Critical-Introduction-for-Understanding-Sexual-Violence-and-Methods-of-Resistance. *"Circles of Hell": Domestic, Public and State Violence Against Women in Egypt*. Alex Ortiz, "Egypt's New President Visits Sexual Assault Victim in Hospital," CBS News, June 11, 2014, www.cbsnews.com/news/egypts-new-president-visits-sexual-assault-victim-in-hospital/. "El-Sisi Visits Tahrir Sexual Assault Victim, Apologises to Egypt's Women," *Ahram Online*, June 11, 2014, http://english.ahram.org.eg/NewsAFCON/2019/103444.aspx.

25. Mohamed Abdellah and Mahmoud Mourad, "Eight Years After Uprising, Egyptians Say Freedoms Have Eroded," Reuters, January 24, 2019, www.reuters.com/article/us-egypt-anniversary-uprising/eight-years-after-uprising-egyptians-say-freedoms-have-eroded-idUSKCN1PI1ZJ.

26. Details of the events surrounding Rania Fahmy's case, and related statistics, come from the following sources: "Egyptian Female Wins Her Case Against a Harasser in Determination to Fight Sexual Harassment," Egyptian Streets, February 22, 2018, https://egyptianstreets.com/2018/02/22/egyptian-female-wins-her-case-against-sexual-harasser/. *Study on Ways and Methods to Eliminate Sexual Harassment in Egypt*, UN

Women et al., accessed January 24, 2021, https://web.law.columbia.edu/sites/default
/files/microsites/gender-sexuality/un_womensexual-harassment-study-egypt-final-en.pdf.
Basil el-Dabh, "99.3% of Egyptian Women Experienced Sexual Harassment: Report,"
Daily News Egypt, April 28, 2013, www.dailynewsegypt.com/2013/04/28/99-3-of-egyptian
-women-experienced-sexual-harassment-report/. Marian Reda, "Girl Wins First Case
Against Harasser in Upper Egypt," *Egypt Today*, February 22, 2018, www.egypttoday
.com/Article/1/43616/Girl-wins-first-case-against-harasser-in-Upper-Egypt. Al-Masry Al-
Youm, "Women's Council Honors 1st Upper Egyptian Woman to Take Sexual Assaulter to
Court," *Egypt Independent*, March 7, 2018, www.egyptindependent.com/womens-council
-honors-1st-upper-egyptian-woman-to-take-sexual-assaulter-to-court/.

27. Details of the events surrounding Amal Fathy's case come from the following sources: "Two-Year Sentence Upheld for Egyptian Activist Who Posted Critical
Video," Reuters, December 30, 2018, www.reuters.com/article/us-egypt-court/two-year
-sentence-upheld-for-egyptian-activist-who-posted-critical-video-idUSKCN1OT0L6.
Scott Lucas and Giovanni Piazzese, "Egypt and Amal Fathy: One Woman's Story Highlights National Wave of Repression and Sexual Violence," The Conversation, November
16, 2018, https://theconversation.com/egypt-and-amal-fathy-one-womans-story-highlights
-national-wave-of-repression-and-sexual-violence-106890. Dave Burke, "Husband of
Woman Jailed for Complaining About Sexual Harassment Reveals Heartbreaking Impact on Son, 3," *Daily Mirror*, October 10, 2018, www.mirror.co.uk/news/world-news
/husband-woman-jailed-complaining-sexual-13394804. *Egypt: Prosecution and Detention
of Human Rights Defender Amal Fathy*, Frontline Defenders, May 14, 2018, www.frontline
defenders.org/sites/default/files/urgent_appeal_egypt_prosecution_and_detention_of
_human_rights_defender_amal_fathy_14_may.pdf. "Precautionary Measures Against
Amal Fathy Lifted," Frontline Defenders, accessed October 25, 2020, www.frontline
defenders.org/en/case/detention-amal-fathy.

28. "Judicial Harassment of Mozn Hassan," Frontline Defenders, accessed October 25, 2020, www.frontlinedefenders.org/en/case/judicial-harassment-mozn-hassan.
"Stop the Campaign of Repression Against Mozn Hassan and All Human Rights Defenders in Egypt," Global Fund for Women, accessed October 25, 2020, www.global
fundforwomen.org/mozn-hassan-stop-repression-human-rights-defenders-egypt/. Amira El-
Fekki and Jared Malsin, "Egypt's Broad Security Law Targets Women Decrying Sexual Harassment," *Wall Street Journal*, September 6, 2018, www.wsj.com/articles/egypt-cracks-down
-on-women-who-decry-sexual-harassment-1536148800.

29. Sudarsan Raghavan and Heba Farouk Mahfouz, "In Egypt, a #MeToo Complaint
Can Land a Woman in Jail," *Washington Post*, October 25, 2018, www.washingtonpost
.com/world/in-egypt-a-metoo-complaint-can-land-a-woman-in-jail/2018/10/24/3a2fe5a0
-d6db-11e8-a10f-b51546b10756_story.html.

30. May El Shamy, in interview with Meighan Stone, May 8, 2020. Unless otherwise attributed, all quotations from May El Shamy throughout this chapter come from
this interview. She also provided narrative about the incident with her manager and subsequent events. Additional details about the events described here come from the following sources: Yehia Soliman, interview with Meighan Stone, May 8, 2020. May El
Shamy, Facebook, as seen in Randa Darwish, "Sexual Harassment Scandal Hits Youm7,
Egypt's Largest Newspaper," *Al Bawaba*, September 4, 2018, www.albawaba.com/loop
/sexual-harassment-scandal-hits-youm7-egypt's-largest-newspaper-1181532. Raghavan and

Mahfouz, "In Egypt, a #MeToo Complaint Can Land a Woman in Jail." Mai Shams El-Din, "Untold Stories of Sexual Harassment in Egypt's Newsrooms," *Mada Masr*, August 26, 2016, www.madamasr.com/en/2016/08/26/feature/society/untold-stories-of-sexual-harassment-in-egypts-newsrooms/. "Prosecution Suspends Investigation into Sexual Assault Accusations Against Youm7 Chief Editor," *Mada Masr*, November 11, 2018, www.madamasr.com/en/2018/11/11/news/u/prosecution-suspends-investigation-into-sexual-assault-accusations-against-youm7-chief-editor/.

31. Jeremy Sharp, *Egypt: Background and U.S. Relations*, Congressional Research Service, updated May 27, 2020, 25, https://fas.org/sgp/crs/mideast/RL33003.pdf. Ivanka Trump (@IvankaTrump), "Egyptian president Al-Sisi delivered an important speech," Twitter, April 4, 2019, https://twitter.com/ivankatrump/status/1113786931358457856?lang=en.

32. "Egypt," USAID, accessed October 25, 2020, www.usaid.gov/egypt.

33. "NGOs Identify Human Rights Abusers, Corrupt Actors for Sanctions Under U.S. Bill," Human Rights First, September 13, 2017, www.humanrightsfirst.org/press-release/ngos-identify-human-rights-abusers-corrupt-actors-sanctions-under-us-bill. Ryan Browne, "US Releases $195M in Military Aid to Egypt That Was Previously Withheld over Human Rights Concerns," CNN, July 25, 2018, www.cnn.com/2018/07/25/politics/us-military-aid-egypt/index.html. Sharp, *Egypt*, 26.

34. Bochra Belhaj Hmida, in an interview with Meighan Stone, February 24, 2020. Unless otherwise attributed, all quotations from Bochra Belhaj Hmida throughout this chapter come from this interview.

35. Frédéric Bobin, "Bochra Belhaj Hmida, militante de la Tunisie 'universelle,'" *Le Monde*, December 23, 2018, www.lemonde.fr/idees/article/2018/12/23/bochra-belhaj-hmida-militante-de-la-tunisie-universelle_5401540_3232.html. Imen Yacoubi, "Sovereignty from Below: State Feminism and Politics of Women Against Women in Tunisia," *Arab Studies Journal* 24, no. 1 (2016): 263, www.jstor.org/stable/44746854?seq=1#metadata_info_tab_contents. Nanako Tamaru, Olivia Holt-Ivry, and Marie O'Reilly, *Beyond Revolution: How Women Influenced Constitution Making in Tunisia*, Inclusive Security, March 2018, www.inclusivesecurity.org/wp-content/uploads/2018/03/Beyond-Revolution_Constitution-Making-in-Tunisia.pdf. *Assaulted and Accused: Sexual and Gender-Based Violence in Tunisia*, Amnesty International, 2015, www.amnestyusa.org/files/tunisia-assaulted-and-accused-report.pdf.

36. Bochra Belhaj Hmida, interview with Meighan Stone.

37. "Tunisia: A Step Forward for Women's Rights," Human Rights Watch, November 12, 2015, www.hrw.org/news/2015/11/12/tunisia-step-forward-womens-rights. *Tunisia's Constitution of 2014*, Constitute Project, generated July 20, 2020, www.constituteproject.org/constitution/Tunisia_2014.pdf.

38. "Tunisia: Landmark Action on Women's Rights," Human Rights Watch, April 30, 2014, www.hrw.org/news/2014/04/30/tunisia-landmark-action-womens-rights.

39. "Where Are the Women in Tunisia's Presidential Race?," Qantara, September 9, 2019, https://en.qantara.de/content/where-are-the-women-in-tunisias-presidential-race.

40. "Tunisia Moves Closer to Achieving Gender Equality in Politics," UN Women, June 28, 2016, www.unwomen.org/en/news/stories/2016/6/tunisia-moves-closer-to-achieving-gender-equality-in-politics. "Tunisian Women Free to Marry Non-Muslims."

41. "Tunisia Passes Historic Law to End Violence Against Women and Girls." *Enquête nationale sur la violence a l'egard des femmes en Tunisie*, Office National de la Famille et de la Population and Spanish Agency for International Development Cooperation, December 2010, 37, www.unwomen.org/en/news/stories/2017/8/news-tunisia-law-on-ending-violence -against-women.

42. Bobin, "Bochra Belhaj Hmida."

43. "Tunisian PM-Designate Unveils Lineup of New Gov't," Xinhua, February 16, 2020, www.xinhuanet.com/english/2020-02/16/c_138787353.htm.

44. Amal Bint Nadia, in interview with Meighan Stone, February 22, 2020. Unless otherwise attributed, all quotations from Amal Bint Nadia throughout this chapter come from this interview.

45. Ghaya Ben Mbarek, "'The Sexual Harasser Does Not Legislate,' Demonstrators Chant in Front of Prime Ministry," *Meshkal*, December 15, 2019, https://meshkal .org/?p=644. "Tunisian Women Perform Viral Feminist Anthem, 'The Rapist Is You!,'" Agence France Presse, December 14, 2019, video, www.youtube.com/watch?v=kDM7 BC4SUzc&list=ULMm9Yy0Xu6KI&index=37097.

Chapter Four. Nigeria

1. Torinmo Salau, "Nigeria's #MeToo Moment," *BRIGHT Magazine*, June 18, 2019, https://brightthemag.com/nigeria-metoo-moment-women-sexual-assault-arewametoo -157444542fb7. Khadijah Adamu, "That Day . . . ," *Anything Everything* (blog), August 10, 2017, https://darknessandblues.wordpress.com/2017/08/20/that-day/.

2. "Nigeria," Girls Not Brides, accessed October 30, 2020, www.girlsnotbrides.org /where-does-it-happen/atlas/Nigeria. "Nigeria Girl, Beaten and Denied Education, Among Thousands of Divorced Children," AP, June 27, 2014, www.cbsnews.com/news/nigeria-girl -among-thousands-of-divorced-children/. Amanda Holpuch, "Stolen Daughters: What Happened After #BringBackOurGirls?," *The Guardian*, October 22, 2018, www.theguard ian.com/tv-and-radio/2018/oct/22/bring-back-our-girls-documentary-stolen-daughters -kidnapped-boko-haram.

3. "Nigeria's President Buhari: My Wife Belongs in Kitchen," BBC, October 14, 2016, www.bbc.com/news/world-africa-37659863. *Global Gender Gap Report 2020*, World Economic Forum, 2019, www3.weforum.org/docs/WEF_GGGR_2020.pdf. "25 Years After the Historic Beijing Women's Conference, Violence Against Women and Girls Still Common in Nigeria, Says UNICEF," UNICEF, March 4, 2020, www.unicef.org/nigeria/press-releas es/25-years-after-historic-beijing-womens-conference-violence-against-women-and-girls.

4. Fakhrriyyah Hashim, in interview with Meighan Stone, June 15, 2020. Unless otherwise attributed, all quotations from Fakhrriyyah Hashim throughout this chapter come from this interview. She also provided narrative for some of the events related in the chapter.

5. "How #ArewaMeToo Empowered Northern Nigerian Women to Share Their Stories of Sexual Abuse: 10 Questions with Fakhrriyyah Hashim," Myrihla, April 30, 2019, https://myrihla.com/2019/04/30/how-arewametoo-empowered-northern-nigerian-women -to-share-their-stories-of-sexual-abuse-10-questions-with-fakhrriyyah-hashim/. Salau, "Nigeria's #MeToo Moment." Sada Malumfashi, "Nigeria: #ArewaMeToo—Northern Nigerian Women Call Out Abusers," AllAfrica, February 14, 2019, https://allafrica.com /stories/201902140472.html.

6. Data from the International Telecommunication Union, "Individuals Using the Internet (% of Population)—Nigeria," World Bank, accessed February 22, 2021, https://data.world bank.org/indicator/IT.NET.USER.ZS?locations=NG. Linus Unah, "The #MeToo Movement Has Reached Muslim-Majority Northern Nigeria," Al Jazeera, March 31, 2019, www.aljazeera .com/features/2019/3/31/the-metoo-movement-has-reached-muslim-majority-northern-nigeria.

7. Hassana Maina, in interview with Meighan Stone, December 6, 2019. Unless otherwise attributed, all quotations from Hassana Maina throughout this chapter come from this interview. She also provided narrative for some of the events related in the chapter.

8. Salau, "Nigeria's #MeToo Moment." Fatiatu Inusah, "#MeToo Storms Conservative Northern Nigeria Where Women Had No Voice," Face 2 Face Africa, February 22, 2019, https://face2faceafrica.com/article/metoo-storms-conservative-northern-nigeria-where -women-had-no-voice. Motolani Alake, "#ArewaMeToo: Women from Northern Nigeria Speak Up on Sexual Abuse," *The Pulse*, February 18, 2019, www.pulse.ng/news/local /arewametoo-rape-pedophilia-child-marriage-sexual-harassment-and-sexual-violence/yg69ftw.

9. Inusah, "#MeToo Storms Conservative Northern Nigeria." "#ArewaMeToo Campaigner Maryam Awaisu Arrested," *Guardian Nigeria*, February 19, 2019, https://guardian .ng/news/arewametoo-campaigner-maryam-awaisu-arrested/. "#ArewaMeToo Activist, Maryam Awaisu, Freed—Amnesty International," *The Punch*, February 20, 2019, https:// punchng.com/arewametoo-activist-maryam-awaisu-freed-amnesty-international/. Rick Gladstone and Megan Specia, "Nigeria's Police Brutality Crisis: What's Happening Now," *New York Times*, November 14, 2020, www.nytimes.com/article/sars-nigeria-police.html.

10. "Nigeria: Police Must Release #ArewaMeToo Activist Maryam Awaisu Immediately and Unconditionally," Amnesty International, February 19, 2019, www.amnesty.org/en /latest/news/2019/02/nigeria-police-must-release-arewametoo-activist-maryam-awaisu -immediately/. "Maryam Awaisu Released Hours After Arrest," *Guardian Nigeria*, February 20, 2019, https://guardian.ng/news/maryam-awaisu-released-hours-after-arrest/.

11. Salau, "Nigeria's #MeToo Moment."

12. Unah, "The #MeToo Movement Has Reached Muslim-Majority Northern Nigeria." Melissa Mordi, "The Amazons Behind #Arewametoo, the Hashtag Against Sexual Abuse in North Nigeria," *Guardian Nigeria*, May 2, 2019, https://guardian.ng/features /gender-politics/the-amazons-behind-arewametoo-the-hashtag-against-sexual-abuse-in -north-nigeria/. Amatallah Saulawa, "A Look at the Nigerian #ArewaMeToo Movement and the Need to Distinguish It," Amaliah.com, April 29, 2019, www.amaliah.com/post/54999 /look-nigerian-arewametoo-movement-need-distinguish.

13. Julie Turkewitz, "Nigerian Women Say 'MeToo.' Critics Say 'Prove It,'" *New York Times*, November 2, 2019, www.nytimes.com/2019/11/02/world/africa/nigerian -women-me-too-sexual-abuse-harassment.html.

14. Busola Dakolo, interviews with Meighan Stone, December 6, 2019, and June 16, 2020. Unless otherwise attributed, all quotations from Busola Dakolo throughout this chapter come from these interviews.

15. Nduka Orjinmo, "Enoch Adeboye Sexism Row: Why the Nigerian Pastor Is So Popular," BBC, August 12, 2020, www.bbc.com/news/world-africa-53488921. Nick Shindo Street, "How a Pentecostal Law Professor Has Helped Reshape Nigerian Politics," *Washington Post*, April 10, 2015, www.washingtonpost.com/news/acts-of-faith /wp/2015/04/10/how-a-pentecostal-law-professor-has-helped-reshape-nigerian-politics/.

16. Chude Jideonwo, "Full Interview: Pastor Biodun Fatoyinbo Raped Me—Busola Dakolo," YNaija, June 28, 2019, video, www.youtube.com/watch?v=YLFQ5rQzi3U.

17. Turkewitz, "Nigerian Women Say 'MeToo.'" Biodun Fatoyinbo (@biodunfatoyinbo), "My Confidence in the Lord Remains Unwavering," Instagram, July 1, 2019, www.instagram.com/p/BzXkF8hBnSv/?utm_source=ig_embed. "COZA's Biodun Fatoyinbo: Nigeria Outrage as Rape Accused Pastor Returns," BBC, August 5, 2019, www .bbc.com/news/world-africa-49234844. Samson Toromade, "Another Former COZA Member Accuses Pastor Fatoyinbo of Rape," *The Pulse*, July 4, 2019, www.pulse.ng /news/metro/fatoyinbo-another-ex-coza-member-accuses-pastor-of-rape/3db5c3r. Daniel Erezi, "Fatoyinbo Threatens to Sue Accusers over Rape Allegations," *Guardian Nigeria*, June 28, 2019, https://guardian.ng/news/fatoyinbo-threatens-to-sue-accusers-in-rape -allegations/. Nellie Peyton, "Nigeria Has #MeToo Moment After Popular Pastor Is Accused of Rape," Reuters, July 1, 2019, www.reuters.com/article/us-nigeria-women-rape /nigeria-has-metoo-moment-after-popular-pastor-is-accused-of-rape-idUSKCN1TW3KE.

18. Eno Adeogun, "Nigerian Pastor Biodun Fatoyinbo Steps Down over Rape Allegations," Premier Christian News, July 2, 2019, https://premierchristian.news/en/news /article/nigerian-pastor-biodun-fatoyinbo-steps-down-over-rape-allegations. Ruth Maclean and Eromo Egbejule, "How 'Nigeria's #MeToo Moment' Turned Against Rape Accuser," *The Guardian*, August 6, 2019, www.theguardian.com/global-development/2019/aug/06 /nigeria-metoo-moment-accuser-busola-dakolo.

19. "Busola Dakolo Formally Reports Fatoyinbo to Police," PM News Nigeria, July 4, 2019, www.pmnewsnigeria.com/2019/07/04/busola-dakolo-formally-reports-fatoyinbo -to-police/. Maclean and Egbejule, "How 'Nigeria's #MeToo Moment' Turned Against Rape Accuser."

20. "COZA's Biodun Fatoyinbo: Nigeria Outrage."

21. Timileyin Omilana, "There Are Pressure to Bury My Rape Case Against Pastor Fatoyinbo, Says Busola Dakolo," *Guardian Nigeria*, June 4, 2020, https://guardian.ng /news/there-are-pressure-to-bury-my-rape-case-against-pastor-fatoyinbo-says-busola -dakolo/. QueenEsther Iroanusi, "Senate Removes Time Limit on Rape Charge, Prescribes Life Jail for Kidnapping," *Premium Times*, July 14, 2020, www.premiumtimesng.com/news /top-news/402828-updated-senate-removes-time-limit-on-rape-charge-prescribes-life-jail -for-kidnapping.html.

22. Bayo Wahab, "Protesters Storm COZA Church in Lagos, Screaming 'No to Rape,'" *The Pulse*, June 30, 2019, video, www.pulse.ng/news/local/protesters-storm-coza-church -in-lagos-screaming-no-to-rape/2t42x6d. "COZA: Nigerians Protests in Abuja, Lagos over Alleged Rape," TalkWorld Nigeria, accessed October 30, 2020, www.talkworld.com.ng /protests-rock-coza-in-abuja-lagos-over-alleged-rape/.

23. Kiki Mordi, in interview with Meighan Stone, December 9, 2019. Unless otherwise attributed, all quotations from Kiki Mordi throughout this chapter come from this interview. She also provided narrative regarding events surrounding her documentary.

24. Kiki Mordi, reporter, *Sex for Grades: Undercover Inside Nigerian and Ghanaian Universities—BBC Africa Eye Documentary*, October 9, 2019, video, www.youtube.com /watch?v=we-F0Gi0Lqs&list=PL6Hy_nEYDqvkEYhXnO8yhd8xPiW2l-1AG&index=29.

25. Anonymous, in interview with Meighan Stone, 2019.

26. Mordi, *Sex for Grades*.

27. "Aisha Buhari Wants Urgent Action to Address Sexual Harassment Against Students," *Premium Times*, October 8, 2019, www.premiumtimesng.com/news/more-news/356501 -aisha-buhari-wants-urgent-action-to-address-sexual-harassment-against-students.html. QueenEsther Iroanusi, "Senate Re-Introduces Anti-Sexual Harassment Bill," *Premium Times*, October 9, 2019, www.premiumtimesng.com/news/top-news/356764-senate-re -introduces-anti-sexual-harassment-bill.html.

28. Bukola Adebayo and Stephanie Busari, "Lecturer Demanded Sex in Return for Better Grades, Nigerian Student Says," CNN, May 23, 2018, www.cnn.com/2018/05/23 /africa/sex-for-grades-university-nigeria-intl/index.html. Sahara News, "OAU Professor Demands to Have Sex Five Times to Pass a Female Student," April 10, 2018, video, www .youtube.com/watch?v=XWKLIPXkYuY.

29. Archive of the President of the 8th Senate (@SP8thNGRSenate), "UPDATE: The Nigerian Senate has passed a Motion on the growing trend of sexual harassment," Twitter, May 30, 2018, https://twitter.com/SP8thNGRSenate/status/1001819810496380930. Bukola Adebayo, "Nigerian Professor in Sex for Grades Scandal Gets Prison Term," CNN, December 17, 2018, www.cnn.com/2018/12/17/africa/nigerian-professor-jailed-in -sexual-assault-case-intl/index.html. Titlope Fadare, "As Outrage Trails BBC Sex-for-Grades Expose, Nigeria's Senate Reintroduces Sexual Harassment Bill," *Order Paper*, October 9, 2019, www.orderpaper.ng/as-outrage-trails-bbc-sex-for-grades-expose-nigerias-senate -reintroduces-sexual-harassment-bill/.

30. Henry Umoru, "ASUU, NANS, Other Women Rights Advocacy Groups Clash at the Senate over Sexual Harassment Bill," *Vanguard*, February 17, 2020, www .vanguardngr.com/2020/02/asuu-nans-other-women-rights-advocacy-groups-clash-at-the -senate-over-sexual-harassment-bill/. "Amid Sex-for-Grades Scandal, Bill to Stop Sexual Harassment Reappears in Senate," *The Pulse*, October 9, 2019, www.pulse.ng/news/local /sex-for-grades-anti-sexual-harassment-bill-reappears-in-senate/7dbrtf9.

31. "Nigeria's 'Sex for Grades' Inquiry Starts," *Daily News Ghana*, November 15, 2019, https://dailynewsgh.com/2019/11/15/nigerias-sex-for-grades-inquiry-starts/. Emmanuel Akinwotu, "Nigeria Launches First Sex Offender Register," *The Guardian*, November 25, 2019, www.theguardian.com/global-development/2019/nov/25/nigeria-first-sex-offender -register. "UNILAG Suspends Another Lecturer Indicted in Sex for Grades Scandal," *The Pulse*, October 9, 2019, www.pulse.ng/news/local/sex-for-grades-unilag-suspends -another-indicted-lecturer/cpz4fff. "Sex for Grade Video Work of Devil, New Facebook Page Quotes Lecturer as Saying," *Punch Nigeria*, October 12, 2019, https://punchng.com /sex-for-grade-video-work-of-devil-new-facebook-page-quotes-lecturer-as-saying/.

32. Marc Matera, Misty L. Bastian, and S. Kingsley, *The Women's War of 1929: Gender and Violence in Colonial Nigeria* (New York: Palgrave Macmillan, 2012). Felicia Ihuoma Abaraonye, "The Women's War of 1929 in South-Eastern Nigeria," in *Women and Revolution: Global Expressions*, ed. M. J. Diamond (Dordrecht: Springer Netherlands, 1998), 109.

33. Omiko Awa, "Lady Oyinkansola Abayomi: An Amazon, Trailblazer," *Guardian Nigeria*, February 16, 2020, https://guardian.ng/saturday-magazine/transition/lady -oyinkansola-abayomi-an-amazon-trailblazer/.

34. "Haija Gambo Sawaba," *The Punch*, April 7, 2019, www.pressreader.com/nigeria /the-punch/20190407/282488595102539. Elizabeth Ofosuah Johnson, "This Nigerian Woman Survived Forced Marriage at 13 to Become a Fierce Political Activist in the 1950s,"

Face2Face Africa, March 8, 2019, https://face2faceafrica.com/article/this-nigerian-woman -survived-forced-marriage-at-13-to-become-a-fierce-political-activist-in-the-1950s.

35. Tunde Fatunde, "Does the New Sexual Harassment Bill Unfairly Target Academics?," *University World News, Africa Edition*, August 20, 2020, www.universityworldnews .com/post.php?story=20200820081902475. Umoru, "ASUU, NANS, Other Women Rights Advocacy Groups Clash."

36. Violence Against Persons Prohibition Act, hosted by International Labour Organization, accessed October 30, 2020, www.ilo.org/dyn/natlex/docs/ELECTRONIC /104156/126946/F-1224509384/NGA104156.pdf.

37. "CSOs Demand Domestication of Child Rights, Violence Against Persons Prohibition Acts," *Vanguard*, October 1, 2020, www.vanguardngr.com/2020/10/csos-demand -domestication-of-child-rights-violence-against-persons-prohibition-acts/.

38. Nike Adebowale, "11 States in Northern Nigeria Yet to Pass Child Rights Law—UNICEF Official," *Premium Times*, May 11, 2019, www.premiumtimesng.com/news /more-news/329511-12-states-in-northern-nigeria-yet-to-pass-child-rights-law-unicef -official.html. Rotimi Olawale, "A Major Win for Out-of-School Nigerian Girls," Malala .org, May 8, 2018, https://blog.malala.org/a-major-win-for-out-of-school-nigerian-girls-608 3773d0799.

39. Kunle Adebajo, "Fact Check: No, It Is Not True Nigeria Has Recorded Only 18 Convictions in Rape Cases," International Center for Investigative Reporting, July 3, 2019, www .icirnigeria.org/fact-check-no-it-isnt-true-nigeria-has-recorded-only-18-convictions-in-rape -cases/.

40. Eromo Egbejule, "Welcome to Mirabel: The First Centre Supporting Rape Survivors in Nigeria," *The Guardian*, February 25, 2016, www.theguardian.com/world/2016/feb/25 /welcome-to-mirabel-the-first-centre-supporting-survivors-in-nigeria.

41. "Monthly Ranking of Women in National Parliaments," IPU Parline, accessed October 30, 2020, https://data.ipu.org/women-ranking?month=10&year=2020.

42. Many of the events recounted in the passage that follows come from our interview with Hassana Maina and from the following source: Sada Malumfashi, "Young Women Lead a Movement Against Sexual Violence and Patriarchy in Northern Nigeria," Women's Media Center, June 30, 2020, https://womensmediacenter.com/women-under-siege /young-women-lead-a-movement-against-sexual-violence-and-patriarchy-in-northern -nigeria.

43. "People Calling Me Lesbian to Stop My Fight Against Sexual Abuse—Taheer, Sokoto #ArewaMeToo Movement Leader," *The Punch*, December 1, 2019, https://punchng .com/people-calling-me-lesbian-to-stop-my-fight-against-sexual-abuse-taheer-sokoto -arewametoo-movement-leader/.

44. Sadiya Taheer, "Was Beaten Up by the Nigerian Police for Standing Against Violence," November 27, 2019, video, www.youtube.com/watch?v=QR98xJIvcpc&feature =youtu.be.

45. Damilare Famuyiwa, "Busola Dakolo Says She's Going to Appeal Judgement of Rape Case Against Fatoyinbo," *The Pulse*, November 14, 2019, www.pulse.ng/news/local/busola -dakolo-says-fatoyinbo-is-not-free-just-yet/664k29n. Omilana, "There Are Pressure to Bury My Rape Case." Stephen Azubuike, "Busola Dakolo: 2 Reasons Her Civil Suit Suffered Technical Knockout," *Stephen Legal* (blog), November 17, 2019, https://stephenlegal.ng /busola-dakolo-2-reasons-her-civil-suit-suffered-technical-knockout/.

46. Aniete Ewang, "Nigerians Should Say No to Social Media Bill," Human Rights Watch, November 26, 2019, www.hrw.org/news/2019/11/26/nigerians-should-say -no-social-media-bill#. "Egypt: Spate of 'Morality' Prosecutions of Women," Human Rights Watch, August 17, 2020, www.hrw.org/news/2020/08/17/egypt-spate-morality -prosecutions-women. "Egypt to Regulate Popular Social Media Users," BBC, July 17, 2018, www.bbc.com/news/world-middle-east-44858547. Asif Shahzad, "New Internet Rules to Give Pakistan Blanket Powers of Censorship," Reuters, November 19, 2020, www.reuters.com/article/pakistan-socialmedia-censorship/new-internet-rules-to-give -pakistan-blanket-powers-of-censorship-idUSL8N2I53OW.

47. Paul Currion, "Decolonising Aid, Again," New Humanitarian, July 13, 2020, www.thenewhumanitarian.org/opinion/2020/07/13/decolonisation-aid-humanitarian -development-racism-black-lives-matter. Rory Horner, "Towards a New Paradigm of Global Development? Beyond the Limits of International Development," *Progress in Human Geography* 44, no. 3 (2020): 415–436, https://doi.org/10.1177/0309132519836158.

48. David Pilling, "Why George W. Bush Is Africa's Favorite U.S. President," *Financial Times*, July 17, 2019, www.ft.com/content/72424694-a86e-11e9-984c-fac8325aaa04. George Ingram, *Adjusting Assistance to the 21st Century: A Revised Agenda for Foreign Assistance Reform*, Brookings Institution, July 2014, www.brookings.edu/wp-content /uploads/2016/06/ingram-aid-reform-final2.pdf.

49. "The Hands Off Team," Hands Off Initiative, 2019, www.handsoffinitiative.org /about-us/. Ololade Ganikale, in interviews with Meighan Stone, December 10, 2019, and February 26, 2020. Unless otherwise attributed, all quotations from Ololade Ganikale throughout this chapter come from these interviews.

50. Torinmo Salau, "Market Harassment Is Not a Hoax, There's Data to Prove It," *Guardian Nigeria*, February 28, 2019, https://guardian.ng/features/market-harassment-is -not-a-hoax-theres-data-to-prove-it/. Damilola Marcus, in interview with Meighan Stone, August 29, 2020. Unless otherwise attributed, all quotations from Damilola Marcus throughout this chapter come from this interview.

51. Kelechukwu Iruoma, "'Stop Touching Us': Women Protest Against Harassment at Nigeria's Street Markets," NPR, April 11, 2019, www.npr.org/sections/goatsandsoda /2019/04/11/711388869/stop-touching-us-women-protest-against-harassment-at-nigerias -street-markets.

52. MarketMarch, "Laws & Policy Enforcements Against Sexual Harrassment and Bullying," Change.org, accessed October 30, 2020, www.change.org/p/government -laws-policy-enforcements-against-sexual-assault-in-lagos-markets?recruiter=923922188 &utm_source=share_petition&utm_medium=copylink&utm_campaign=tap_basic_share. Iruoma, "'Stop Touching Us.'"

53. Motolani Alake, "Pulse Chats with Omoge Dami: The Feminist Who Wants to 'March on the Market,'" *The Pulse*, November 19, 2018, www.pulse.ng/lifestyle/food-travel /pulse-chats-with-omoge-dami-the-feminist-who-wants-to-march-on-the-market/g0w7jqc.

54. "Bill Against Violence Passes 2nd Reading at Bauchi Assembly," *Nigerian News Direct*, June 10, 2020, https://nigeriannewsdirect.com/181397-2/.

55. "About Skoll," Skoll Foundation, accessed October 30, 2020, https://skoll.org/about /about-skoll/.

56. Busola Dakolo (@busoladakolo), "It is now officially one year," Instagram, June 4, 2020, www.instagram.com/p/CBBAluyJ1UI/?igshid=jk8t6j0cal72.

57. Bukola Adebayo, "Nigerian Senate Passes Sexual Harassment Bill," CNN, July 8, 2020, www.cnn.com/2020/07/08/africa/nigeria-sexual-harassment-bill/index.html.

58. Precious "Mamazeus" Nwogu, "Nigerian Journalist Kiki Mordi Snags Emmy Nomination for 'Sex for Grades' Documentary," *The Pulse*, August 19, 2020, www.pulse .ng/entertainment/movies/kiki-mordi-snags-first-emmy-nomination-for-sex-for-grades -documentary/erwdhm9.

Chapter Five. Pakistan

1. Meesha Shafi (@itsmeeshashafi), "Sharing this because I believe that by speaking out about my own experience of sexual harassment, I will break the culture of silence," Twitter, April 19, 2018, https://twitter.com/itsmeeshashafi/status/986918710991519744?lang=en.

2. "Meesha Says She Was Harassed on Multiple Occasions by Ali Zafar," *Dawn*, December 10, 2019, www.dawn.com/news/1521345.

3. Ali Zafar (@AliZafarsays), "I am deeply aware and in support of the global #Me-Too movement," Twitter, April 19, 2018, https://twitter.com/AliZafarsays/status/986969 628869046272.

4. Leena Ghani, quoted in Shahab Ansari and Arshad Dogar, "More Women Accuse Ali Zafar of Harassment," *News International*, April 21, 2018, www.thenews.com.pk /print/307171-more-women-accuse-ali-zafar-of-harassment. Leena Ghani (@Leena-Ghani), "Thank you @itsmeeshashafi for your courage," as seen in "More Women Step Forward to Accuse Ali Zafar of Sexual Harassment," *Dawn*, April 20, 2018, https://images.dawn.com /news/1179895.

5. "Maham Javaid," Human Rights Watch, accessed October 25, 2020, www.hrw .org/about/people/maham-javaid. "Meesha Shafi Isn't the Only One, More Women Come Forward with Sexual Harassment Allegations Against Ali Zafar," *Indian Express*, April 20, 2018, https://indianexpress.com/article/entertainment/music/ali-zafar-sexual -harassment-5145120/.

6. "More Women Step Forward to Accuse Ali Zafar of Sexual Harassment."

7. Osman Khalid Butt (@aClockworkObi), "A woman breaks her silence about abuse, withstands character assassination & further abuse on social media, her story turns into memes & tone-deaf jokes that trivialize the issue, she fears ostracization— but suuuuure, she did it for the cheap publicity," Twitter, April 19, 2018, https:// twitter.com/aClockworkObi/status/987001646633930753. Urwa Hocane (@ VJURWA), "More power to you!," Twitter, April 2019, https://twitter.com/VJURWA /status/986994084542930945. Momina Mustehsan (@MominaMustehsan), "#MeToo needs a response #ImSorry from the offenders. Nothing will change until they acknowledge, take responsibility and make amends," Twitter, April 20, 2018, https://twitter.com /MominaMustehsan/status/987351835311771650. Ayesha Omar to Geo News, quoted in "I Too Have Been a Victim of Serious Harassment: Ayesha Omar," *Dawn*, April 21, 2018, https:// images.dawn.com/news/1179907/i-too-have-been-a-victim-of-serious-harassment-ayesha -omar.

8. "Meesha Shafi's Legal Team Receives Ali Zafar's Rs1 Billion Legal Notice," Geo News, April 25, 2018, www.geo.tv/latest/192646. Meesha Shafi (@itsmeeshashafi), "I have appointed Barrister @pansota1 and @nighatdad as my legal counsels," Twitter, April 24, 2018, as seen in "A Timeline of the Meesha Shafi-Ali Zafar Controversy," *Dawn*, May 12, 2018, https://images.dawn.com/news/1179925.

9. "Five Questions on #MeToo in Pakistan: Nighat Dad," Council on Foreign Relations, July 15, 2019, www.cfr.org/blog/five-questions-metoo-pakistan-nighat-dad.

10. Fauzia Viqar, in interview with Meighan Stone, October 15, 2018. Unless otherwise attributed, all quotations from Fauzia Viqar throughout this chapter come from this interview.

11. Rukhshanda Naz, in interview with Meighan Stone, October 14, 2018. Unless otherwise attributed, all quotations from Rukhshanda Naz throughout this chapter come from this interview.

12. Suzanne Goldenberg, "A Question of Honour," *The Guardian*, May 26, 1999, https://www.theguardian.com/world/1999/may/27/gender.uk1.

13. According to Rukhshanda Naz, in interview with Meighan Stone.

14. Haseeb Bhatti, "CJ Says He's Sorry If Anyone Hurt over Length of Skirt Remark," *Dawn*, January 24, 2018, www.dawn.com/news/1384990/cj-says-hes-sorry-if-anyone-hurt-over-length-of-skirt-remark.

15. Saroop Ijaz, "First Woman in Pakistan Nominated as High Court Chief Justice," Human Rights Watch, August 1, 2018, www.hrw.org/news/2018/08/01/first-woman-pakistan-nominated-high-court-chief-justice. Myra Imran, "Only 5.8% Judges in Pakistan Are Women: HRCP," *News International*, March 5, 2016, www.thenews.com.pk/print/102929-Only-58-judges-in-Pakistan-are-women-HRCP. Xari Jalil, "Women Lawyers Want to Be Heard in Bar Elections," *Dawn*, September 26, 2020, www.dawn.com/news/1581626/women-lawyers-want-to-be-heard-in-bar-elections.

16. For example, see transcript of "Outlawed in Pakistan," *Frontline*, May 18, 2013, www.pbs.org/wgbh/frontline/film/outlawed-in-pakistan/transcript/. Saroop Ijaz, "Blaming the Victim for Sexual Violence in Pakistan," Human Rights Watch, September 14, 2020, www.hrw.org/news/2020/09/14/blaming-victim-sexual-violence-pakistan.

17. "Five Questions on #MeToo in Pakistan: Nighat Dad."

18. Nighat Dad, in interviews with Meighan Stone, October 18, 2018, and October 1, 2020; "#MeToo in Pakistan's Courts, Streets, and Online: A Conversation with Nighat Dad," Women and Foreign Policy Roundtable Series, Council on Foreign Relations, June 4, 2019. Unless otherwise attributed, all quotations from Nighat Dad throughout this chapter come from these interviews.

19. Rachel Vogelstein, Jamille Bigio, Gayle Tzemach Lemmon, Meighan Stone, Alexandra Bro, Becky Allen, and Jody Heymann, *Women and the Law: Leveling the Global Economic Playing Field*, Council on Foreign Relations, 2018, 37, https://cdn.cfr.org/sites/default/files/report_pdf/Essay_Compendium_Vogelstein_Bigio_Women_Law_OR.pdf. Abira Ashfaq, "Voices from Prison and a Call for Repeal: The Hudood Laws of Pakistan," *New Politics* X, no. 4 (2006), https://newpol.org/issue_post/voices-prison-and-call-repeal-hudood-laws-pakistan/. "Pakistan: Reform Hudood Laws Now," Human Rights Watch, November 14, 2006, www.hrw.org/news/2006/11/14/pakistan-reform-hudood-laws-now. Anita Weiss, *Moving Forward with the Legal Empowerment of Women in Pakistan*, United States Institute of Peace, 2012, www.usip.org/sites/default/files/resources/SR305.pdf. "Pakistan Court Takes Up Appeal in Gang-Rape Case," *New York Times*, June 28, 2005, www.nytimes.com/2005/06/28/world/asia/pakistan-court-takes-up-appeal-in-gangrape-case.html. Samantha Kroffie, "Duty or Faith?: The Evolution of Pakistani Rape Laws and Possibility for Non-Domestic Redress for Victims," *Emory Law Review* 30, no. 4 (2016):

565–595, https://law.emory.edu/eilr/content/volume-30/issue-4/comments/duty-faith-pakistani-rape-non-domestic-redress.html.

20. The Protection Against Harassment of Women at the Workplace Act, 2010 (Act No. IV of 2010), website of the International Labour Organization, accessed January 25, 2021, www.ilo.org/dyn/natlex/natlex4.detail?p_lang=en&p_isn=86175. Hassan Niazi, "Understanding Pakistan's Sexual Harassment Law—Part III," *Express Tribune*, December 16, 2019, https://tribune.com.pk/article/92002/understanding-pakistans-sexual-harassment-law-part-iii.

21. Section 509 of the Pakistan Penal Code, 2010, www.senate.gov.pk/uploads/documents/1363267161_658.pdf.

22. Hassan Niazi, "Understanding Pakistan's Sexual Harassment Law—Part 1," *Express Tribune*, November 8, 2019, https://tribune.com.pk/article/90571/understanding-pakistans-sexual-harassment-law-part-1.

23. Ayesha Khan and Sana Naqvi, "Dilemmas of Representation: Women in Pakistan's Assemblies," *Asian Affairs* 51, no. 2 (2020): 286–306, www.tandfonline.com/doi/pdf/10.1080/03068374.2020.1748414. "PML-F's Abbasi 'Forgives' MPA Behind Misogynistic Remarks," *Dawn*, January 23, 2017, www.dawn.com/news/1310237.

24. Data from the International Labour Organization, "Labor Force Participation Rate, Female (% of Female Population Ages 15+) (Modeled ILO Estimate)—Pakistan," World Bank, accessed October 25, 2020, https://data.worldbank.org/indicator/SL.TLF.CACT.FE.ZS?locations=PK. David Cuberes and Marc Teignier, "Gender Inequality and Economic Growth: A Critical Review," *Journal of International Development* 26, no. 2 (2014): 260–276, cited in Ferhan Salman, "Pakistan," in *Women, Work, and Economic Growth: Leveling the Playing Field*, ed. Kalpana Kochhar, Sonali Jain-Chandra, and Monique Newiak, International Monetary Fund, 2017, www.elibrary.imf.org/view/IMF071/23146-9781513516103/23146-9781513516103/ch08b.xml#ch08Bref6. Sakiko Tanaka and Maricor Muzones, "Policy Brief on Female Labor Force Participation in Pakistan," Asian Development Bank, 2016, www.adb.org/publications/policy-brief-female-labor-force-participation-pakistan. Meighan Stone, "Pakistan's Imran Khan Promises End to Discriminatory Laws," Council on Foreign Relations, August 1, 2018, www.cfr.org/blog/pakistans-imran-khan-promises-end-discriminatory-laws.

25. Hamna Zubair, in interview with Meighan Stone, September 21, 2020. Unless otherwise attributed, all quotations from Hamna Zubair throughout this chapter come from this interview.

26. Shiza Malik, "Pakistan's #MeToo Movement Gains Momentum as Teachers at Elite Girls School Face Abuse Accusations," Vice India, July 13, 2020, www.vice.com/en/article/7kpwk4/pakistans-me-too-movement-gains-momentum-as-teachers-at-elite-girls-school-face-abuse-accusations.

27. Malik, "Pakistan's #MeToo Movement Gains Momentum." Zuha Siddiqui, "Harassment Scandal at Girls' School Spurs Pakistan #MeToo Movement," *The National*, July 24, 2020, www.thenationalnews.com/world/asia/harassment-scandal-at-girls-school-spurs-pakistan-metoo-movement-1.1053732. Xari Jalil, "Harassment Scandal at School in Lahore Raises Alarm over Safety," *Dawn*, June 30, 2020, www.dawn.com/news/1565976.

28. Jalil, "Harassment Scandal at School in Lahore Raises Alarm over Safety."

29. Meesha Shafi (@itsmeeshashafi), "Proud to see all the women/girls break their silence," Twitter, June 30, 2020, https://twitter.com/itsmeeshashafi/status/1277821973259792384.

Shahab Omer, "LGS Suspends Principal, Administrator and Coordinator over Sexual Harassment Scandal," *Pakistan Today*, June 30, 2020, www.pressreader.com/pakistan/pakistan-today-lahore/20200701/281621012610809. Murad Raas (@DrMuradPTI), "I will deal with the case in Lahore Grammar School," Twitter, June 30, 2020, https://twitter.com/DrMuradPTI/status/1277896899694153728.

30. "Lahore Schools Harassment Scandal: Action Can't Be Taken Without Written Complaint, Says Minister," *News International*, July 4, 2020, www.thenews.com.pk/print/681800-lahore-schools-harassment-scandal-action-can-t-be-taken-without-written-complaint-says-minister.

31. Shiza Malik, in interviews with Meighan Stone, September 21, 2020, and October 1, 2020. Unless otherwise attributed, all quotations from Shiza Malik throughout this chapter come from these interviews.

32. Jalil, "Harassment Scandal at School in Lahore Raises Alarm over Safety."

33. Jalil, "Harassment Scandal at School in Lahore Raises Alarm over Safety."

34. Siddiqui, "Harassment Scandal at Girls' School Spurs Pakistan #MeToo Movement."

35. Siddiqui, "Harassment Scandal at Girls' School Spurs Pakistan #MeToo Movement."

36. Salman Masood and Mike Ives, "Rapes of Woman and 5-Year-Old Fuel Outrage in Pakistan," *New York Times*, September 11, 2020, www.nytimes.com/2020/09/11/world/asia/pakistan-rape-5-year-old-lahore-karachi.html. "Prime Suspect in Lahore Motorway Gang-Rape Case Abid Malhi Arrested in Major Breakthrough," *News International*, October 12, 2020, www.thenews.com.pk/latest/728367-prime-suspect-in-lahore-motorway-gang-rape-case-abid-ali-arrested. "Pakistan Outcry over Police Victim-Blaming of Gang-Raped Mother," BBC, September 19, 2020, www.bbc.com/news/world-asia-54186609. AFP, "Pakistani Police Chief Sparks Outrage by Blaming Gang-Rape Victim," *The National*, September 11, 2020, www.thenationalnews.com/world/asia/pakistani-police-chief-sparks-outrage-by-blaming-gang-rape-victim-1.1076293. "Tariq Jameel's Comments on Motorway Gang-Rape Incident Create Controversy," *Daily Times*, September 19, 2020, https://dailytimes.com.pk/668441/tariq-jameels-comments-on-motorway-gang-rape-incident-create-controversy/.

37. Shireen Mazari (@ShireenMazari1), "For an officer to effectively blame," Twitter, September 10, 2020, https://twitter.com/ShireenMazari1/status/1304018447395819522.

38. "Pakistan PM Imran Khan Calls for 'Chemical Castration' of Rapists," Al Jazeera, September 14, 2020, www.aljazeera.com/news/2020/9/14/pakistan-pm-imran-khan-calls-for-chemical-castration-of-rapists. Photo by Fareed Khan, AP, cited in Maria Usman, "Pakistan's Prime Minister Calls for Rapists to Be Hanged or Castrated After Mother Gang-Raped," CBS News, September 16, 2020, www.cbsnews.com/news/pakistan-prime-minister-rapists-hanged-castrated-after-gang-rape/.

39. Saira Asher, "Aurat March: Pakistani Women Face Violent Threats Ahead of Rally," BBC, March 7, 2020, www.bbc.com/news/world-asia-51748152.

40. Mehr Tarar, "Aurat March of Pakistan: The Decoding of Mera Jism Meri Marzi or My Body, My Choice," *Gulf News*, March 5, 2020, https://gulfnews.com/world/asia/pakistan/aurat-march-of-pakistan-the-decoding-of-mera-jism-meri-marzi-or-my-body-my-choice-1.1583397878153. Shehryar Warraich, "How Dare They Demand?," *News International*, March 8, 2020, www.thenews.com.pk/tns/detail/624737-how-dare-they. Talal Raza, "Understanding Hatred Against #Aurat March in Pa-

kistan," Digital Rights Monitor, March 15, 2019, www.digitalrightsmonitor.pk /understanding-hatred-against-aurat-march-in-pakistan/.

41. Sarah Price, "Aurat March 2019: Her Blues Are Everyone's Jazz," *Express Tribune*, March 9, 2019, https://tribune.com.pk/story/1926213/aurat-march-2019-blues-everyones -jazz. Mehek Saeed, "Aurat March 2018: Freedom over Fear," *News International*, March 2018, www.thenews.com.pk/magazine/instep-today/290411-aurat-march-2018-freedom-over-fear.

42. Saeed, "Aurat March 2018."

43. Salman Zafar, "'Khud Khana Garam Karlo': Pakistani Men's Kryptonite," *Express Tribune*, March 16, 2018, https://tribune.com.pk/article/64936/khud-khana -garam-karlo-pakistani-mens-kryptonite.

44. Shehzil Malik, in interview with Meighan Stone, October 2, 2020. Unless otherwise attributed, all quotations from Shehzil Malik throughout this chapter come from this interview.

45. AFP, "AFP Fact Checks Viral Image of TV Anchor with 'Controversial' Placard at Aurat March," *Express Tribune*, March 10, 2020, https://tribune.com.pk/story/2173377/1 -afp-fact-checks-viral-image-tv-anchor-controversial-placard-aurat-march. Hyra Basit, "Aurat March Backlash and the Continuum of Misogyny from the Street to Facebook Pages," Digital Rights Foundation, March 22, 2018, https://digitalrightsfoundation.pk /aurat-march-backlash-and-the-continuum-of-misogyny-from-the-street-to-facebook-pages/.

46. "Aurat March 2019 Set to Take Place in Major Cities of Pakistan Today," *The Nation* (Pakistan), March 8, 2019, https://nation.com.pk/08-Mar-2019/aurat-march-2019-to-be-held-in -pakistans-major-cities-today. Price, "Aurat March 2019." Imran Gobal, "'Aurat March' Held Nationwide to Mark International Women's Day," *Dawn*, March 8, 2020, www.dawn.com /news/1539318/aurat-march-held-nationwide-to-mark-international-womens-day.

47. Xari Jalil, "Aurat March Displays Street Power," *Dawn*, March 9, 2019, www.dawn .com/news/1468486/aurat-march-displays-street-power.

48. Jalil, "Aurat March Displays Street Power."

49. Sher Ali Khalti, "PCSW Chairperson Terminated," *News International*, May 25, 2019, www.thenews.com.pk/print/475917-pcsw-chairperson-terminated. Jamshed Kazi (@ JKaziunwomen), "Dismayed to hear of the sudden removal of @fauziaviqar as Chairperson," Twitter, May 24, 2019, https://twitter.com/JKaziunwomen/status/1131990701883961344. "PCSW Head's Removal Draws Activists' Ire," *Dawn*, May 26, 2019, www.dawn.com /news/1484578/pcsw-heads-removal-draws-activists-ire.

50. "PCSW Head's Removal Draws Activists' Ire."

51. Rana Bilal, "LHC Dismisses Meesha Shafi's Appeal in Harassment Case Against Ali Zafar," *Dawn*, October 11, 2019, www.dawn.com/news/1510271/lhc-dismisses -meesha-shafis-appeal-in-harassment-case-against-ali-zafar.

52. Sabrina Toppa, "They Accused a Pakistani Megastar of Sexual Harassment. Then They Were Sued for Defamation," *Time*, October 20, 2020, https://time.com/5900710 /pakistan-me-too-movement-lawsuits/. "Unreasonable Bill," editorial, *Dawn*, September 17, 2020, www.dawn.com/news/1580114.

53. Humna Raza (@HumnaRaza), Twitter, since deleted, October 9, 2020, https:// twitter.com/HumnaRaza/status/1314498436876689408.

54. "UN Women, KP Ombudsperson Launch Toolkit to Eliminate Workplace Harassment," *Dawn*, June 27, 2020, www.dawn.com/news/1565510/un-women -kp-ombudsperson-launch-toolkit-to-eliminate-workplace-harassment. Habib Asgher

and Saman Ahsan, "Working Together to Fight Sexual Harassment and Abuse in the Workplace with Provincial Offices of Ombudsperson," UN Women, August 16, 2020, https://asiapacific.unwomen.org/en/news-and-events/stories/2020/08/working-together-to-fight-sexual-harassment-and-abuse-in-the-workplace.

55. K. Alan Kronstadt, "Pakistan-U.S. Relations," Congressional Research Service, July 15, 2019, https://crsreports.congress.gov/product/pdf/IF/IF11270. See also "Foreign Aid Explorer," USAID, March 1, 2021, https://explorer.usaid.gov/aid-trends.html.

56. "Pakistan to Remain on Global Terror Financing 'Grey' List," Al Jazeera, October 23, 2020, www.aljazeera.com/news/2020/10/23/pakistan-to-remain-on-global-terror-financing-grey-list.

57. "Five Questions on #MeToo in Pakistan: Nighat Dad."

58. "Five Questions on #MeToo in Pakistan: Nighat Dad."

59. *Global Gender Gap Report 2017*, World Economic Forum, 2017, 11, www3.weforum.org/docs/WEF_GGGR_2017.pdf.

60. Aurat March, "Aurat March Demand 1—End sexual harassment and violence in schools and homes," Facebook, March 7, 2020, www.facebook.com/AuratMarch Karachi/photos/a.2662852043947458/2662852160614113. Sarah Price, Yumna Aftab, and Asfa Sultan, "#AuratMarch2020: Celebrities Use Their Influence for the Greater Good," *Express Tribune*, March 9, 2020, https://tribune.com.pk/story/2172383/auratmarch2020-celebrities-use-influence-greater-good.

61. Wajih Ahmad Sheikh, "LHC Moved for Permanent Ban on Aurat March," *Dawn*, February 25, 2020, www.dawn.com/news/1536477/lhc-moved-for-permanent-ban-on-aurat-march. "IHC Rejects Petition Seeking Ban on Aurat March," *Express Tribune*, March 6, 2020, https://tribune.com.pk/story/2170450/1-ihc-reserves-verdict-maintainability-petition-aurat-march. "Petition Against the Upcoming Aurat March Filed by a Woman," *Daily Times*, February 29, 2020, https://dailytimes.com.pk/567395/petition-against-the-upcoming-aurat-march-filed-by-a-woman/. Alia Chughtai, "Pakistan's Women's March: Shaking Patriarchy 'to Its Core,'" Al Jazeera, March 8, 2020, www.aljazeera.com/features/2020/3/8/pakistans-womens-march-shaking-patriarchy-to-its-core.

62. Aisha Mahmood, "Extremist Mob Vandalises Mural of Two Women Painted by Aurat March Organizers," *Business Recorder*, March 4, 2020, www.brecorder.com/news/576922/lal-masjid-clerics-vandalise-mural-of-two-women-painted-by-aurat-march-organizers. Tooba Syed (@Tooba_SD), "Our existence, our politics, our art, our labour will not be rendered invisible by a handful of right wing goons," Twitter, March 3, 2020, https://twitter.com/Tooba_Sd/status/1234890242383020032.

63. Shiza Malik, in interview with Meighan Stone, October 1, 2020. Mariam Azeem, "The Aurat March and Pakistan's Struggle for Women's Rights," International Center on Nonviolent Conflict, August 4, 2020, www.nonviolent-conflict.org/blog_post/the-aurat-march-and-pakistans-struggle-for-womens-rights/. "Aurat March: Thousands Hit Streets for Gender Equality," *Express Tribune*, March 8, 2020, https://tribune.com.pk/story/2171752/aurat-march-held-across-pakistan-mark-international-womens-day. Aurat Azadi March Islamabad (@AuratAzadiMarch), "Mullahs are stoning the participants of #AuratAzadiMarch," Twitter, March 8, 2020, https://twitter.com/AuratAzadiMarch/status/1236633372329467904.

64. Imran Gabol et al., "'Aurat March' Held Nationwide to Mark International Women's Day," *Dawn*, March 8, 2020, www.dawn.com/news/1539318/aurat-march-held-nation wide-to-mark-international-womens-day. "Aurat March: Thousands Hit Streets."

65. Munizae Jahangir (@MunizaeJahangir), "#AuratAzadiMarch in Lahore marches on, Asma Jahangir legal aid cell chanting slogans," Twitter, March 8, 2020, https://twitter.com /MunizaeJahangir/status/1236556942912487424. "Fauzia Viqar at Aurat March 2020 in Lahore," Voicepk.net, March 8, 2020, video, www.youtube.com/watch?v=Qe6ONZWR-bY. Sadaf Alvi (@TheGrumpyDoctor), "#AuratAzadiMarch," Twitter, March 8, 2020, https://twitter.com/TheGrumpyDoctor/status/1236571879634337793. Aurat March Lahore (@AuratMarch), "Jagi Jagi Aurat Jagi," Twitter, March 8, 2020, https://twitter.com /AuratMarch/status/1236602782246940672.

Chapter Six. Sweden

1. Jodi Kantor and Megan Twohey, "Harvey Weinstein Paid Off Sexual Harassment Accusers for Decades," *New York Times*, October 5, 2017, www.nytimes.com/2017/10/05 /us/harvey-weinstein-harassment-allegations.html. Jenny Nordberg, "Yes, It Happens in Sweden, #Too," *New York Times*, December 15, 2017, www.nytimes.com/2017/12/15/opinion /sunday/sweden-sexual-harassment-assault.html.

2. "Cissi Wallin: Därför outade jag Fredrik Virtanen (fälld artikel)" [Cissi Wallin: That's why I outed Fredrik Virtanen (article dropped)], *Resumé*, November 24, 2017, www.resume .se/insikt/helgintervjuer/cissi-wallin-darfor-outade-jag-fredrik-virtanen-falld-artikel/.

3. Cissi Wallin (@CissiWallin), "Den mäktige medieman som drogade och våldtog mig 2006 heter Fredrik Virtanen," Instagram, October 16, 2017, www.instagram.com/p /BaT0d-bHRTr/.

4. "Cissi Wallin i unik intervju om Virtanen: Hans skydd är att vara i förnekelse," *SVT Nyheter*, August 27, 2018, www.svt.se/nyheter/inrikes/cissi-wallin-i-unik-intervju -om-virtanen-hans-skydd-ar-att-vara-i-fornekelse.

5. Alyssa Milano (@Alyssa_Milano), "If you've been sexually harassed or assaulted write 'me too' as a reply to this tweet," Twitter, October 15, 2017, https://twitter.com /Alyssa_Milano/status/919659438700670976.

6. Cissi Wallin (@CissiWallin), "The powerful media man," Instagram, October 16, 2017, www.instagram.com/p/BaT0d-bHRTr/?hl=en.

7. "A Feminist Government," Government Offices of Sweden, accessed July 15, 2020, www.government.se/government-policy/a-feminist-government. Ricardo Hausmann, Laura D. Tyson, and Saadia Zahidi, *Global Gender Gap Report 2006*, World Economic Forum, November 23, 2006, www.weforum.org/reports/global-gender-gap-report-2006.

8. Sofia Helin, interviewed by Rachel Vogelstein, December 20, 2019. Unless otherwise attributed, all quotations from Sofia Helin in this chapter come from these interviews.

9. Jenny Nordberg, "Yes, It Happens in Sweden, #Too."

10. Ida Östensson, interviewed by Rachel Vogelstein, November 13, 2019. Unless otherwise attributed, all quotations from Ida Östensson in this chapter come from this interview. She also provided narrative about some of the events recounted in the chapter.

11. Government Offices of Sweden, "Consent: The Basic Requirement of New Sexual Offence Legislation," press statement, April 26, 2018, www.government .se/press-releases/2018/04/consent—the-basic-requirement-of-new-sexual-offence -legislation/.

12. Malena Rydell, interviewed by Rachel Vogelstein, November 15, 2019. Unless otherwise attributed, all quotations from Malena Rydell in this chapter come from this interview. She also provided narrative about some of the events recounted in the chapter.

13. E. Hallhagen and M. Rydell. "Därför blev #tystnadtagning så stort" [Why #tystnad tagning became so large], *Svenska Dagbladet*, November 12, 2017, www.svd.se/darfor-blev -tystnadtagning-sa-stort/av/malena-rydell. "Välkomment till Svenska Dagbladet" [Welcome to a new year with SvD], *Svenska Dagbladet*, accessed July 15, 2020, https://kundservice.svd .se/omsvd/.

14. TT, "Löfven: Här måste det göras något riktigt radikalt" [Löfven: Something really radical must be done here], *Svenska Dagbladet*, November 9, 2017, www.svd.se /stefan-lofven-har-maste-det-goras-nagot-riktigt-radikalt.

15. Caroline Snellman, interviewed by Rachel Vogelstein, November 14, 2019. Unless otherwise attributed, all quotations from Caroline Snellman in this chapter come from this interview.

16. E. Hallhagen and M. Rydell, "Det manliga 'geniet' får bete sig som ett svin" [The male "genius" may behave like a pig], *Svenska Dagbladet*, November 18, 2017, www.svd.se /det-manliga-geniet-far-bete-sig-som-ett-svin.

17. Hillevi Ganetz, Karin Hansson, Maria Sandgren, and Malin Sveningsson, "Legitimising a Feminist Agenda: The #metoo Petitions in Sweden 2017–2018," *Nordic Journal of Media Studies* 2, no. 1 (2020): 121–132, https://doi.org/10.2478/njms-2020-0011.

18. Sofia Börjesson, "Metoo-uppropens 7 krav till jämställdhetsminister Åsa Regnér" [MeToo's 7 demands to Minister for Gender Equality Åsa Regnér], *Femina*, March 6, 2018, www .femina.se/livsstil/metoo-uppropens-7-krav-till-jamstalldhetsminister-asa-regnr/711952.

19. Elin Andersson, interviewed by Rachel Vogelstein, November 14, 2019. Unless otherwise attributed, all quotations from Elin Andersson in this chapter come from this interview.

20. "Lydia" (anonymous), interviewed by Rachel Vogelstein, January 15, 2020. Unless otherwise attributed, all quotations from Lydia in this chapter, as well as narrative regarding her experiences, come from this interview.

21. Karis Hustad, "Sweden's #Teknisktfel Movement Exposes Sexual Harassment in the Tech Industry," *The World*, June 11, 2018, www.pri.org/stories/2018-06-11 /swedens-teknisktfel-movement-exposes-sexual-harassment-tech-industry.

22. "Så skriver utländska medier om svenska #metoo" [This is how foreign media write about Swedish #metoo], *Dagens Nyheter*, November 24, 2018, www.dn.se/nyheter/varlden /sa-skriver-utlandska-medier-om-svenska-metoo/.

23. Matilda Gustavsson, interviewed by Rachel Vogelstein, December 11, 2019. Unless otherwise attributed, all quotations from Matilda Gustavsson in this chapter come from this interview.

24. Evelyn Jones and Matilda Voss Gustavsson, "Man with Swedish Academy Ties Accused of Sexual Assault," *Dagens Nyheter*, November 21, 2017, www.dn.se /kultur-noje/18-kvinnor-kulturprofil-har-utsatt-oss-for-overgrepp/.

25. Christina Anderson, "In Nobel Scandal, a Man Is Accused of Sexual Misconduct. A Woman Takes the Fall," *New York Times*, April 12, 2018, www.nytimes.com/2018/04/12 /world/europe/sara-danius-swedish-nobel-scandal.html. Jon Henly, "Sexual Abuse Scandal Engulfs Nobel Literature Prize Body," *The Guardian*, April 13, 2018, www.theguardian .com/world/2018/apr/12/sara-danius-resigns-swedish-academy-nobel-prizes.

26. Andrew Brown, "The Ugly Scandal That Cancelled the Nobel Prize," *The Guardian*, July 17, 2018, www.theguardian.com/news/2018/jul/17/the-ugly-scandal

-that-cancelled-the-nobel-prize-in-literature. Klas Östergren, interviewed by Rachel Vogelstein, January 21, 2020.

27. Anderson, "In Nobel Scandal, a Man Is Accused of Sexual Misconduct."

28. David Keaton and Jan Olson, "Outrage in Sweden After Two Women Are Pressured to Leave Nobel Group," *Bloomberg Press*, April 13, 2018, www .bloomberg.com/news/articles/2018-04-13/swedish-culture-minister-backs-ex-nobel -body-head. "Litteratursverige om Nobelpriset: Svenska Akademien har missbrukat sitt förtroende," *Dagens Nyheter*, May 4, 2018, www.dn.se/kultur-noje/litteratursverige -om-nobelpriset-svenska-akademien-har-missbrukat-sitt-fortroende/.

29. Erin Reimel, "This Is the Important Reason Women in Sweden Are Wearing Pussy-Bow Blouses," *Glamour*, April 14, 2018, www.glamour.com/story/this-is-the -important-reason-women-in-sweden-are-wearing-pussybow-blouses.

30. Nobel Foundation, "The Nobel Foundation Supports the Swedish Academy's Decision to Postpone the Nobel Prize in Literature," press release, May 4, 2018, http://meltwater .pressify.io/publication/5aec06e7386baf00045db476/552bd85dccc8e20c00e7f979.

31. Isaac Stanley-Becker, "Famed Opera Singer Blames #Metoo for Her Husband's Suicide: 'You Can Break a Person,'" *Washington Post*, July 30, 2018, www.washingtonpost.com /news/morning-mix/wp/2018/07/30/famed-swedish-opera-singer-blames-metoo-for-her -husbands-suicide-you-can-break-a-person/.

32. Andrew Brown, "Public Fights, Resignations and a Sex Scandal: What's Going On with the Nobel Prize?," *The Guardian*, April 14, 2018, www.theguardian.com/books/2018 /apr/14/nobel-prize-swedish-academy.

33. Catherine Edwards, "Sweden in Focus: One Year on, What Did #Metoo Achieve in Sweden?," *The Local*, December 10, 2018, www.thelocal.se/20181210 /one-year-on-what-did-metoo-achieve-in-sweden.

34. Government of Sweden, Ministry of Foreign Affairs, "Strategy for Sweden's Development Cooperation for Global Gender Equality and Women's and Girls' Rights 2018–2022," November 20, 2018, www.government.se/4acfa2/contentassets/3e6be18734b94807b98 a7b4d4c970d81/strategygenderequalityandwomensrights-002.pdf.

35. Kristina Lindh, "Cissi Wallin: Varit jobbigt även för mitt samvete," *Svenska Dagbladet*, March 7, 2019, www.svd.se/cissi-wallin-varit-jobbigt-aven-for-mitt-samvete.

36. "Uppdrag granskning #metoo och Fredrik Virtanen," SVT Play, September 5, 2018, video, www.youtube.com/watch?v=BmXjlgM1qXY.

37. "Swedish #MeToo Activist Told to Pay Damages to Man She Accused of Rape," *The Local*, December 9, 2019, www.thelocal.se/20191209/swedish-metoo-activist-told-to-pay -damages-to-man-she-accused-of-rape.

38. Fredrik Virtanen, *Utan Nåd* (Oslo: Gloria Forlag AS, 2019).

39. Cissi Wallin, *Allt som var mitt: Historien som inte får berättas* [All that was mine: The story that must not be told] (Cissi Wallin Produktion AB, 2020), 117–202. Lindh, "Cissi Wallin: Varit jobbigt även för mitt samvete."

Chapter Seven. Global Agenda

1. Michelle Bachelet, interviewed by Rachel Vogelstein and Meighan Stone, April 23, 2020. Unless otherwise attributed, all quotes from Michelle Bachelet in this chapter come from this interview.

2. Omar Rashid, "Unnao rape survivor accident: BJP MLA Kuldeep Singh Sengar among 10 named in FIR," *The Hindu*, July 29, 2019, www.thehindu.com/news/national /unnao-rape-survivor-accident-bjp-mla-kuldeep-singh-sengar-among-10-named-in-fir /article28748925.ece. Elian Peltier, "Former U.K. Lawmaker Jailed for 2 Years in Sexual Assaults," *New York Times*, September 15, 2020, www.nytimes.com/2020/09/15/world /europe/charlie-elphicke-sexual-assault-prison.html.

3. Dan Bilefsky and Elian Peltier, "France Considers Fines for Catcalls as Women Speak Out on Harassment," *New York Times*, October 17, 2017, www.nytimes.com/2017/10/17 /world/europe/france-harassment-twitter-weinstein.html?module=inline. Moroccan Violence Against Women Bill, Law no. 103-13, www.moroccoworldnews.com/2018/04/244641 /unenglish-translation-of-moroccos-law-103-13-on-elimination-of-violence-against -women/. Ethiopian Labour Proclamation No. 377/2003, www.ilo.org/dyn/travail /docs/327/Proclamation. See also *Ethiopia's Compliance with the Convention on the Elimination of All Forms of Discrimination Against Women*, submitted by the Advocates for Human Rights, January 2019, www.theadvocatesforhumanrights.org/uploads/ethiopia_tahr _cedaw_final_4.pdf.

4. Adriana Carranca, "The Women-Led Opposition to Brazil's Far-Right Leader," *The Atlantic*, November 2, 2018, www.theatlantic.com/international/archive/2018/11/bra zil-women-bolsonaro-haddad-election/574792/. "Record Number of Women on the Ballot in Lebanon's First Parliamentary Elections Since 2009," UN Women, May 23, 2018, www.unwomen.org/en/news/stories/2018/5/news-record-number-of-women-on-the-ballot -in-lebanon. Carrie Kahn, "In Mexico's Elections, Women Are Running in Unprecedented Numbers," National Public Radio, June 30, 2018, www.npr.org/2018/06/30/624055891 /in-mexicos-elections-women-are-running-in-unprecedented-numbers. Drew Desilver, "A Record Number of Women Will Be Serving in the New Congress," Pew Research Center, December 18, 2018, www.pewresearch.org/fact-tank/2018/12/18/record-number-wom en-in-congress/. Leslie Shapiro et al., "Women Running for Office: Which Ones Won the 2018 Midterms," *Washington Post*, November 6, 2018, www.washingtonpost.com/graph ics/2018/politics/women-congress-governor/. Grace Sparks, "A Record Number of Women Are Running for Senate, but Percentage Is Still Low," CNN Politics, May 24, 2018, www .cnn.com/2018/05/24/politics/record-women-running-for-senate-office-election-2018/index .html. "Sri Lanka Vote: New Law Sees More Women Standing," Al Jazeera, February 10, 2018, www.aljazeera.com/news/2018/2/10/sri-lanka-vote-new-law-sees-more-women-standing.

5. International Labour Organization C190—Violence and Harassment Convention, 2019 (No. 190), www.ilo.org/dyn/normlex/en/f?p=NORMLEXPUB:12100:0:NO:P12100 _ILO_CODE:C190. See also *A Quantum Leap for Gender Equality, for a Better Future of Work for All*, International Labour Organization, 2019, www.ilo.org/wcmsp5/groups /public/---dgreports/---dcomm/---publ/documents/publication/wcms_674831.pdf. "Uruguay First to Ratify ILO Violence and Harassment Convention," International Labour Organization, June 15, 2020, www.ilo.org/global/about-the-ilo/newsroom/news /WCMS_747820/lang--en/index.htm.

6. Haleh Esfandiari, *Reconstructed Lives: Women and Iran's Islamic Revolution* (Princeton, NJ: Woodrow Wilson Center Press, 1997), 94–125. Sergey Davydov, *Internet in Russia: A Study of the Runet and Its Impact on Social Life* (Zurich: Springer International Publishing, 2020), 83–100. Hiba Zayadin (@HZayadin), "In a remarkable show of courage, Saudi

women are taking to Twitter to share their experiences with sexual harassment and to demand an end to the discriminatory male guardianship system," Twitter, April 15, 2020, https:// twitter.com/hzayadin/status/1250344414448209927. See also "Saudi Women Are Publicly Calling Out Their Sexual Harassers Online," *New Arab*, April 15, 2020, https://english .alaraby.co.uk/english/news/2020/4/15/saudi-women-expose-sexual-harassers-on-twitter.

7. Plan International, *Free to Be Online?: A Report on Girl's and Young Women's Experiences of Online Harassment*, 2020, https://plan-international.org/publications/freetobe online. "Amnesty reveals alarming impact of online abuse against women," Amnesty International, November 20, 2017, www.amnesty.org/en/latest/news/2017/11/amnesty-reveals -alarming-impact-of-online-abuse-against-women. Sepideh Modrek and Bozhidar Chakalov, "The #MeToo Movement in the United States: Text Analysis of Early Twitter Conversations," *Journal of Medical Internet Research* 21, no. 9 (September 2019), www.ncbi.nlm.nih .gov/pmc/articles/PMC6751092/. See also K. Mendes, J. Ringrose, and J. Keller, "#MeToo and the Promise and Pitfalls of Challenging Rape Culture Through Digital Feminist Activism," *European Journal of Women's Studies* 25, no. 2 (April 29, 2018): 236–246.

8. "Dep. Jair Bolsonaro (PP) Counters Dep. Maria do Rosário on Human Rights Discourse, Recorded by TV Câmara," December 9, 2014, video, www.youtube.com /watch?v=5bquCfAxMDg&feature=emb_title. See also Charlotte Alter, "Brazilian Politician Tells Congresswoman She's 'Not Worthy' of Sexual Assault," *Time*, December 11, 2014, https://time.com/3630922/brazil-politics-congresswoman-rape-comments/. Peter Baker and Neil Vigdor, "'She's Not My Type': Accused Again of Sexual Assault, Trump Resorts to Old Insult," *New York Times*, June 24, 2019, www.nytimes.com/2019/06/24/us/politics /jean-carroll-trump.html. Criminal Code of the Russian Federation, Bill No. 26265-7, Amending Article 116, January 25, 2017, www.loc.gov/law/help/domestic-violence/russia .php. See also "Russia: Bill to Decriminalize Domestic Violence," Human Rights Watch, updated February 7, 2017, www.hrw.org/news/2017/01/23/russia-bill-decriminalize -domestic-violence. See also Shep Melnik, "Analyzing the Department of Education's Final Title IX Rules on Sexual Misconduct," Brookings Institution, June 11, 2020, www.brookings .edu/research/analyzing-the-department-of-educations-final-title-ix-rules-on-sexual-mis conduct/.

9. Jodi Kantor, interviewed by Rachel Vogelstein and Meighan Stone, August 28, 2020. Unless otherwise attributed, all quotes from Jodi Kantor in this chapter come from this interview.

10. Tarana Burke, interviewed by Rachel Vogelstein and Meighan Stone, May 28, 2020. Unless otherwise attributed, all quotes from Tarana Burke in this chapter come from this interview.

11. "The Survivors' Agenda," SurvivorsAgenda.org, accessed October 28, 2020, https:// survivorsagenda.org/agenda/.

12. Ellen Johnson Sirleaf, interviewed by Rachel Vogelstein and Meighan Stone, August 25, 2020. Tina Tchen, interviewed by Rachel Vogelstein and Meighan Stone, November 4, 2019. Unless otherwise attributed, all quotes from Ellen Johnson Sirleaf and Tina Tchen in this chapter come from these interviews.

13. Julia Gillard, interviewed by Rachel Vogelstein and Meighan Stone, March 24, 2020. Unless otherwise attributed, all quotes from Julia Gillard in this chapter come from this interview.

14. Amina Mohammed, interviewed by Rachel Vogelstein and Meighan Stone, October 13, 2020. Unless otherwise attributed, all quotes from Amina Mohammed in this chapter come from this interview.

15. Rebecca Traister, interviewed by Rachel Vogelstein and Meighan Stone, January 7, 2020. Unless otherwise attributed, all quotes from Rebecca Traister in this chapter come from this interview.

16. Hillary Rodham Clinton, "Power Shortage," *The Atlantic*, October 2020, www .theatlantic.com/magazine/archive/2020/10/hillary-clinton-womens-rights/615463/.

17. Phumzile Mlambo-Ngcuka, interviewed by Rachel Vogelstein and Meighan Stone, October 5, 2020. Unless otherwise attributed, all quotes from Phumzile Mlambo-Ngcuka in this chapter come from this interview. Hilary Weaver, "Golden Globes 2018: Black Dresses, Time's Up Pins, Activist Plus-Ones, and Everything Else You Need to Know," *Vanity Fair*, January 7, 2018, www.vanityfair.com/style/2018/01/golden-globes-2018-red -carpet-times-up. *Time* Staff, "700,000 Female Farmworkers Say They Stand with Hollywood Actors Against Sexual Assault," *Time*, November 10, 2017, https://time.com /5018813/farmworkers-solidarity-hollywood-sexual-assault/.

18. *Handbook: Sweden's Feminist Foreign Policy*, Government of Sweden, Ministry of Foreign Affairs, August 23, 2018, www.government.se/4ae557/contentassets/fc115607 a4ad4bca913cd8d11c2339dc/handbook---swedens-feminist-foreign-policy.pdf. See also Rachel Vogelstein, "Five Questions on Feminist Foreign Policy: Margot Wallström," Council on Foreign Relations, November 18, 2019, www.cfr.org/blog/five-questions-feminist -foreign-policy-margot-wallstrom. Rachel Vogelstein and Alexandra Bro, "Sweden's Feminist Foreign Policy, Long May It Reign," *Foreign Policy*, January 30, 2019, https://foreign policy.com/2019/01/30/sweden-feminist-foreignpolicy/.

19. Judith G. Greenberg, Martha Minow, and Dorothy E. Roberts, *Women and the Law* (New York: Foundation Press, 2004). See also Rosemarie Tong, *Women, Sex, and the Law* (Totowa, NJ: Rowman and Allanheld, 1984), and Dacher Keltner, "Sex, Power, and the Systems That Enable Men Like Harvey Weinstein," *Harvard Business Review*, October 13, 2017, https://hbr.org/2017/10/sex-power-and-the-systems-that-enable-men-like-harvey-weinstein.

20. *Women, Business, and the Law 2020*, World Bank Group, 2020, https://openknowl edge.worldbank.org/bitstream/handle/10986/32639/9781464815324.pdf. *The World's Shame: The Global Rape Epidemic*, Equality Now, February 2017, https://d3n8a8pro7vhmx .cloudfront.net/equalitynow/pages/308/attachments/original/1527599090/EqualityNow RapeLawReport2017_Single_Pages_0.pdf?1527599090. *Global Study on Homicide, Gender-Related Killing of Women and Girls*, United Nations Office on Drugs and Crime, 2019, www.unodc.org/documents/data-and-analysis/gsh/Booklet_5.pdf.

21. *The World's Shame: The Global Rape Epidemic*. M. Ilyas Khan, "Pakistan Court Outlaws 'Virginity Tests,'" BBC News, January 5, 2021, www.bbc.com/news /world-asia-55541447.

22. Staff, "Statistics on Rape in India and Some Well-Known Cases," Reuters, December 16, 2019, www.reuters.com/article/us-india-rape-factbox/statistics-on-rape-in-india -and-some-well-known-cases-idUSKBN1YA0UV. "The Criminal Justice System: Statistics," RAINN, accessed January 8, 2021, www.rainn.org/statistics/criminal-justice-system. "Rape Poll Report," NOIPolls, July 25, 2019, https://noi-polls.com/noipolls-rape-poll-report/.

23. TIME'S UP Legal Defense Fund, accessed January 8, 2021, https://timesup foundation.org/work/times-up-legal-defense-fund/.

24. Project Restore, accessed January 8, 2021, www.projectrestore.nz/.

25. Global Survivors Fund, accessed January 8, 2021, www.globalsurvivorsfund.org/. Margot Wallström, interviewed by Rachel Vogelstein and Meighan Stone, March 20, 2020. Unless otherwise attributed, all quotes from Margot Wallström in this chapter come from this interview.

26. South Africa Commission of Truth and Reconciliation, Promotion of National Unity and Reconciliation Act, No. 34 of 1995 (1995–2002), https://ihl-databases.icrc.org /applic/ihl/ihl-nat.nsf/0/AF494D2C3E5803FEC1256AF400524BE5. See also United States Institute of Peace, Truth Commission: South Africa, accessed January 8, 2021, www.usip .org/publications/1995/12/truth-commission-south-africa.

27. *Women, Business, and the Law 2020*.

28. Malala Yousafzai, interviewed by Rachel Vogelstein and Meighan Stone, October 6, 2020. Unless otherwise attributed, all quotes from Malala Yousafzai in this chapter come from this interview.

29. Rachel Vogelstein et al., "Women and the Law: Leveling the Global Economic Playing Field," Council on Foreign Relations, October 2018, www.cfr.org/report/women-and -law. See also "Women's Workplace Equality Index," Council on Foreign Relations, 2020, www.cfr.org/legal-barriers/, and *Women, Business and the Law 2018*, World Bank, 2018, openknowledge.worldbank.org/handle/10986/29498. *Gender Equality: Women's Rights in Review 25 Years After Beijing*, UN Women, 2020, www.unwomen.org/-/media/head quarters/attachments/sections/library/publications/2020/gender-equality-womens -rights-in-review-en.pdf?la=en&vs=934. See also *Progress of the World's Women 2019– 2020*, UN Women, 2019, www.unwomen.org/-/media/headquarters/attachments/sections /library/publications/2019/progress-of-the-worlds-women-2019-2020-en.pdf?la=en &vs=3512. *Women, Business and the Law 2020*. See also Hillary Clinton's speech at the United Nations Fourth World Conference on Women in Beijing, China, 1995, www.un.org /esa/gopher-data/conf/fwcw/conf/gov/950905175653.txt.

30. Women's Democratic Front (WDF), accessed January 26, 2021, https://wdfpk .org/about/history/. *Women in Parliament: 1995–2020—25 Years in Review*, Inter-Parliamentary Union (IPU), 2020, www.ipu.org/resources/publications/reports/2020-03 /women-in-parliament-1995-2020-25-years-in-review. See also *Women in Politics: 2020*, IPU and UN Women, 2020, www.ipu.org/resources/publications/infographics/2020-03 /women-in-politics-2020, and Rachel Vogelstein and Alexandra Bro, "Women's Power Index," Council on Foreign Relations, last updated September 18, 2020, www.cfr.org/article /womens-power-index.

31. Constitution of Tunisia 2014, Article 34 and Article 46, www.constituteproject .org/constitution/Tunisia_2014.pdf

32. *Delivering Through Diversity*, McKinsey & Company, 2018, www.mckinsey.com /business-functions/organization/our-insights/delivering-through-diversity. See also *Pursuing Women's Economic Empowerment*, International Monetary Fund, 2018, www .imf.org/en/Publications/Policy-Papers/Issues/2018/05/31/pp053118pursuing-womens -economic-empowerment.

33. *Feminist Aid: A Call for G7 Leaders to Beat Inequality*, Oxfam, 2019, https:// oxfamilibrary.openrepository.com/bitstream/handle/10546/620755/bp-feminist-aid -g7-090519-en.pdf. See also "Countries with a Gender-Budgeting Government Initiative," International Monetary Fund, last updated January 16, 2017, http://data

.imf.org/?sk=E041EF04-A2F3-492D-B2BF-F581781EB8AA, and Jamille Bigio and Rachel Vogelstein, *Understanding Gender Equality in Foreign Policy*, Council on Foreign Relations, 2020, https://cdn.cfr.org/sites/default/files/report_pdf/discussion-paper_bigio-and-vogelstein_gender-equality_or_0.pdf.

34. Melissa Mancini and Ioanna Roumeliotis, "Sexual Assault Centres Struggle with Limited Funding as More Women Come Forward to Say #MeToo," CBC News, February 10, 2020, www.cbc.ca/news/canada/sexual-assault-centres-funding-services-1.5450099. Kevin Strom et al., "How Much Justice Is Denied? An Estimate of Unsubmitted Sexual Assault Kits in the United States," *Journal of Criminal Justice*, October 20, 2020, https://doi.org/10/1016/j.jcrimjus.2020.101746. Vivian Wang, "Sex Harassment Laws Toughened in New York: 'Finally, This Is Happening,'" *New York Times*, June 20, 2019, www.nytimes.com/2019/06/20/nyregion/sexual-harassment-laws-ny.html. See also Christina Pazzanesse and Colleen Walsh, "The Women's Revolt: Why Now, and Where To," *Harvard Gazette*, December 21, 2017, https://news.harvard.edu/gazette/story/2017/12/metoo-surge-could-change-society-in-pivotal-ways-harvard-analysts-say/.

35. "Aid in Support of Gender Equality and Women's Empowerment," Organization for Economic Cooperation and Development, 2020, www.oecd.org/dac/stats/aidinsupportofgenderequalityandwomensempowerment.htm. Hillary Clinton, interviewed by Rachel Vogelstein and Meighan Stone, August 26, 2020. Unless otherwise attributed, all quotes from Hillary Clinton in this chapter come from this interview.

36. *UN Women Strategic Plan 2018–2021*, UN Women, 2018, www.unwomen.org/en/digital-library/publications/2017/8/un-women-strategic-plan-2018-2021. *UNICEF Annual Report 2019*, UNICEF, 2019, unicef.org/sites/default/files/2020-06/UNICEF-annual-report-2019_2.pdf.

37. "The 17 Goals," United Nations Department of Economic and Social Affairs, accessed January 8, 2021, https://sdgs.un.org/goals.

38. S. Laurel Weldon and Mala Hutun, *The Logics of Gender Justice: State Action on Women's Rights Around the World* (Cambridge, UK: Cambridge University Press, 2018). PeiYao Chen, quoted in "New Research Shows the Power of Feminist Movements Around the World," Simon Fraser University, March 6, 2020, www.prnewswire.co.uk/news-releases/new-research-shows-the-power-of-feminist-movements-around-the-world-806659085.html.

39. *United Nations Development Programme, Annual Report 2019*, UNDP, 2020, https://annualreport.undp.org/assets/UNDP-Annual-Report-2019-en.pdf.

40. *Tackling Social Norms: A Game Changer for Gender Inequalities*, UNDP, 2020, http://hdr.undp.org/sites/default/files/hd_perspectives_gsni.pdf.

41. Megan Garber, "The Logical Fallacy of Christine Blasey Ford's 'Choice,'" *The Atlantic*, September 20, 2018, www.theatlantic.com/entertainment/archive/2018/09/brett-kavanaugh-christine-blasey-ford/570715/.

42. Jodi Kantor and Megan Twohey, "Harvey Weinstein Paid Off Sexual Harassment Accusers for Decades," *New York Times*, October 5, 2017, www.nytimes.com/2017/10/05/us/harvey-weinstein-harassment-allegations.html. Gaby Hinsliff, "'The Rapist Is You!': Why a Chilean Protest Chant Is Being Sung Around the World," *The Guardian*, February 3, 2020, www.theguardian.com/society/2020/feb/03/the-rapist-is-you-chilean-protest-song-chanted-around-the-world-un-iolador-en-tu-camino.

Afterword

1. *COVID-19 and Gender Equality: Countering the Regressive Effects*, McKinsey & Company, July 15, 2020, www.mckinsey.com/featured-insights/future-of-work /covid-19-and-gender-equality-countering-the-regressive-effects#. "Multiple Demands Cause Women to Abandon the Workforce," National Public Radio, October 2, 2020, www.npr.org/sections/coronavirus-live-updates/2020/10/02/919517914/enough-already -multiple-demands-causing-women-to-abandon-workforce. Amanda Taub, "A New COVID-19 Crisis: Domestic Abuse Rises Worldwide," *New York Times*, April 6, 2020, www.nytimes.com/2020/04/06/world/coronavirus-domestic-violence.html. "COVID-19 Global Gender Response Tracker," UNDP, last updated September 21, 2020, https://data .undp.org/gendertracker/.

2. Roya Hakakian, interviewed by Rachel Vogelstein, August 30, 2020.

3. Daniel Politi and Ernesto Londoño, "Argentina Legalizes Abortion, a Milestone in a Conservative Region," *New York Times,* December 30, 2020, www.nytimes. com/2020/12/30/world/americas/argentina-legalizes-abortion.html. Farnaz Fassihi, "Iran Moves to Outlaw Sexual Violence and Harassment of Women," *New York Times,* January 5, 2021, www.nytimes.com/2021/01/05/world/middleeast/iran-sexual-violence-me-too-women.html. Farnaz Fassihi, "A #MeToo Awakening Stirs in Iran," *New York Times,* October 22, 2020, www.nytimes.com/2020/10/22/world/middleeast/iran-metoo -aydin-aghdashloo.html.

INDEX

Rachel Walisko

From the White House and the State Department to the campaign trail, **Rachel Vogelstein** has dedicated her career to elevating the status of women and girls.

For over a decade, Vogelstein was a top counselor to Secretary Hillary Rodham Clinton on domestic and global women's issues, serving as an adviser to her historic 2008 and 2016 presidential campaigns and helping her become the first woman to win a US presidential major party nomination. During the Obama administration, Vogelstein was a member of the White House Council on Women and Girls and an official in the Secretary's Office of Global Women's Issues at the US Department of State, where she developed a groundbreaking foreign policy agenda for women's empowerment.

Vogelstein is currently the Douglas Dillon senior fellow and director of the Women and Foreign Policy program at the Council on Foreign Relations, writing frequently in the *Washington Post*, *Foreign Affairs*, and other leading publications on the most important issues facing women globally. A lawyer by training, she has taught courses on women and foreign policy at Georgetown Law School and Yale Law School's Center for Global Legal Challenges.

Vogelstein has served as an adviser on women's workplace equality at the TIME'S UP Foundation and advanced women's health and reproductive rights as senior counsel at the National Women's Law Center, drafting legislation for the US Congress and amicus briefs to the US Supreme Court. She received the US Secretary of State's Superior Honor Award and a National Association of Women Lawyers Award and has served on the boards of the National Women's History Museum and Planned Parenthood Global.

From helping girls facing Boko Haram to participating in Syria summit negotiations with world leaders, **Meighan Stone** is an outspoken advocate for the rights of women around the world. As president of the Malala Fund from 2014 to 2017, Stone worked with founder and 2014 Nobel Peace Prize laureate Malala Yousafzai to empower girls globally to learn and lead without fear.

Named one of *Fast Company*'s Most Creative People and on *Elle* magazine's "Women in Washington Power List," Stone has led high-level advocacy, international development, and media projects with Bono's ONE Campaign, the United Nations, World Food Programme, World Economic Forum, FIFA World Cup, and at G7 summits and with political campaigns, world leaders, celebrities, and technology corporations. Her writing on global women's issues has appeared in *Time, Fortune, Quartz, The Hill,* and *Foreign Affairs.*

Stone is a senior fellow in the Council on Foreign Relations' Women and Foreign Policy program. Previously, she served as entrepreneurship fellow at the Harvard Kennedy School's Shorenstein Center, where she wrote on refugee policy and collaborated with Harvard faculty to foster social innovation. She serves as board chair of resistance leader Indivisible, on the board of Representative John Lewis's bipartisan Faith and Politics Institute, and as an emeritus board member at Pencils of Promise. As a proud single mom, she could probably use a nap.